EPISODE ONE: NERVOUS IN THE SERVICE

STORY
JEFF McCOMSEY
BILL JEMAS

SCRIPT
JEFF McCOMSEY

LAYOUTS
KURT TIEDE

PENCILS
KURT TIEDE

COLORS
MAXFLAN ARAUJO

COVER
KURT TIEDE

LETTERS
CAROLINE FLANAGAN

EDITOR
ELYSIA LIANG

EPISODE TWO: ALL THE PRESIDENT'S MEN

STORY
JEFF McCOMSEY
BILL JEMAS

SCRIPT
JEFF McCOMSEY

LAYOUTS
KURT TIEDE

PENCILS
KURT TIEDE

COLORS
MAXFLAN ARAUJO

INKS
ALISSON RODRIGUES

COVER
APPLE QINGYANG ZHANG

LETTERS
ELYSIA LIANG
CAROLINE FLANAGAN

EDITOR
ELYSIA LIANG

EPISODE THREE: THE THING THEY CARRIED

STORY
JEFF McCOMSEY
BILL JEMAS

SCRIPT
JEFF McCOMSEY

LAYOUTS
KURT TIEDE

PENCILS
KURT TIEDE

COLORS
MAXFLAN ARAUJO

INKS
ALISSON RODRIGUES

COVER
RUIZ BURGOS

LETTERS
ELYSIA LIANG

EDITOR
ELYSIA LIANG

EPISODE FOUR: HOME OF THE GRAVE

STORY
BILL JEMAS
MICHAEL COAST

SCRIPT
JEFF McCOMSEY
BILL JEMAS

LAYOUTS
YOUNG HELLER
KURT TIEDE
DAVID HILLMAN
BENJAMIN SILBERSTEIN

PENCILS
KURT TIEDE
STAN CHOU
VINCENZO RICCARDI
JAIME SALANGSANG

COLORS
MAXFLAN ARAUJO

INKS
ALISSON RODRIGUES
PATRICIO HERNANDEZ

COVER
RUIZ BURGOS

LETTERS
ELYSIA LIANG

EDITOR
ELYSIA LIANG

EPISODE FIVE: RABRIDGE

STORY
BILL JEMAS

SCRIPT
JEFF McCOMSEY
BILL JEMAS

LAYOUTS
JEFF McCOMSEY
STAN CHOU

PENCILS
KURT TIEDE
JAIME SALANGSANG
ALISSON RODRIGUES

COLORS
MAXFLAN ARAUJO

COVER
DAVID NAKAYAMA

LETTERS
ELYSIA LIANG

EDITOR
ELYSIA LIANG

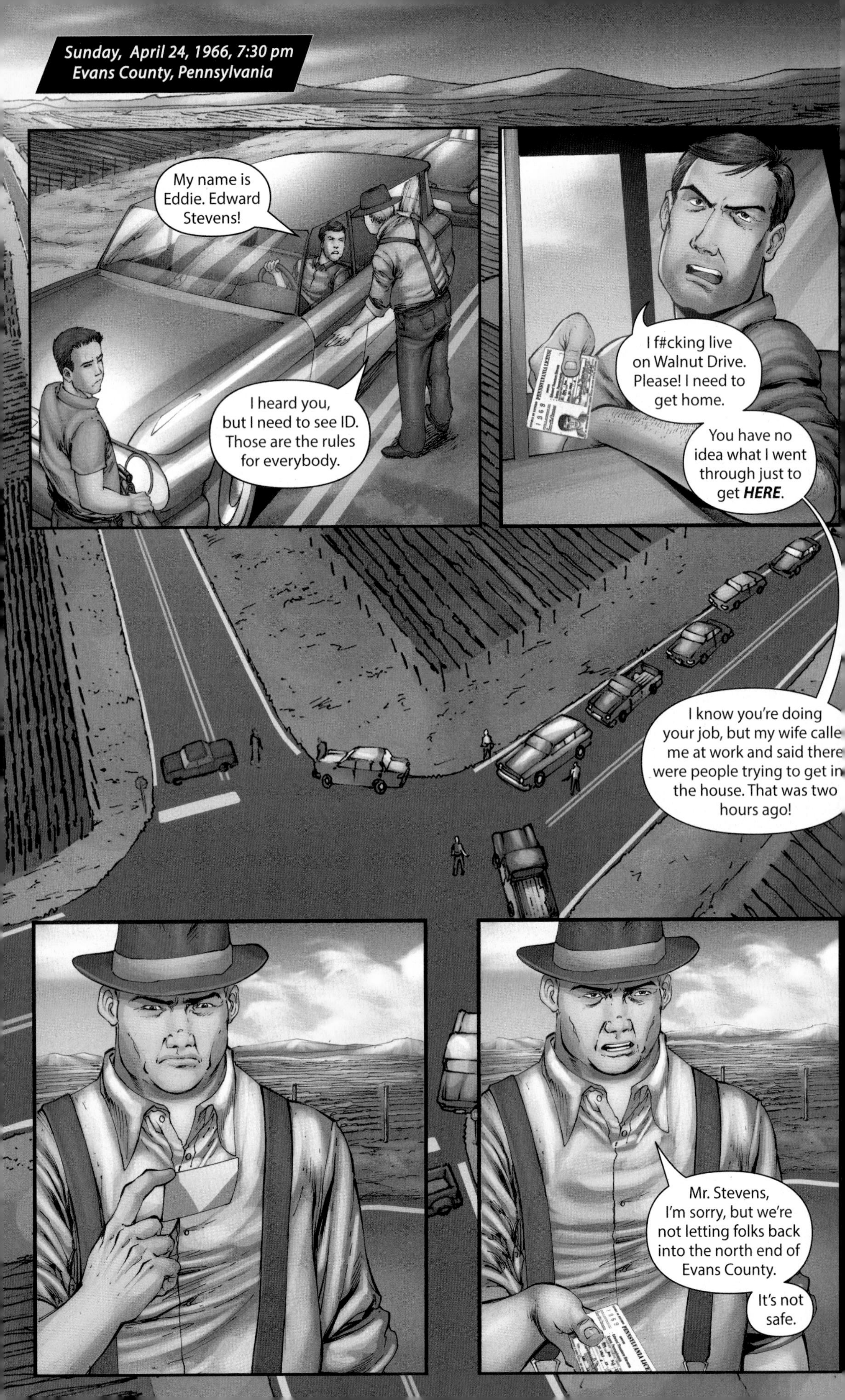
Sunday, April 24, 1966, 7:30 pm
Evans County, Pennsylvania
My name is Eddie. Edward Stevens!
I heard you, but I need to see ID. Those are the rules for everybody.
I f#cking live on Walnut Drive. Please! I need to get home.
You have no idea what I went through just to get **HERE**.
I know you're doing your job, but my wife calle me at work and said there were people trying to get in the house. That was two hours ago!
Mr. Stevens, I'm sorry, but we're not letting folks back into the north end of Evans County.
It's not safe.

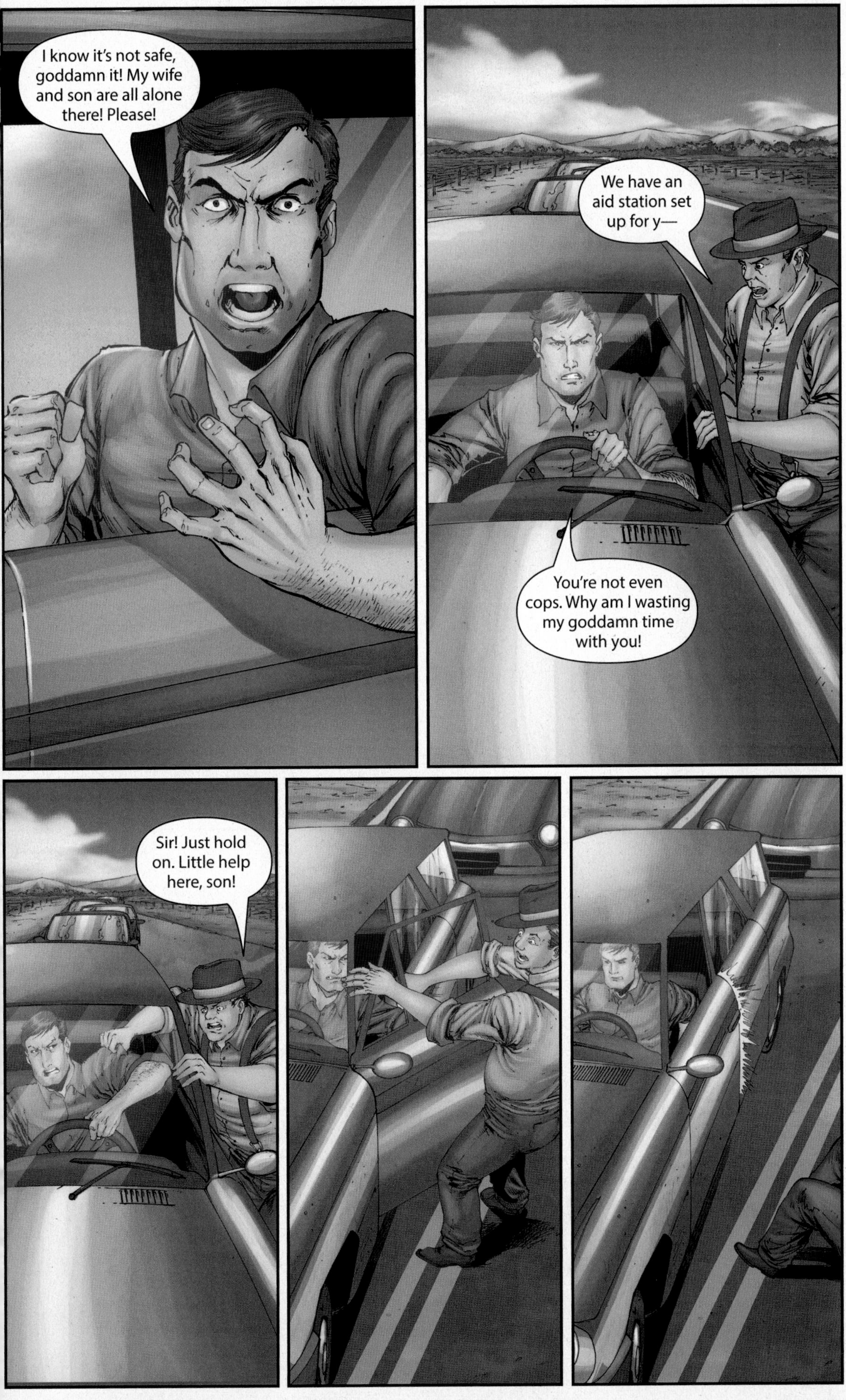
I know it's not safe, goddamn it! My wife and son are all alone there! Please!
We have an aid station set up for y—
You're not even cops. Why am I wasting my goddamn time with you!
Sir! Just hold on. Little help here, son!

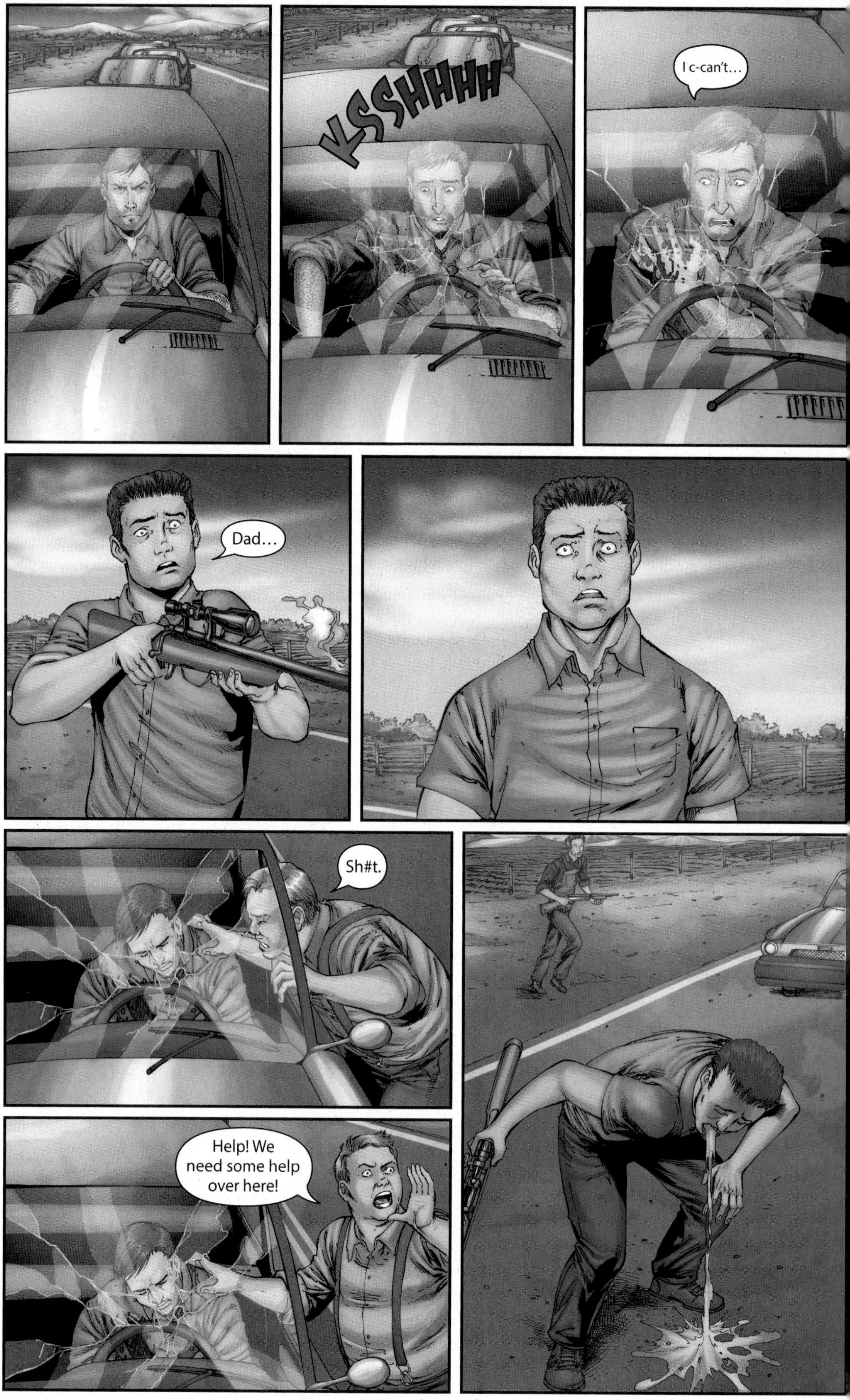
KSSHHHH
I c-can't…
Dad…
Sh#t.
Help! We need some help over here!

ULTIMATE TECHNOLOGY
Buyer's Guide

YOUR GUIDE TO THE BEST
TELEPHONES, TVs, CAMERAS, AND COMPUTERS
PLUS A SNEAK PEEK AT THE SMARTEST CAR IN TOWN.

HONDA S-600

The smartest car in town for the family that has the latest high technology in their home. This car is smart in style with power to spare. It's easy to handle, easy to park, and has spacious luggage compartment for family trips.

$6500; at your local Honda dealership

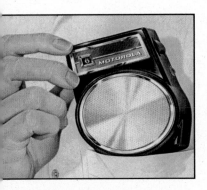

MOTOROLA POCKET RADIO

A shirt-pocket radio with the power and sound you'd expect from a larger set. A six-transistor chassis pinpoints stations and the speaker delivers sound in rich, clear lows, and crisp highs. With battery life up to 100 hours, you can take it on a trip in a custom carrying case.

$14; mail order

AT&T PRINCESS PHONE

America has fallen in love with the new Princess phone. It's little so it fits in those small places where you couldn't fit a telephone before. It's lovely and charms people with its graceful lines and color. It lights so you can find it easily in the dark.

$35; mail order

RCA COLOR TELEVISION

In living color. Get a perfectly fine-tuned picture with brighter highlights every time you watch and circuitry that won't go haywire.

$55; Kaufmann's

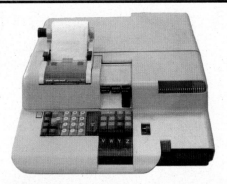

OLIVETTI PROGRAMMA 101

The first computer on your desk. Every company, university, department, laboratory, or institute can now have their own private electronic digital computer. It's only a little larger than a typewriter and doesn't require a skilled operator.

$75; mail order

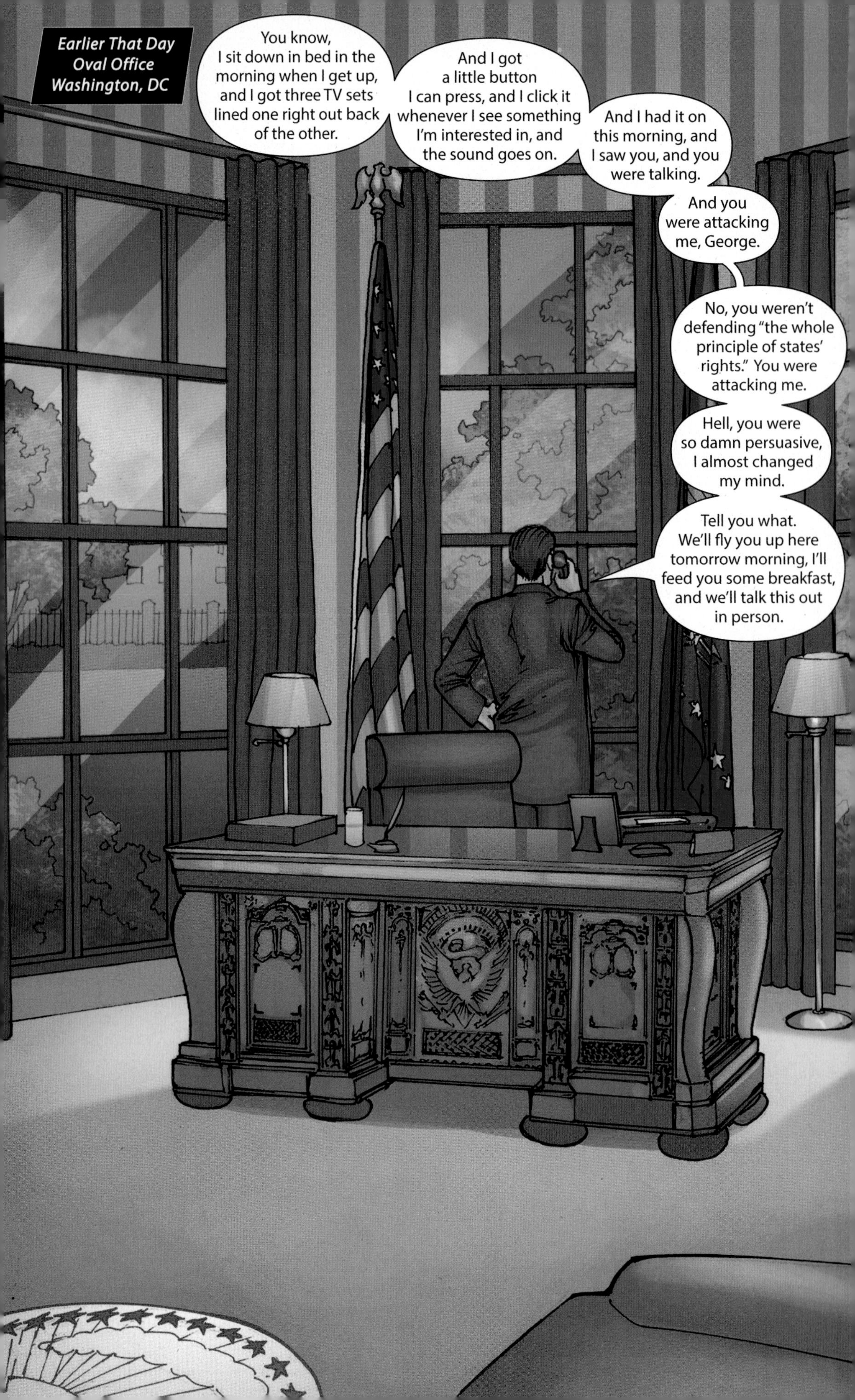
Earlier That Day Oval Office Washington, DC
You know, I sit down in bed in the morning when I get up, and I got three TV sets lined one right out back of the other.
And I got a little button I can press, and I click it whenever I see something I'm interested in, and the sound goes on.
And I had it on this morning, and I saw you, and you were talking.
And you were attacking me, George.
No, you weren't defending "the whole principle of states' rights." You were attacking me.
Hell, you were so damn persuasive, I almost changed my mind.
Tell you what. We'll fly you up here tomorrow morning, I'll feed you some breakfast, and we'll talk this out in person.

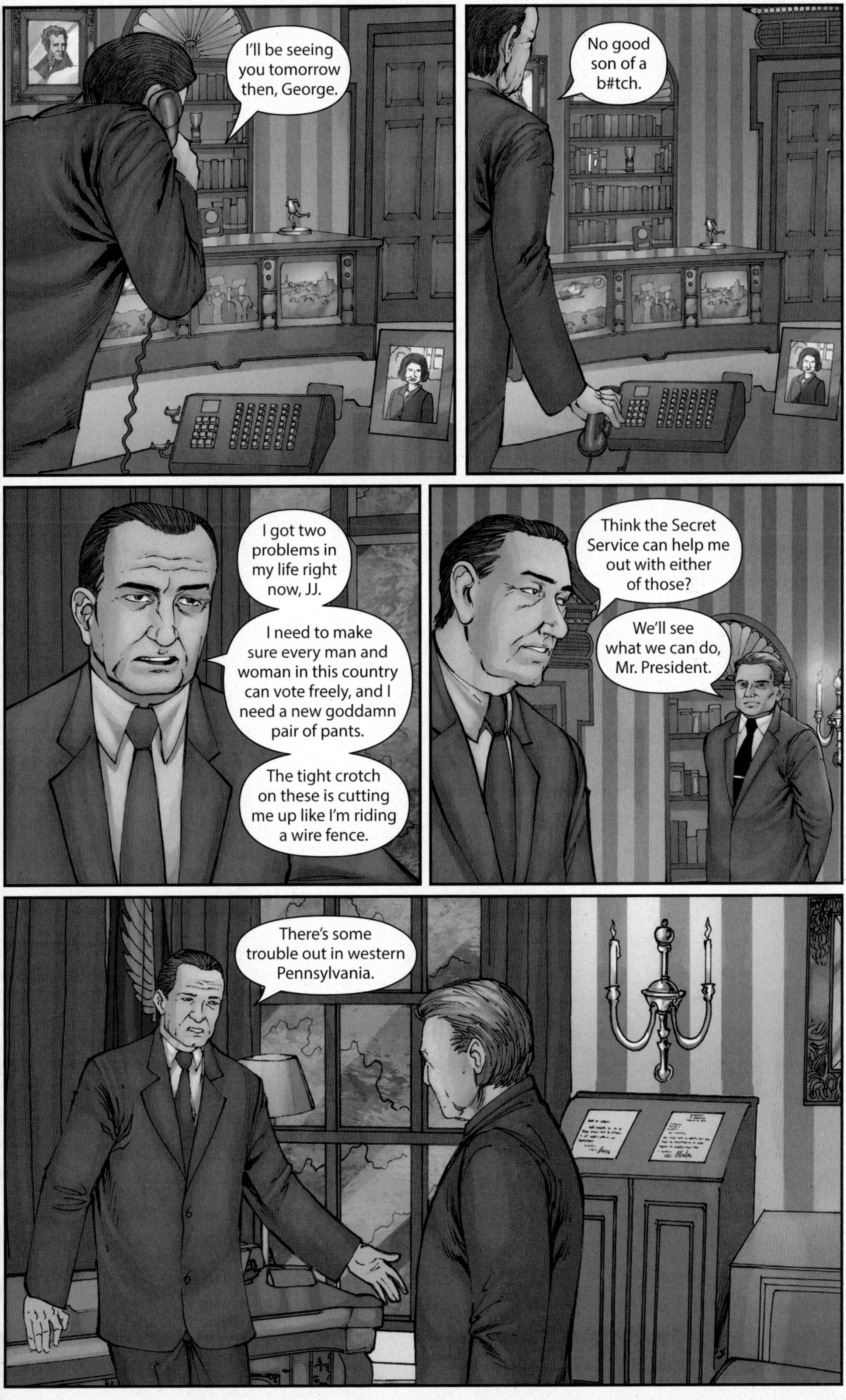
I'll be seeing you tomorrow then, George.
No good son of a b#tch.
I got two problems in my life right now, JJ.
I need to make sure every man and woman in this country can vote freely, and I need a new goddamn pair of pants.
The tight crotch on these is cutting me up like I'm riding a wire fence.
Think the Secret Service can help me out with either of those?
We'll see what we can do, Mr. President.
There's some trouble out in western Pennsylvania.

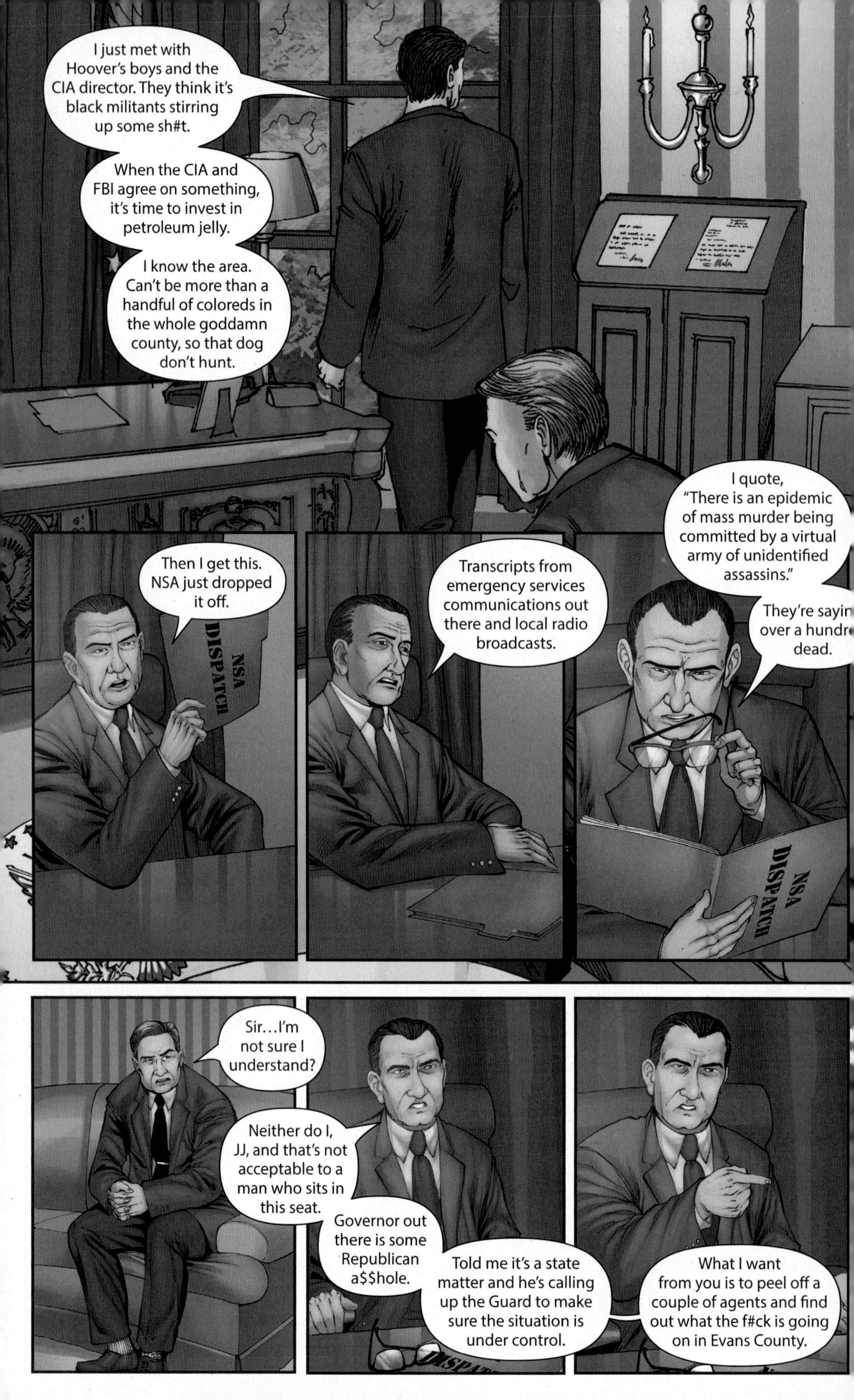
I just met with Hoover's boys and the CIA director. They think it's black militants stirring up some sh#t.
When the CIA and FBI agree on something, it's time to invest in petroleum jelly.
I know the area. Can't be more than a handful of coloreds in the whole goddamn county, so that dog don't hunt.
Then I get this. NSA just dropped it off.
NSA DISPATCH
Transcripts from emergency services communications out there and local radio broadcasts.
I quote, "There is an epidemic of mass murder being committed by a virtual army of unidentified assassins."
They're sayin over a hundr dead.
NSA DISPATCH
Sir…I'm not sure I understand?
Neither do I, JJ, and that's not acceptable to a man who sits in this seat.
Governor out there is some Republican a$$hole.
Told me it's a state matter and he's calling up the Guard to make sure the situation is under control.
What I want from you is to peel off a couple of agents and find out what the f#ck is going on in Evans County.

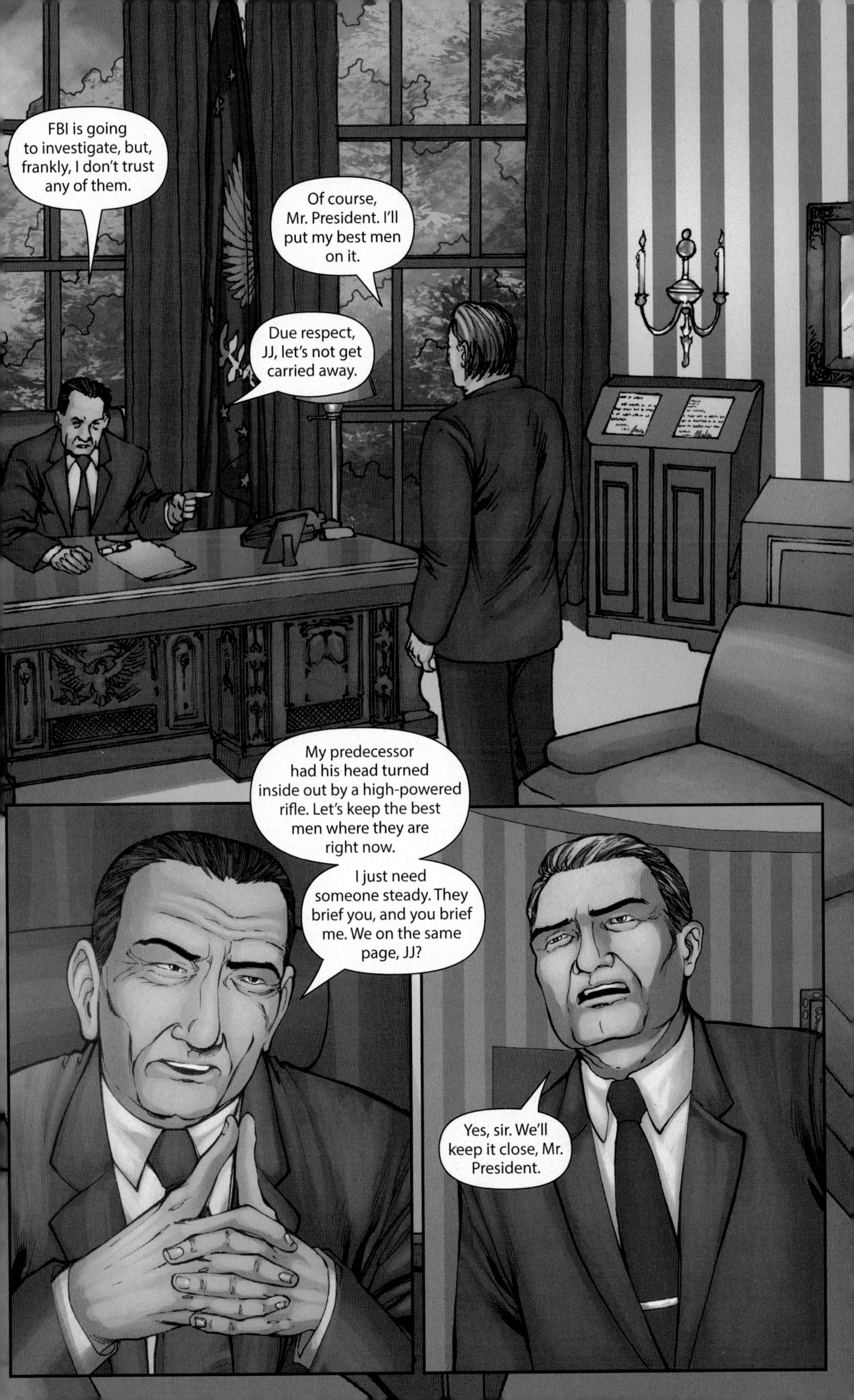
FBI is going to investigate, but, frankly, I don't trust any of them.
Of course, Mr. President. I'll put my best men on it.
Due respect, JJ, let's not get carried away.
My predecessor had his head turned inside out by a high-powered rifle. Let's keep the best men where they are right now.
I just need someone steady. They brief you, and you brief me. We on the same page, JJ?
Yes, sir. We'll keep it close, Mr. President.

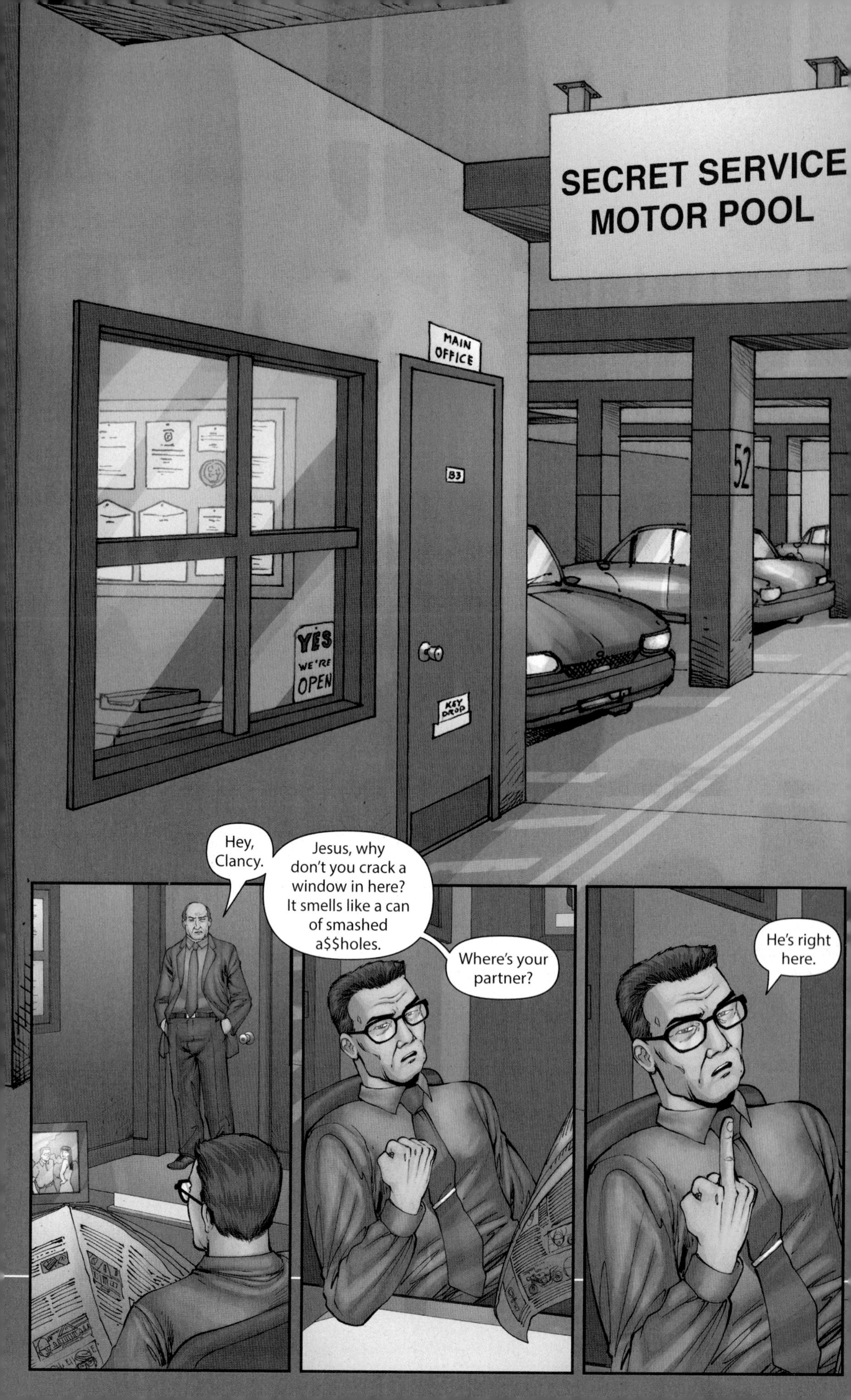
SECRET SERVICE
MOTOR POOL
MAIN OFFICE
B3
YES WE'RE OPEN
KEY DROP
52
Hey, Clancy.
Jesus, why don't you crack a window in here? It smells like a can of smashed a$$holes.
Where's your partner?
He's right here.

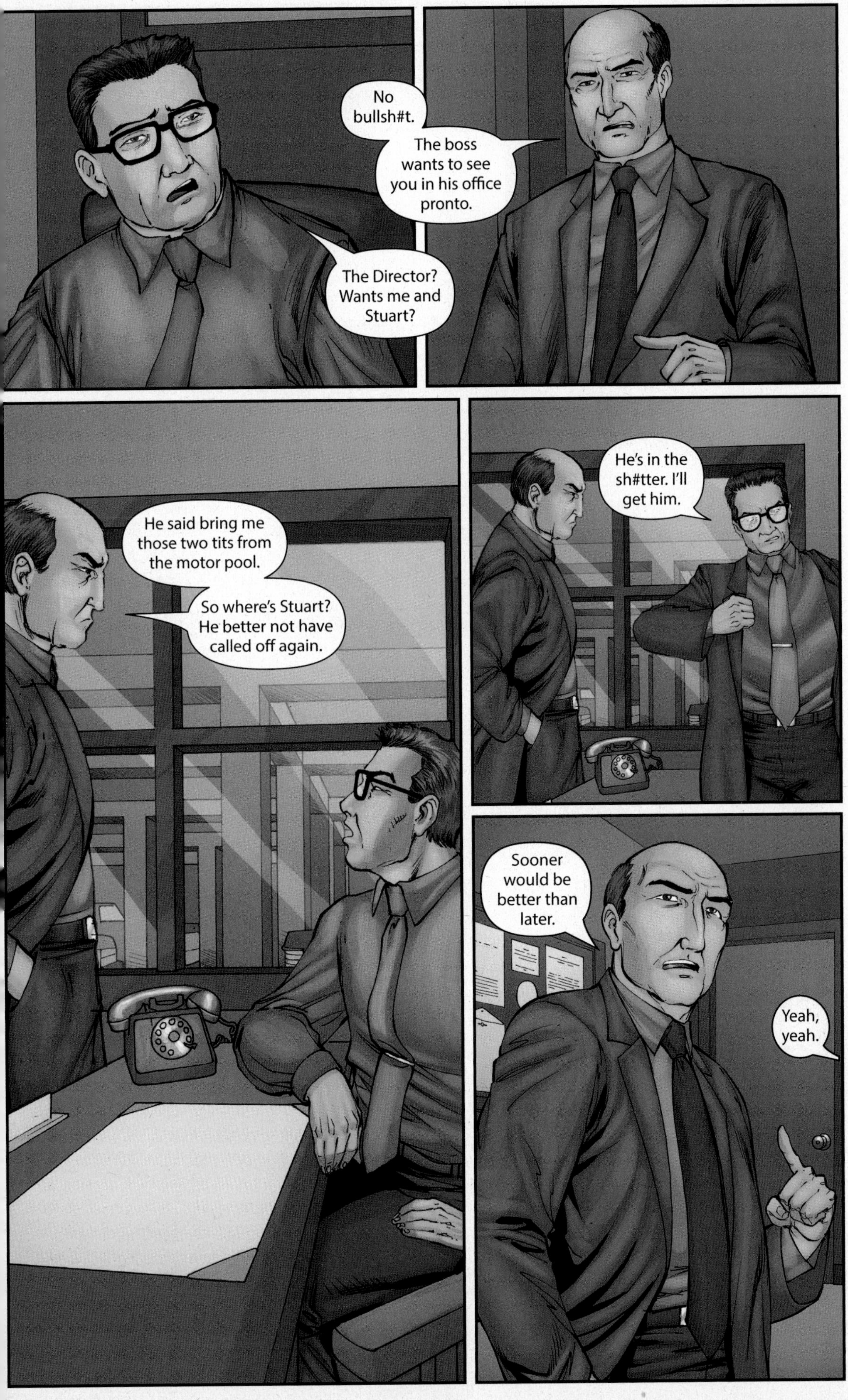

The Director? Wants me and Stuart?
No bullsh#t.
The boss wants to see you in his office pronto.
He said bring me those two tits from the motor pool.
So where's Stuart? He better not have called off again.
He's in the sh#tter. I'll get him.
Sooner would be better than later.
Yeah, yeah.

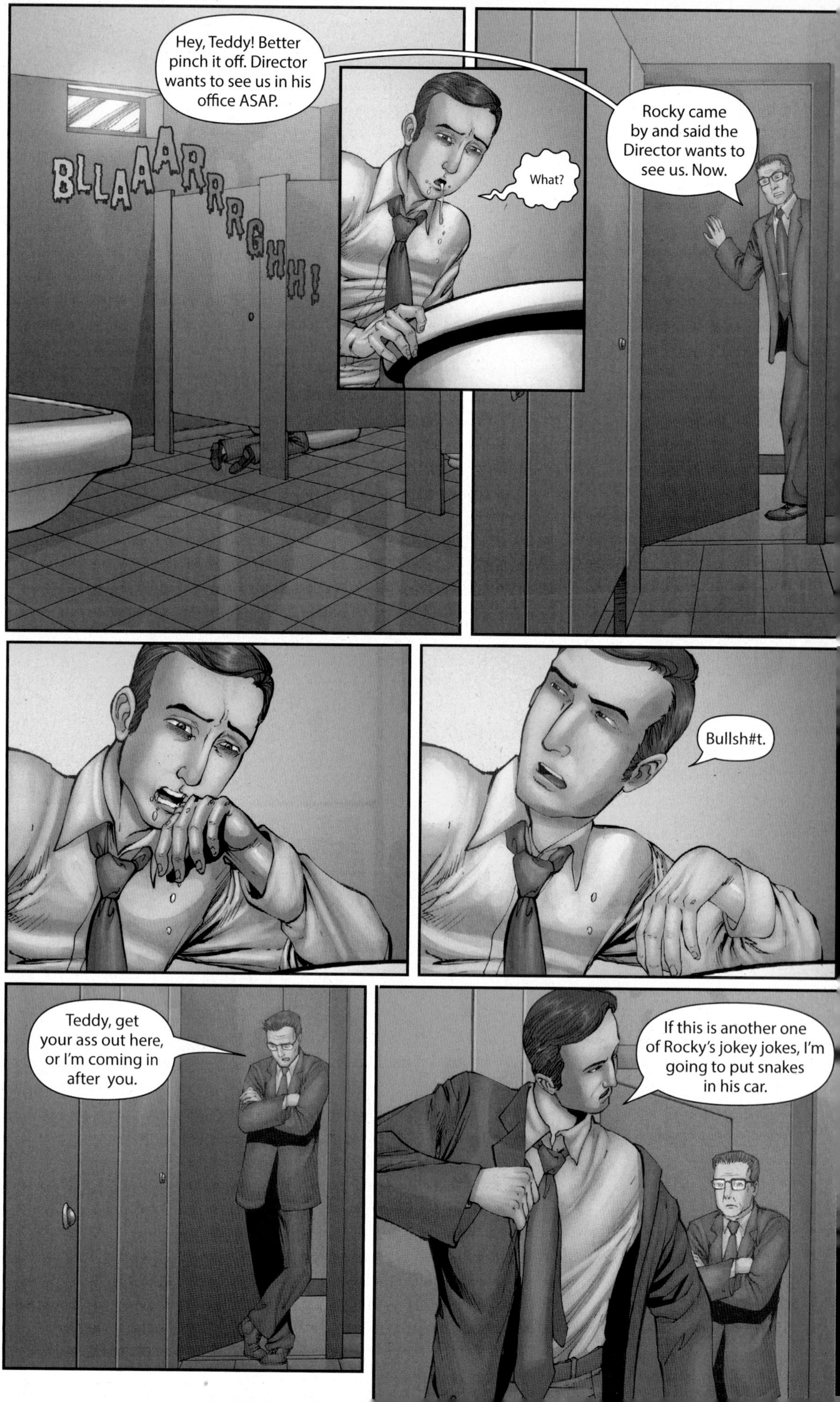
Hey, Teddy! Better pinch it off. Director wants to see us in his office ASAP.
BLLAAARRRGHH!
What?
Rocky came by and said the Director wants to see us. Now.
Bullsh#t.
Teddy, get your ass out here, or I'm coming in after you.
If this is another one of Rocky's jokey jokes, I'm going to put snakes in his car.

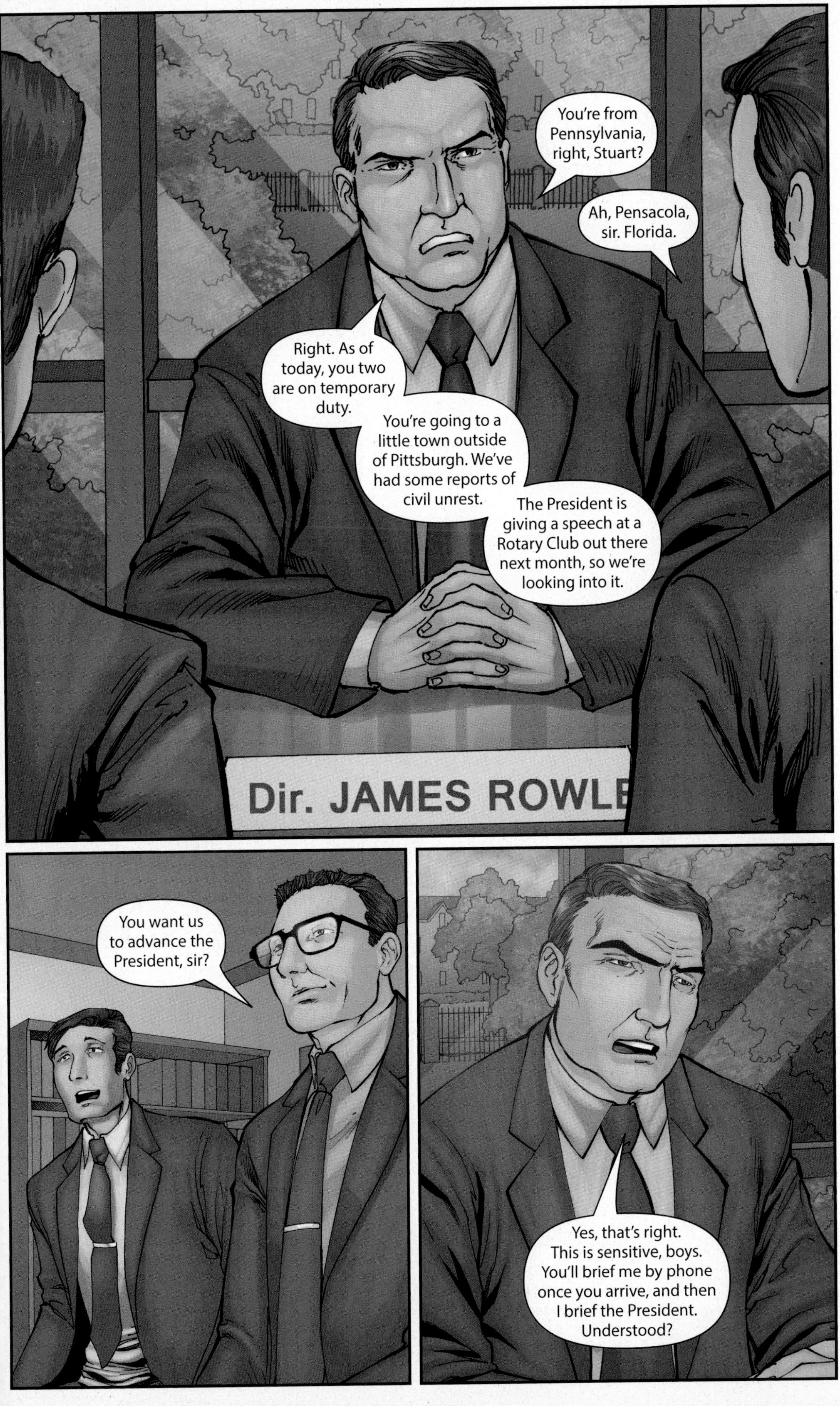
You're from Pennsylvania, right, Stuart?
Ah, Pensacola, sir. Florida.
Right. As of today, you two are on temporary duty.
You're going to a little town outside of Pittsburgh. We've had some reports of civil unrest.
The President is giving a speech at a Rotary Club out there next month, so we're looking into it.
Dir. JAMES ROWLE
You want us to advance the President, sir?
Yes, that's right. This is sensitive, boys. You'll brief me by phone once you arrive, and then I brief the President. Understood?

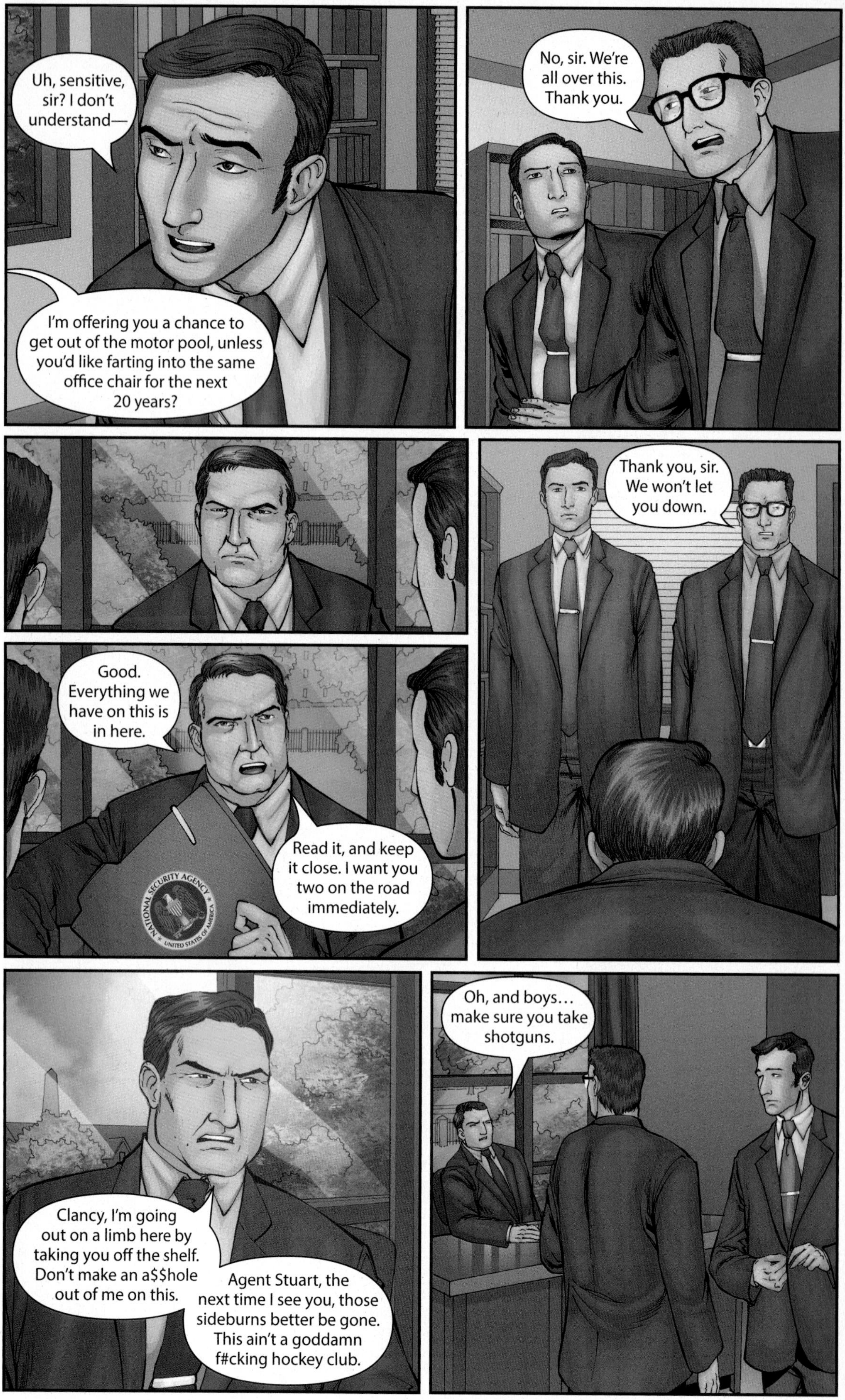
Uh, sensitive, sir? I don't understand—
I'm offering you a chance to get out of the motor pool, unless you'd like farting into the same office chair for the next 20 years?
No, sir. We're all over this. Thank you.
Good. Everything we have on this is in here.
Read it, and keep it close. I want you two on the road immediately.
NATIONAL SECURITY AGENCY
UNITED STATES OF AMERICA
Thank you, sir. We won't let you down.
Clancy, I'm going out on a limb here by taking you off the shelf. Don't make an a$$hole out of me on this.
Agent Stuart, the next time I see you, those sideburns better be gone. This ain't a goddamn f#cking hockey club.
Oh, and boys… make sure you take shotguns.

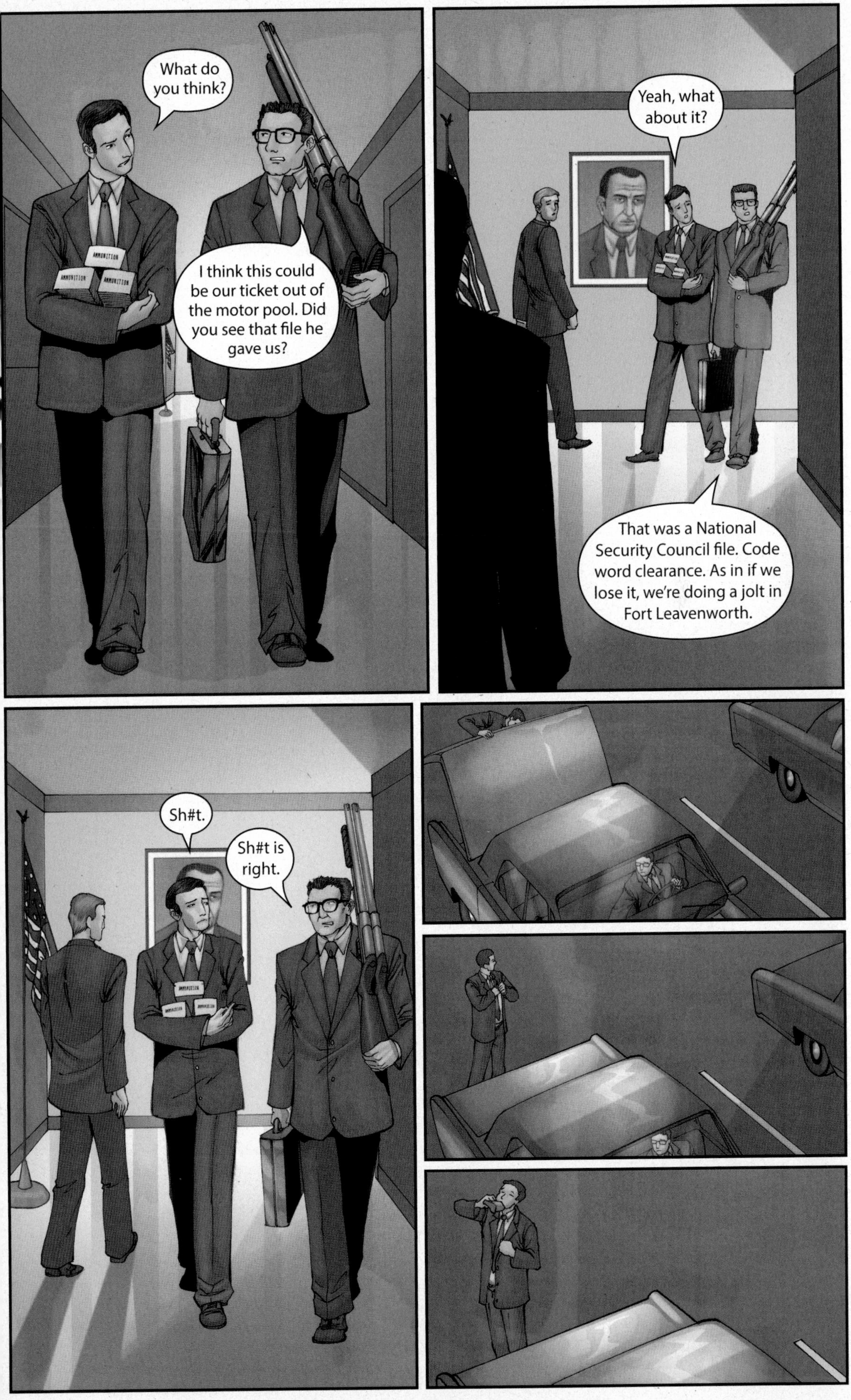
What do you think?
AMMUNITION
AMMUNITION
AMMUNITION
I think this could be our ticket out of the motor pool. Did you see that file he gave us?
Yeah, what about it?
That was a National Security Council file. Code word clearance. As in if we lose it, we're doing a jolt in Fort Leavenworth.
Sh#t.
Sh#t is right.

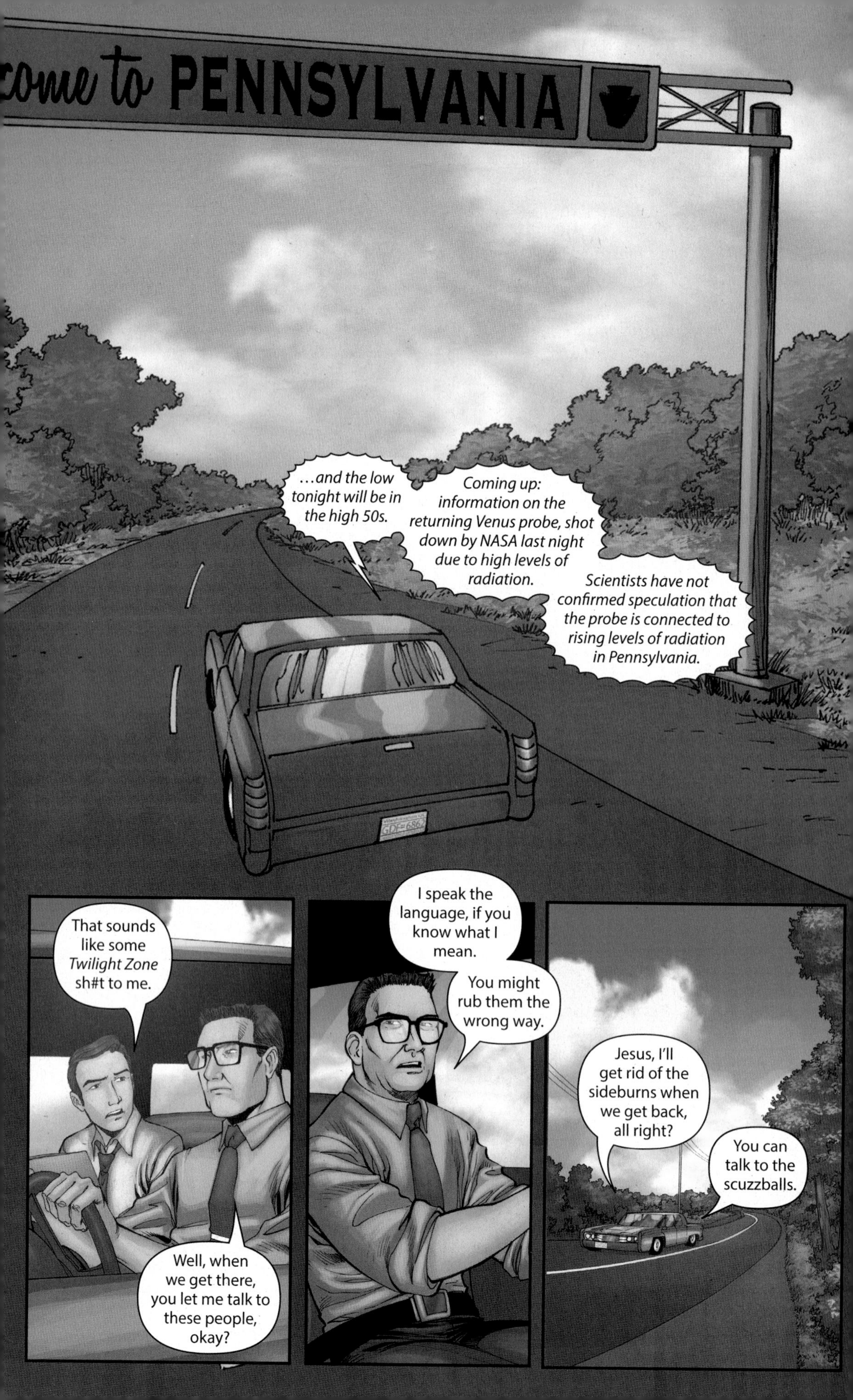
come to PENNSYLVANIA
…and the low tonight will be in the high 50s.
Coming up: information on the returning Venus probe, shot down by NASA last night due to high levels of radiation.
Scientists have not confirmed speculation that the probe is connected to rising levels of radiation in Pennsylvania.
That sounds like some *Twilight Zone* sh#t to me.
Well, when we get there, you let me talk to these people, okay?
I speak the language, if you know what I mean.
You might rub them the wrong way.
Jesus, I'll get rid of the sideburns when we get back, all right?
You can talk to the scuzzballs.

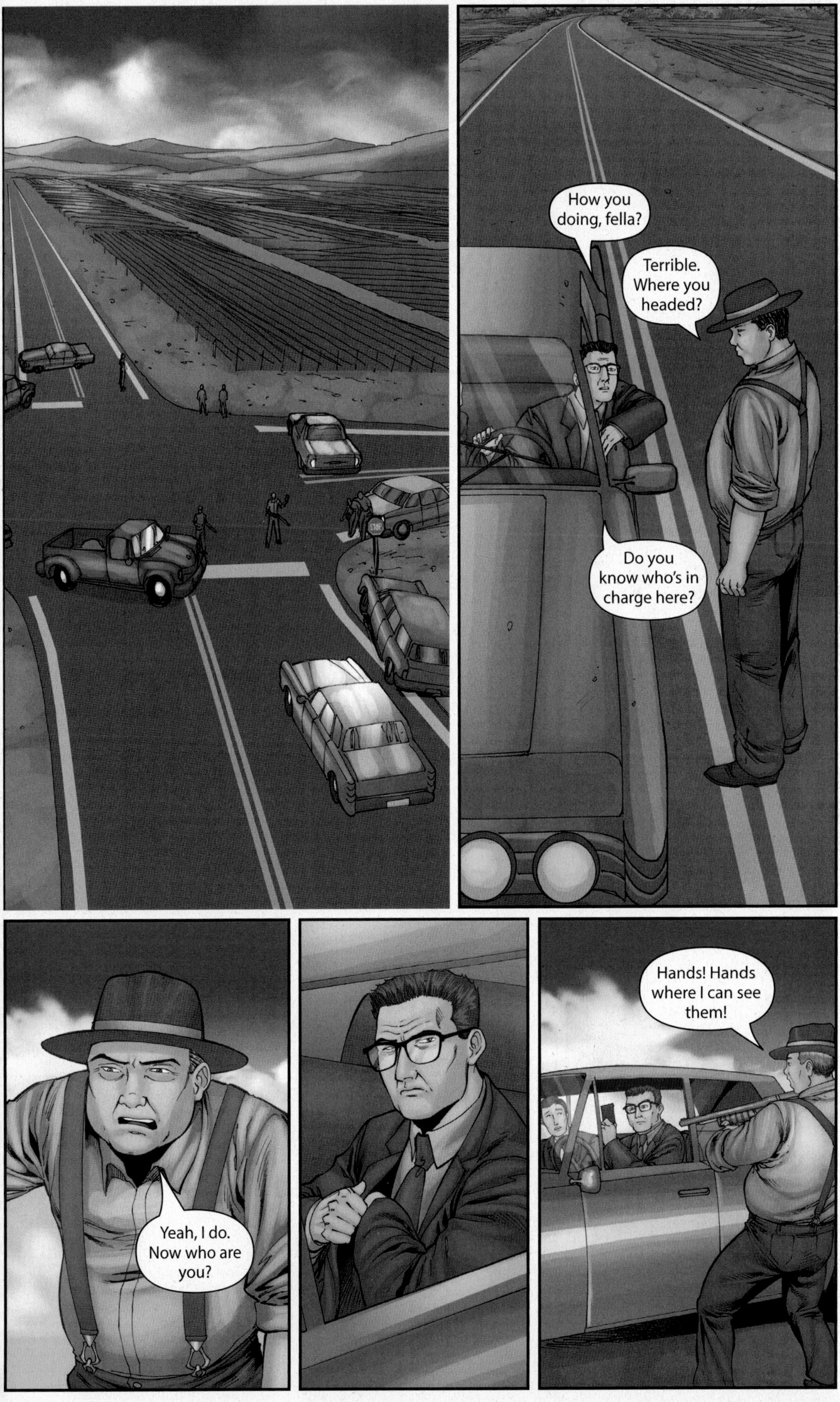
How you doing, fella?
Terrible. Where you headed?
Do you know who's in charge here?
Yeah, I do. Now who are you?
Hands! Hands where I can see them!

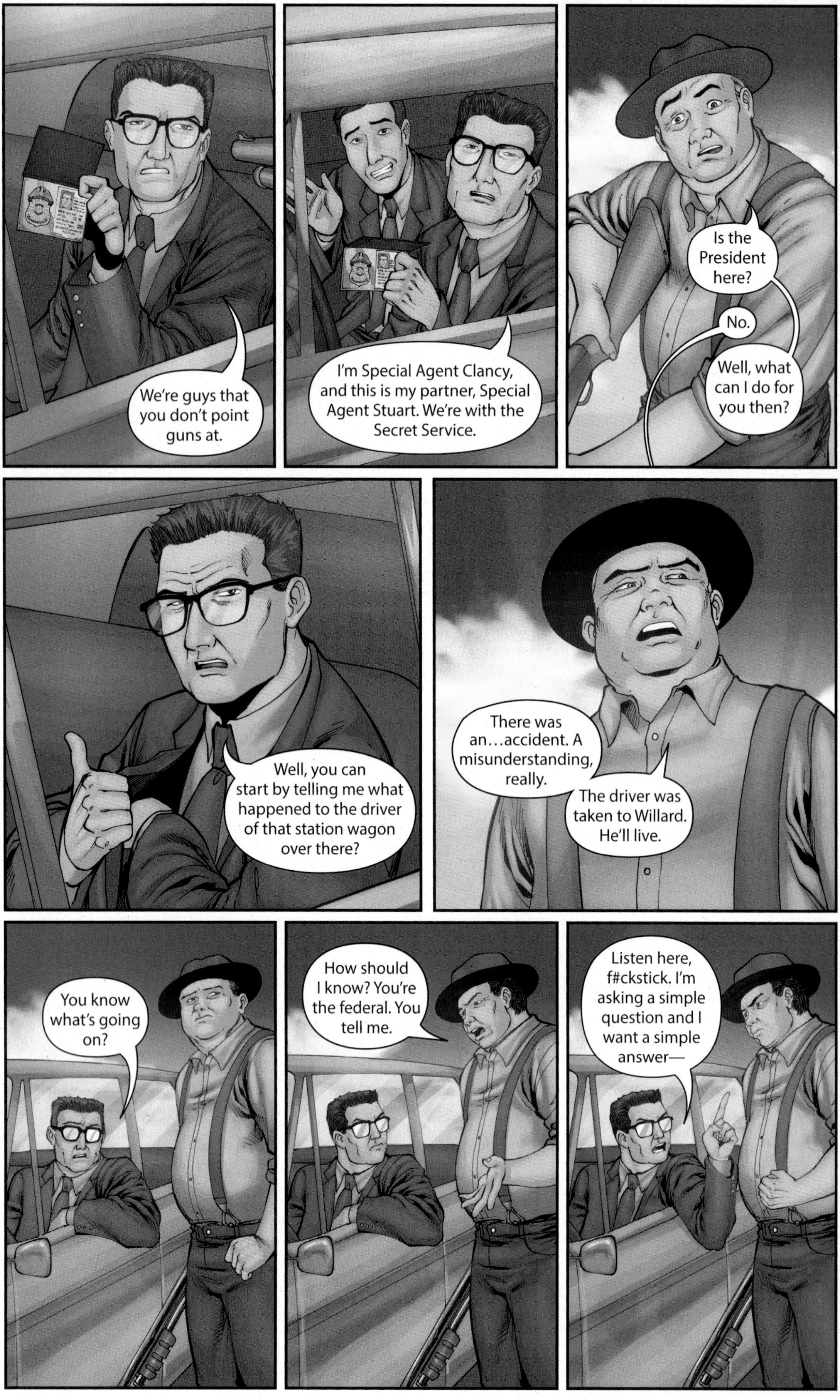

We're guys that you don't point guns at.
I'm Special Agent Clancy, and this is my partner, Special Agent Stuart. We're with the Secret Service.
Is the President here?
No.
Well, what can I do for you then?
Well, you can start by telling me what happened to the driver of that station wagon over there?
There was an…accident. A misunderstanding, really.
The driver was taken to Willard. He'll live.
You know what's going on?
How should I know? You're the federal. You tell me.
Listen here, f#ckstick. I'm asking a simple question and I want a simple answer—

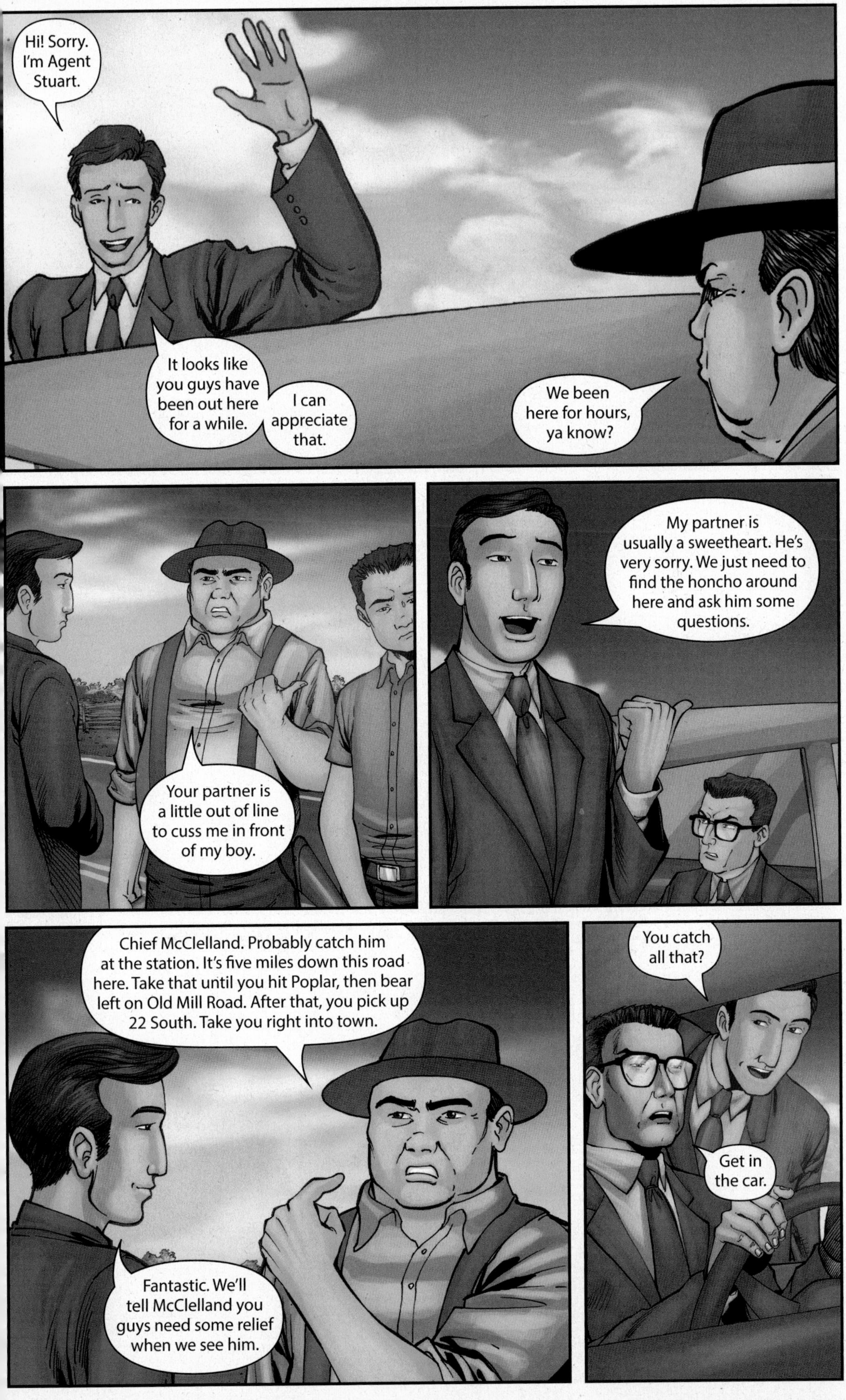
Hi! Sorry. I'm Agent Stuart.
It looks like you guys have been out here for a while.
I can appreciate that.
We been here for hours, ya know?
Your partner is a little out of line to cuss me in front of my boy.
My partner is usually a sweetheart. He's very sorry. We just need to find the honcho around here and ask him some questions.
Chief McClelland. Probably catch him at the station. It's five miles down this road here. Take that until you hit Poplar, then bear left on Old Mill Road. After that, you pick up 22 South. Take you right into town.
Fantastic. We'll tell McClelland you guys need some relief when we see him.
You catch all that?
Get in the car.

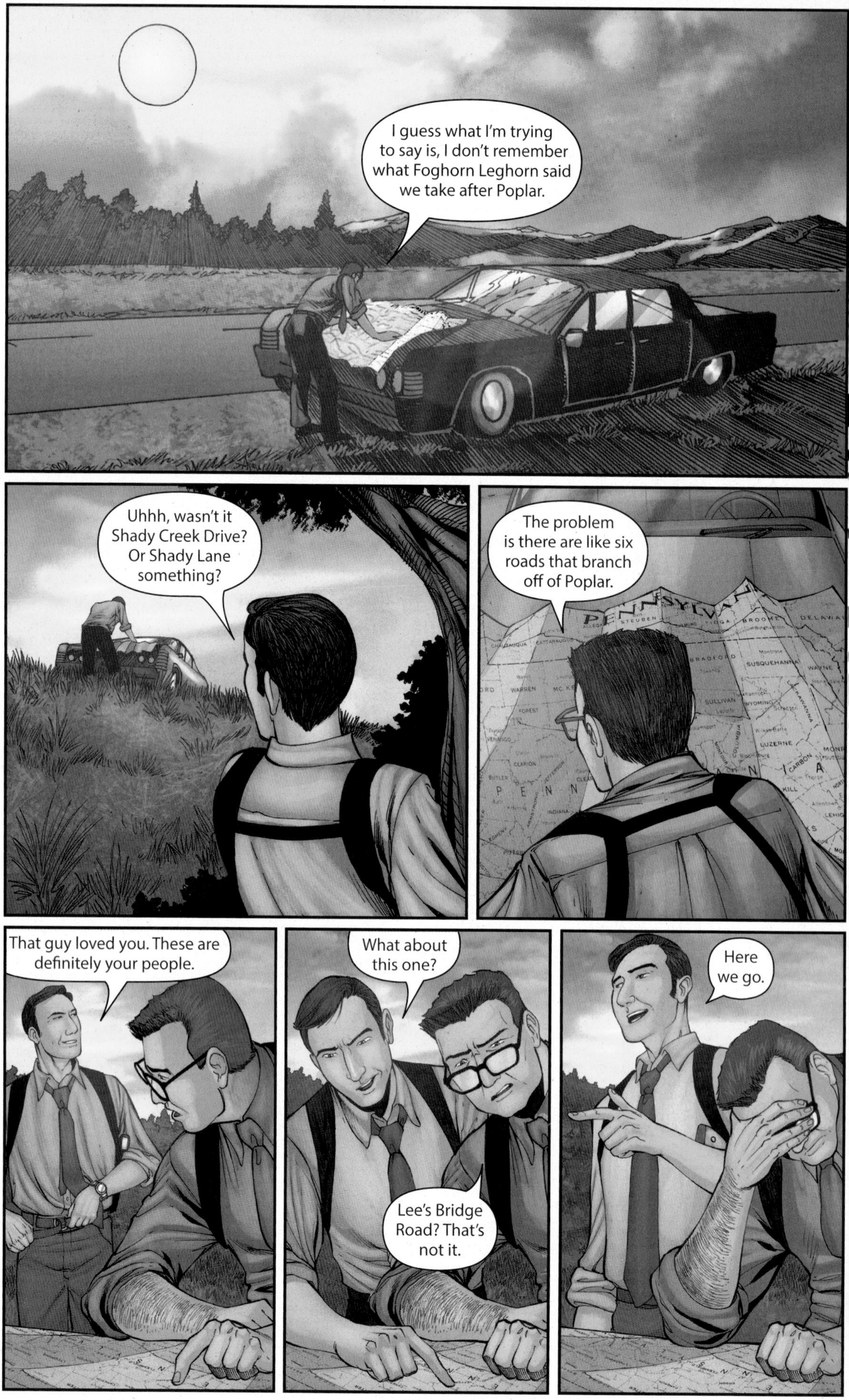
I guess what I'm trying to say is, I don't remember what Foghorn Leghorn said we take after Poplar.
Uhhh, wasn't it Shady Creek Drive? Or Shady Lane something?
The problem is there are like six roads that branch off of Poplar.
That guy loved you. These are definitely your people.
What about this one?
Lee's Bridge Road? That's not it.
Here we go.

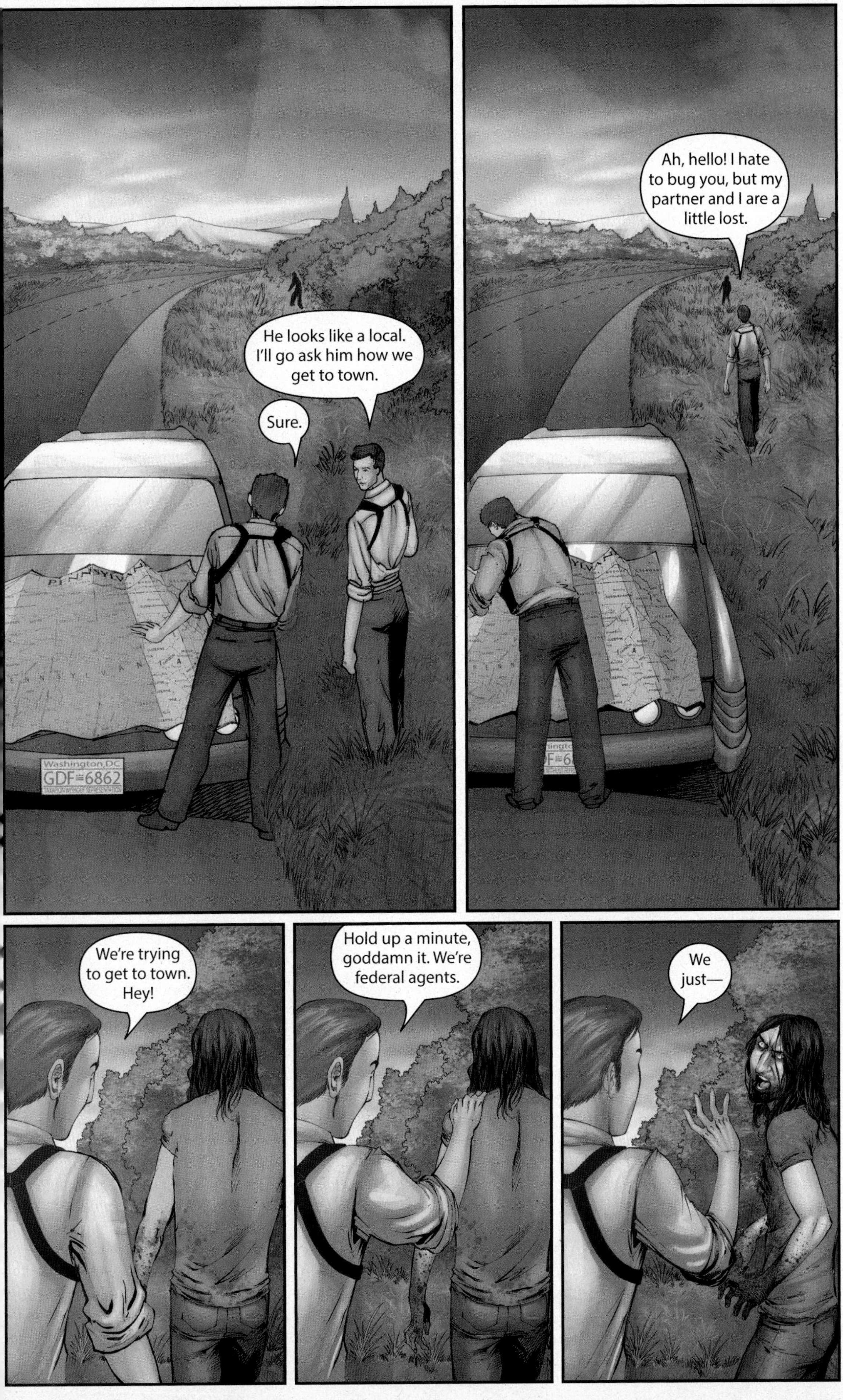
He looks like a local. I'll go ask him how we get to town.
Sure.
Washington,DC
GDF=6862
TAXATION WITHOUT REPRESENTATION
Ah, hello! I hate to bug you, but my partner and I are a little lost.
We're trying to get to town. Hey!
Hold up a minute, goddamn it. We're federal agents.
We just—

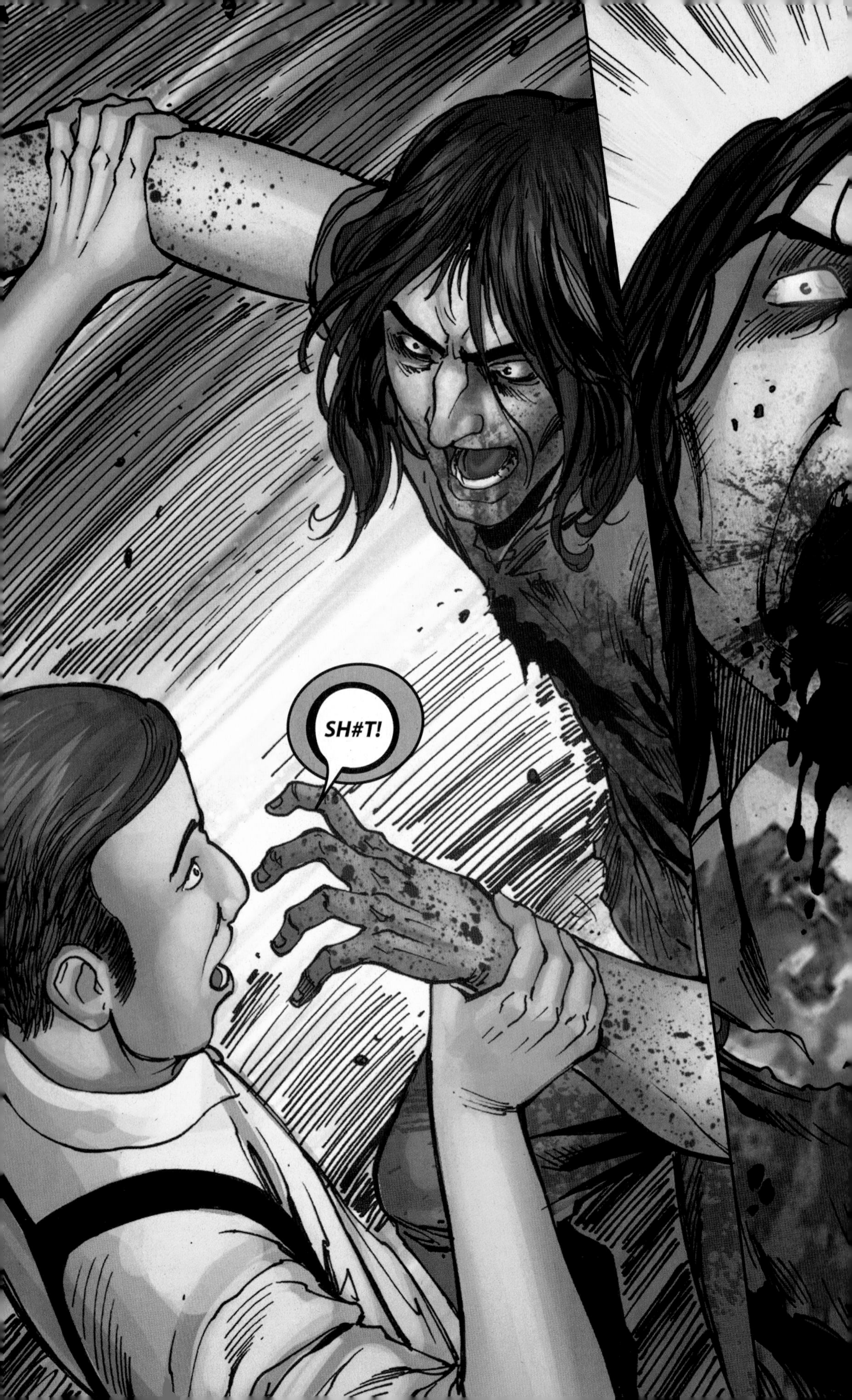
SH#T!

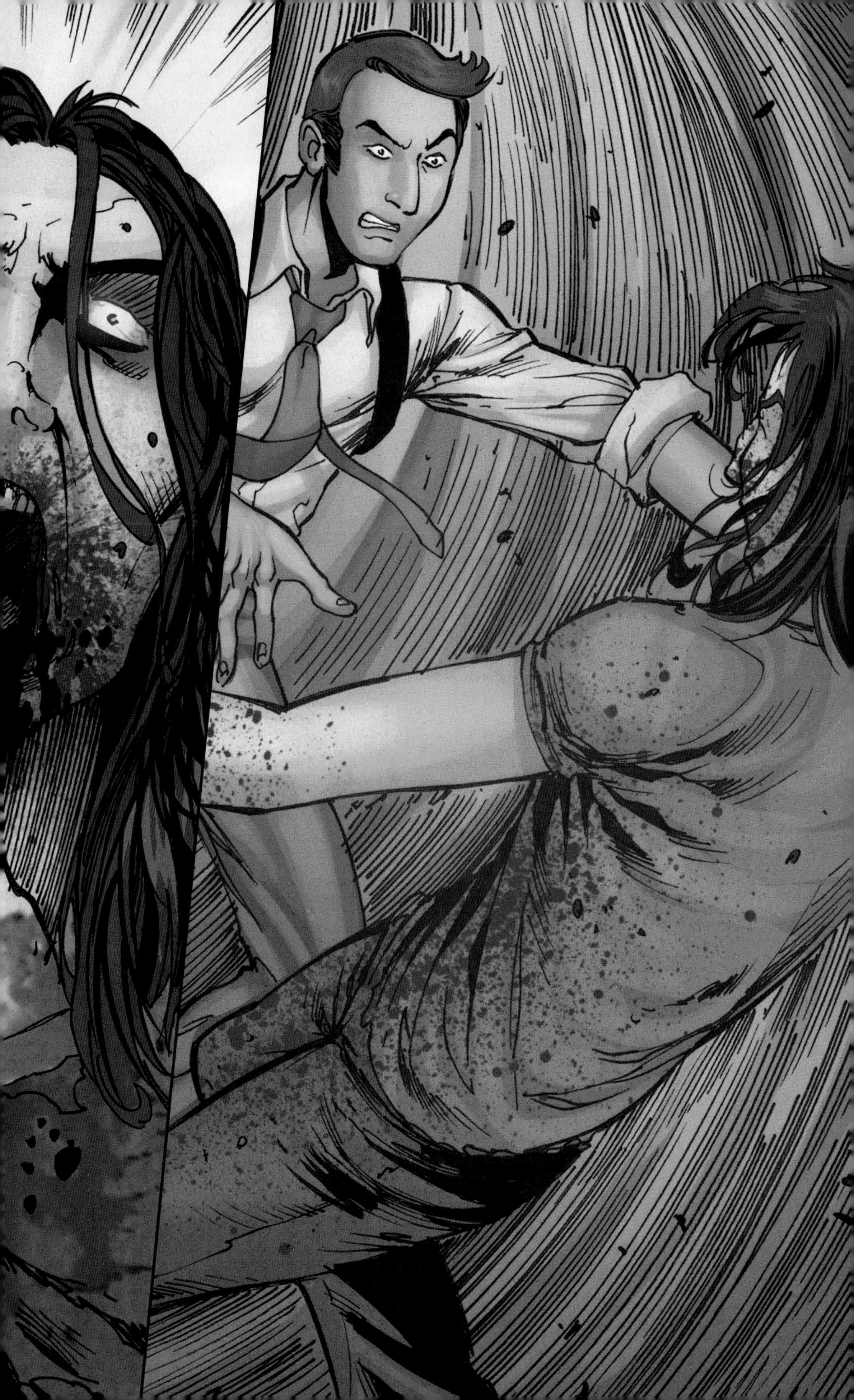

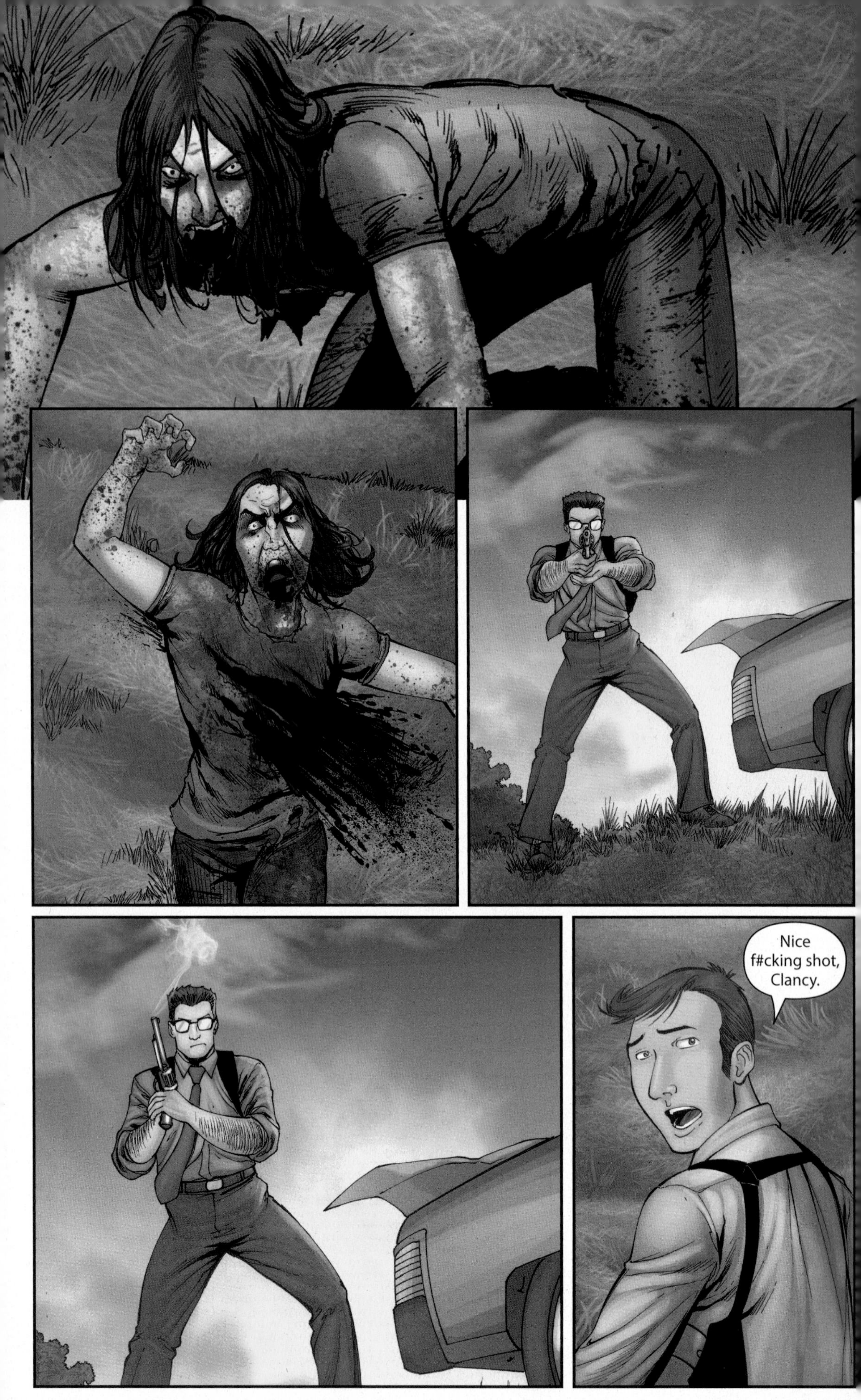
Nice
f#cking shot,
Clancy.

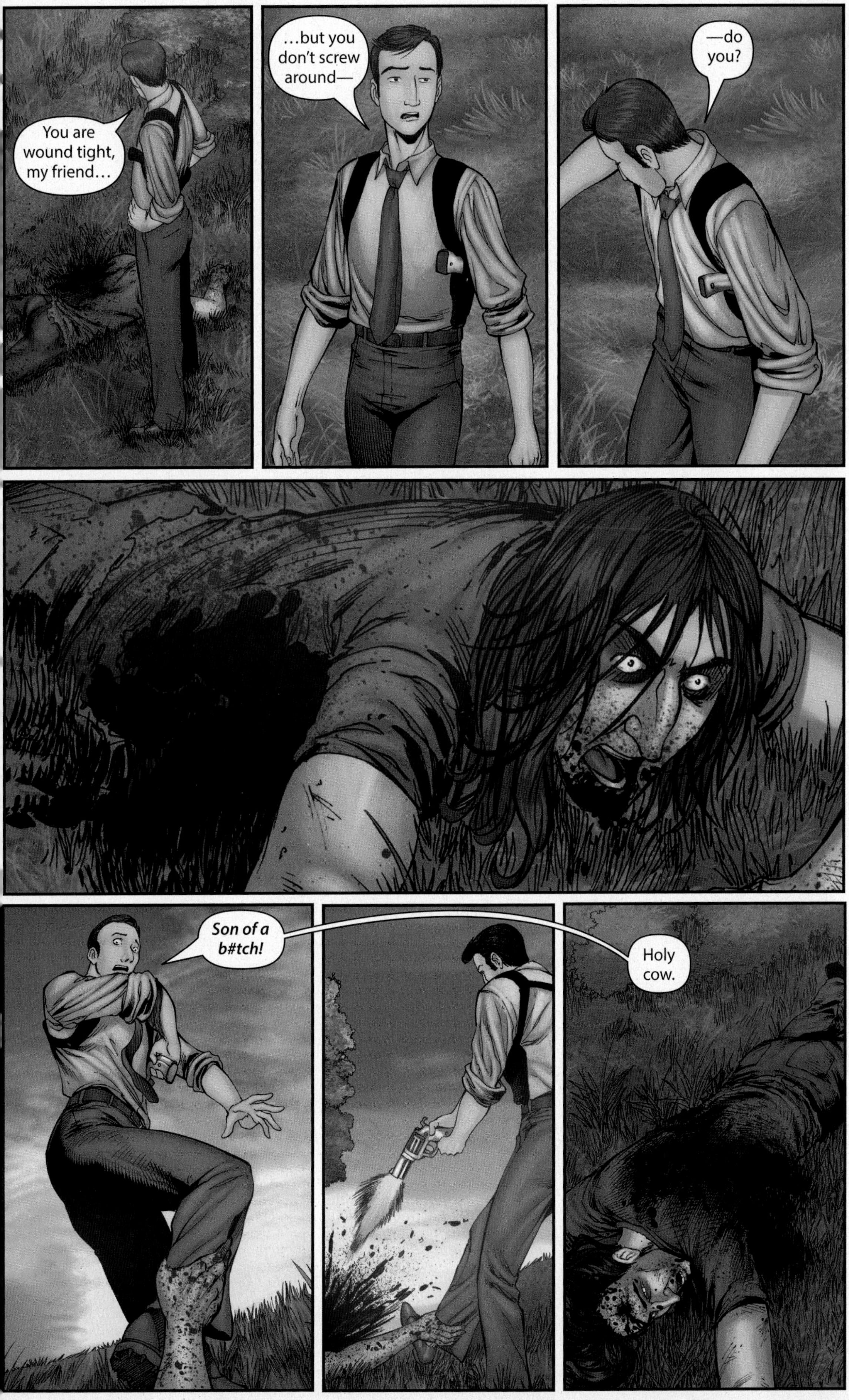
You are wound tight, my friend…
…but you don't screw around—
—do you?
Son of a b#tch!
Holy cow.

2

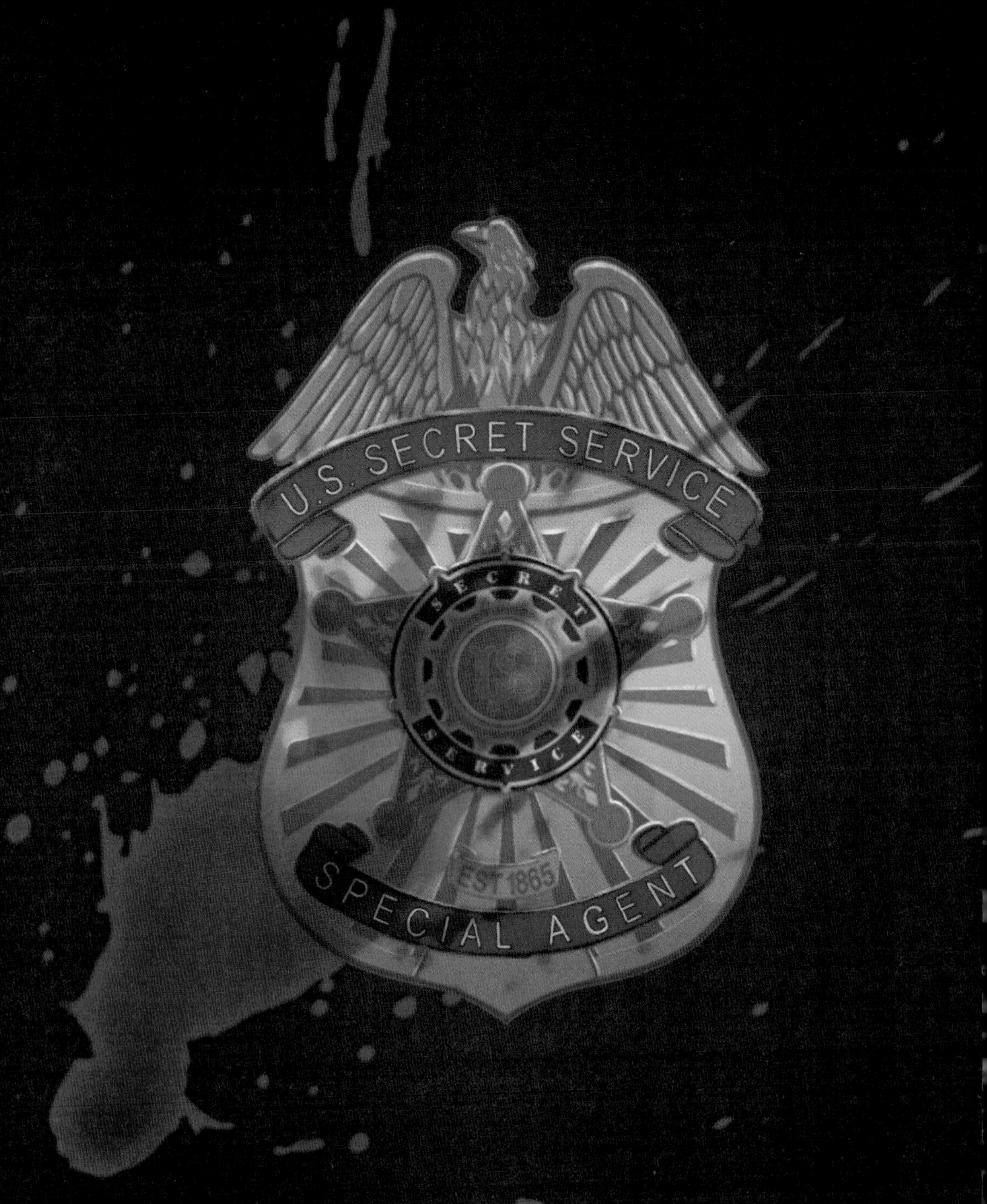
U.S. SECRET SERVICE
SECRET SERVICE
EST 1865
SPECIAL AGENT

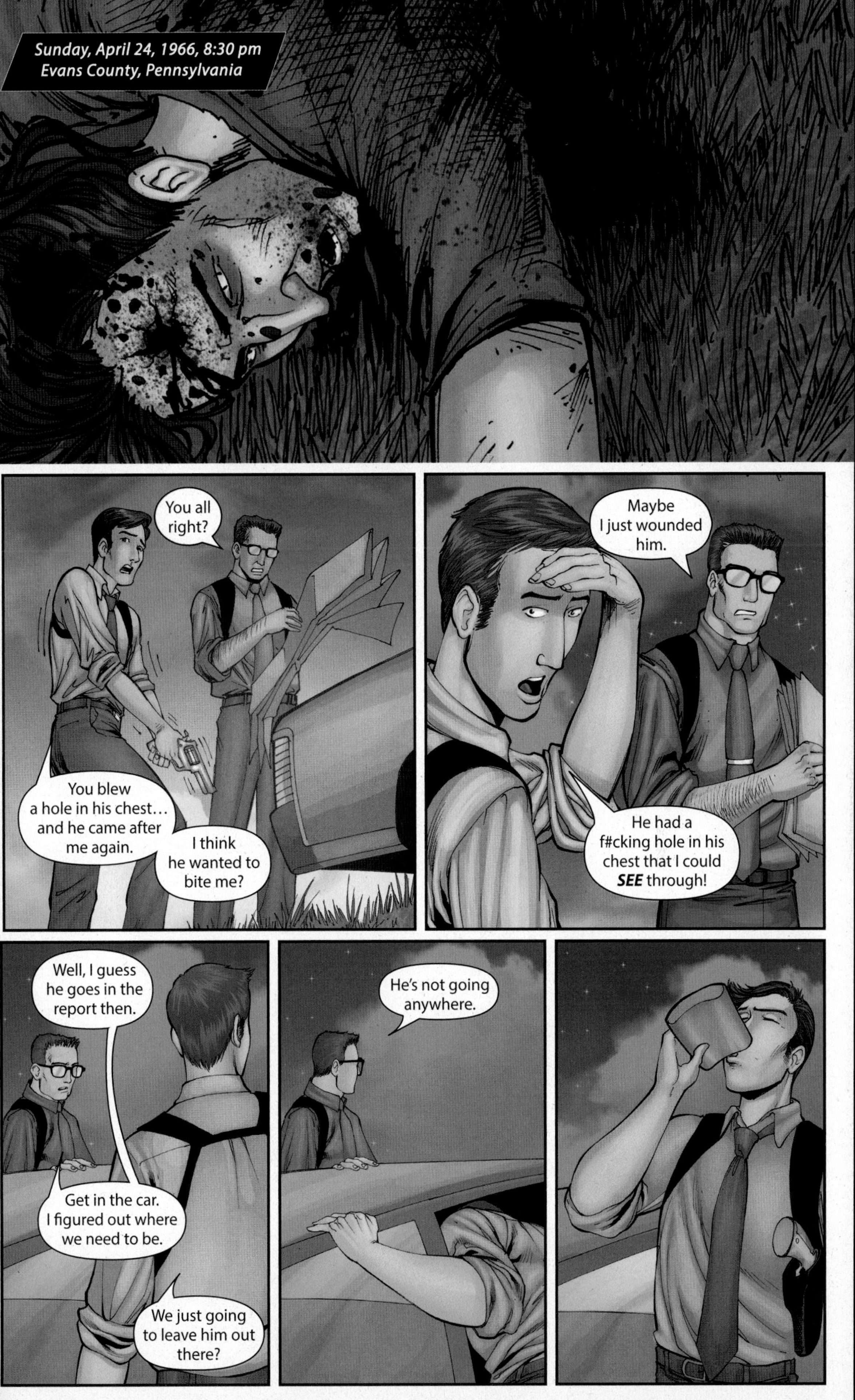
Sunday, April 24, 1966, 8:30 pm
Evans County, Pennsylvania
You all right?
You blew a hole in his chest… and he came after me again.
I think he wanted to bite me?
Maybe I just wounded him.
He had a f#cking hole in his chest that I could ***SEE*** through!
Well, I guess he goes in the report then.
Get in the car. I figured out where we need to be.
We just going to leave him out there?
He's not going anywhere.

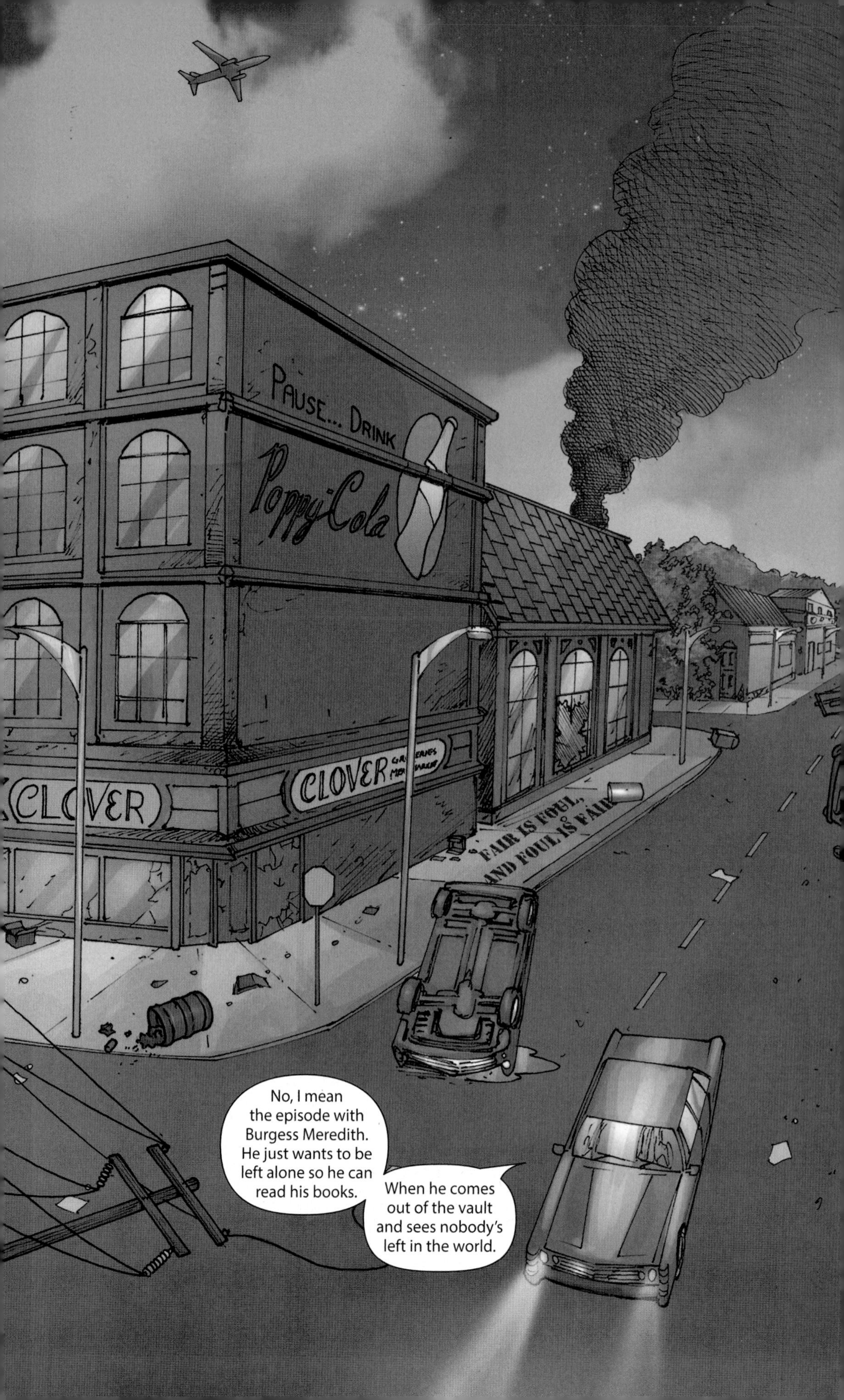

PAUSE... DRINK
Poppy-Cola
CLOVER
CLOVER
FAIR IS FOUL, AND FOUL IS FAIR
No, I mean the episode with Burgess Meredith. He just wants to be left alone so he can read his books.
When he comes out of the vault and sees nobody's left in the world.

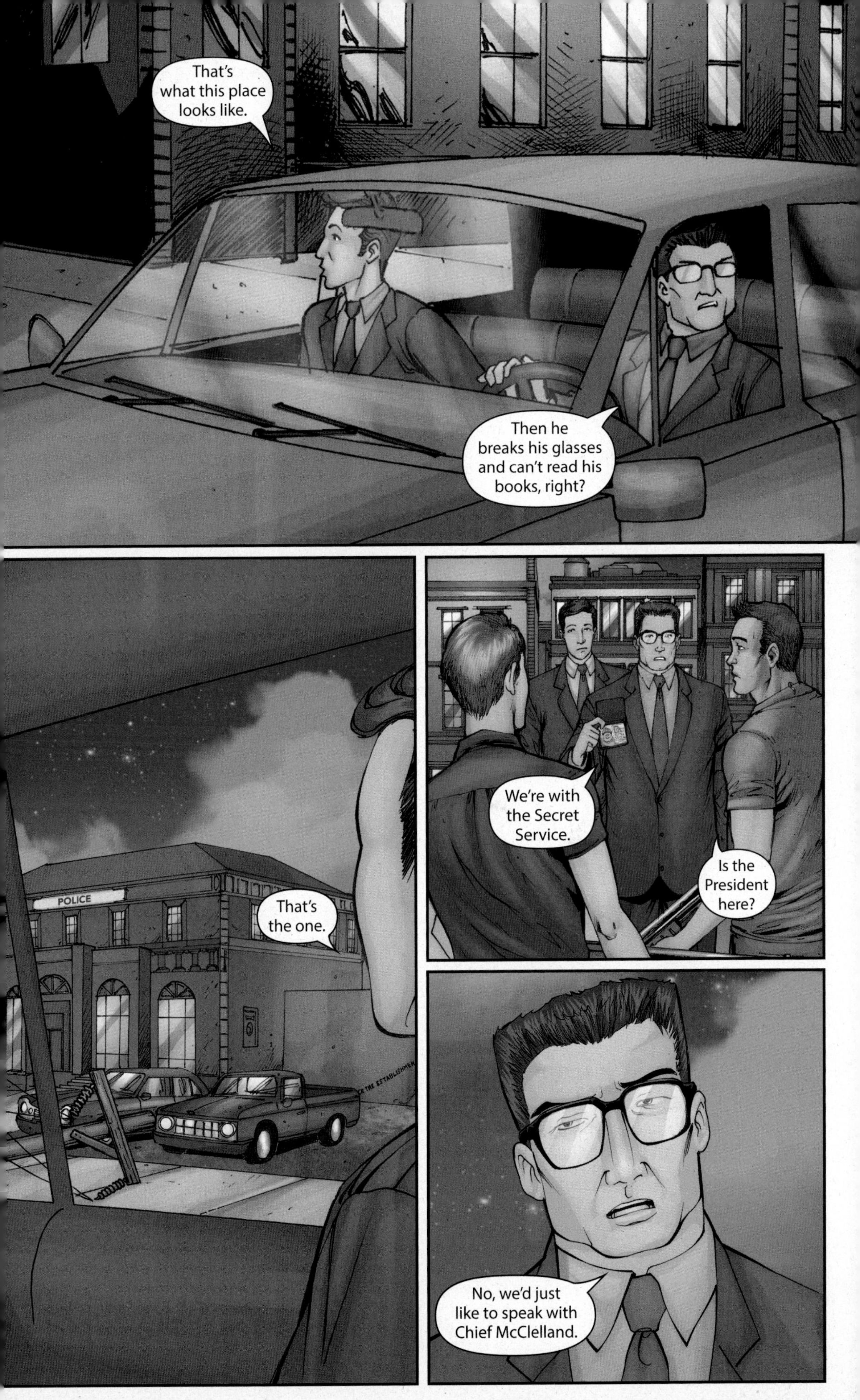
That's what this place looks like.
Then he breaks his glasses and can't read his books, right?
POLICE
That's the one.
We're with the Secret Service.
Is the President here?
No, we'd just like to speak with Chief McClelland.

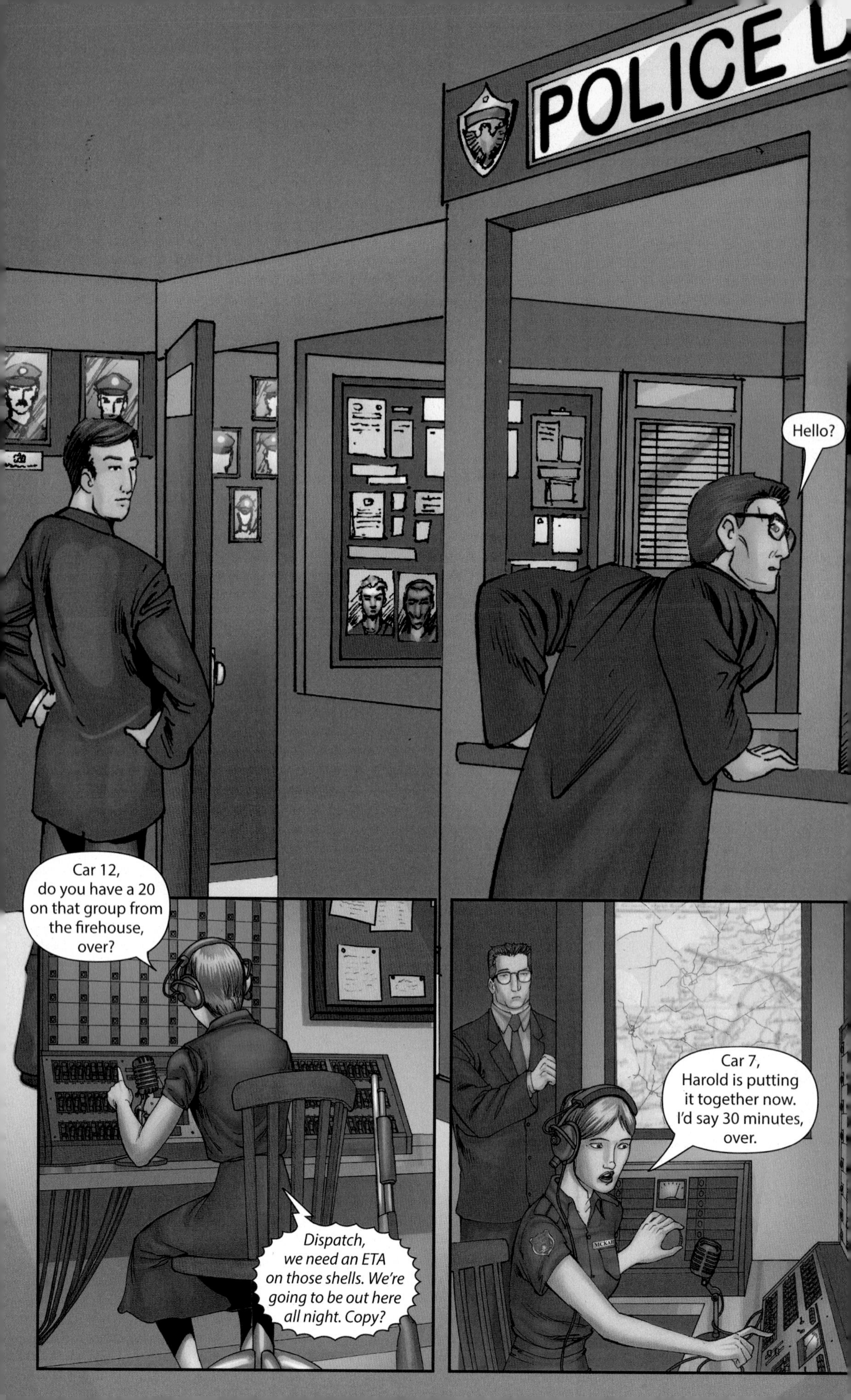
POLICE
Hello?
Car 12,
do you have a 20
on that group from
the firehouse,
over?
Dispatch,
we need an ETA
on those shells. We're
going to be out here
all night. Copy?
Car 7,
Harold is putting
it together now.
I'd say 30 minutes,
over.

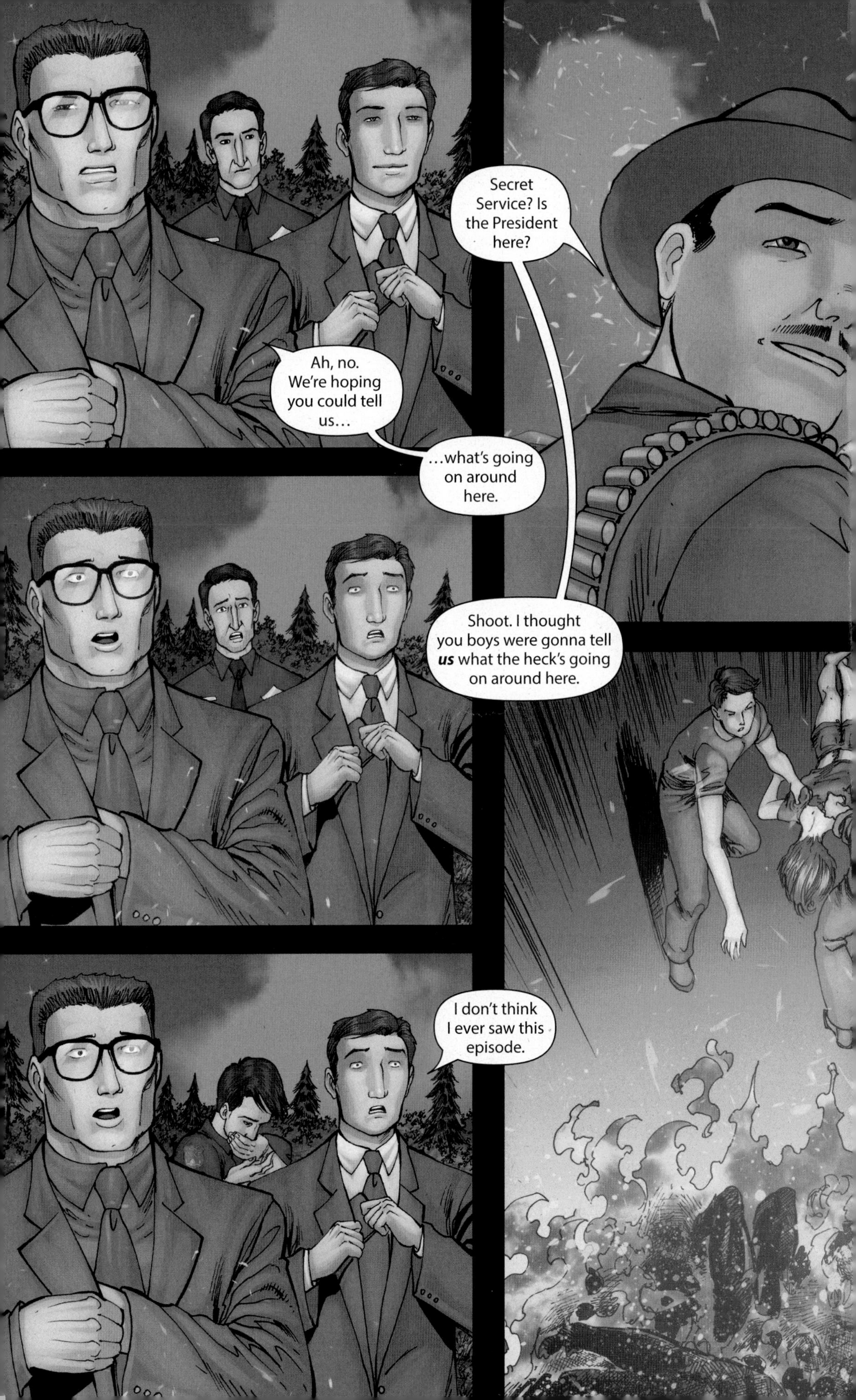
Secret Service? Is the President here?
Ah, no. We're hoping you could tell us…
…what's going on around here.
Shoot. I thought you boys were gonna tell *us* what the heck's going on around here.
I don't think I ever saw this episode.

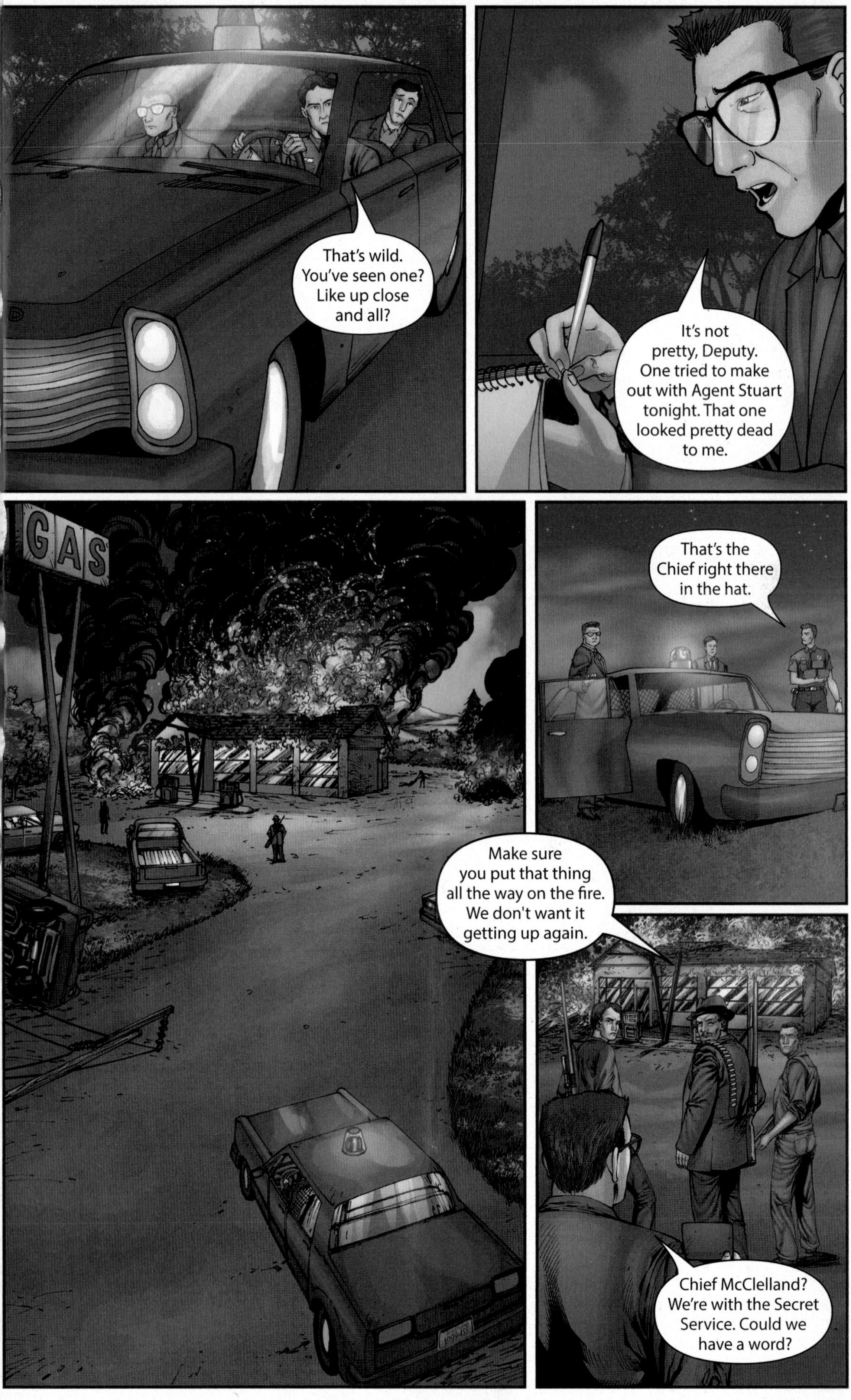
That's wild. You've seen one? Like up close and all?
It's not pretty, Deputy. One tried to make out with Agent Stuart tonight. That one looked pretty dead to me.
GAS
That's the Chief right there in the hat.
Make sure you put that thing all the way on the fire. We don't want it getting up again.
Chief McClelland? We're with the Secret Service. Could we have a word?

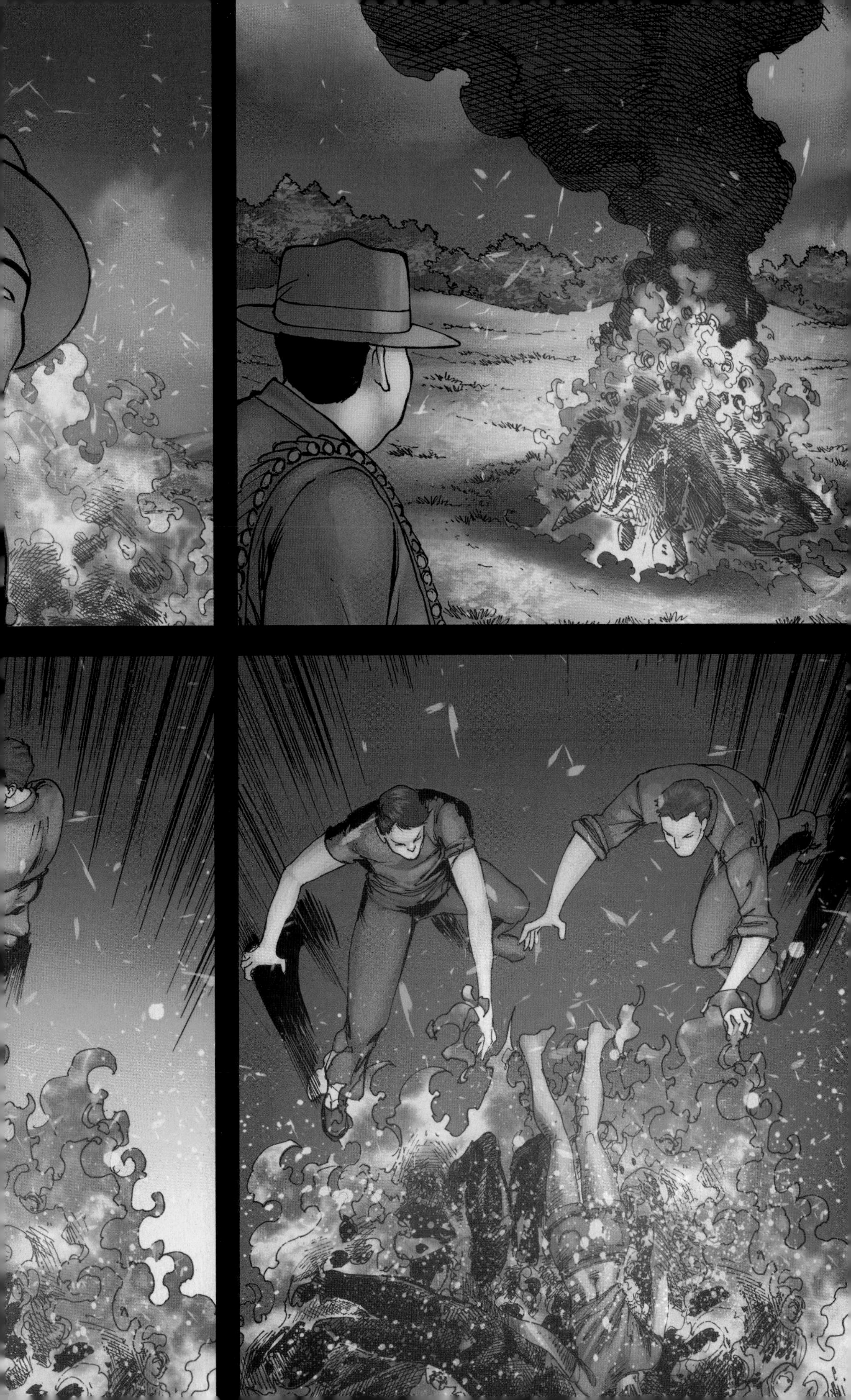

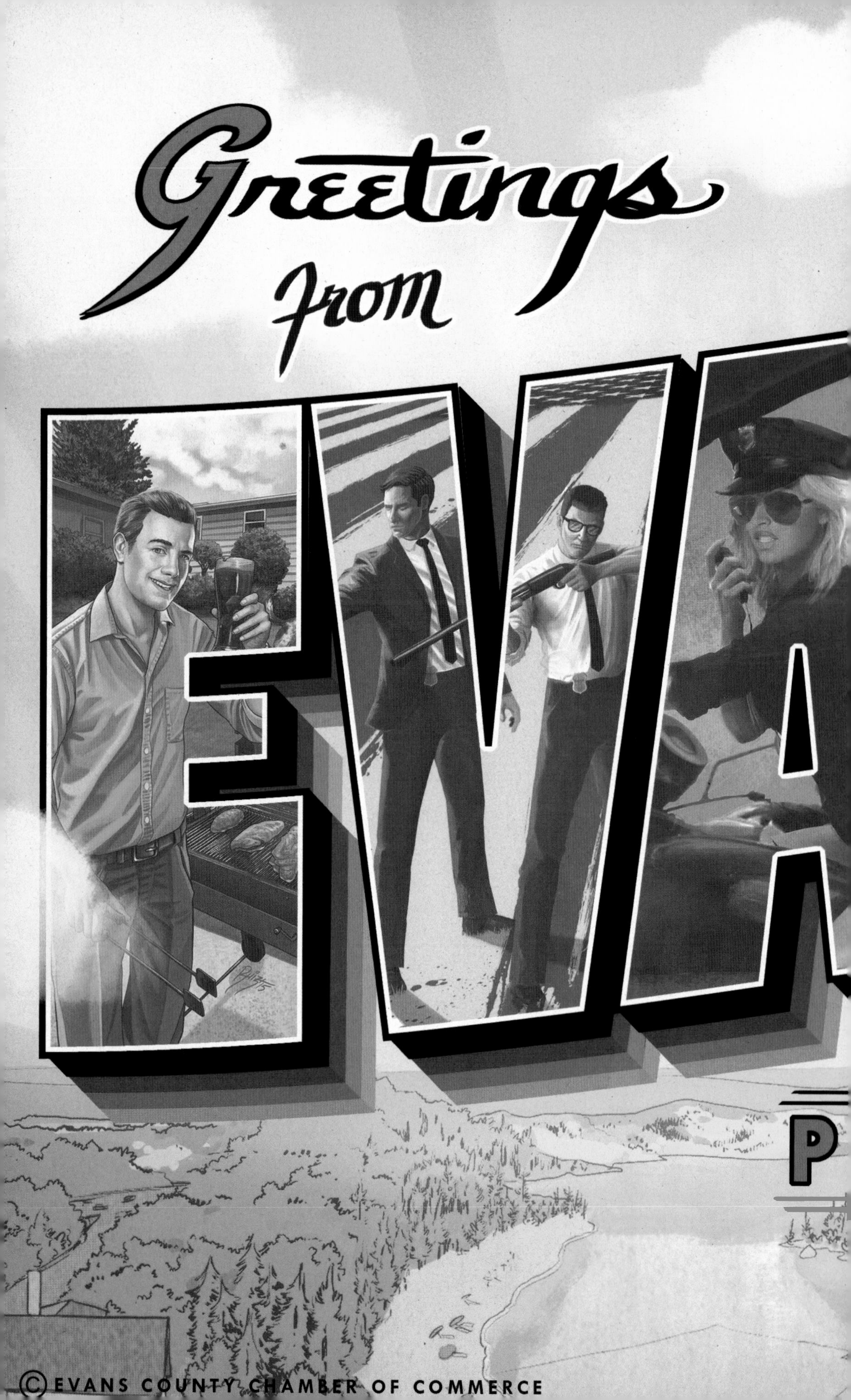
Greetings from
EVA
P
© EVANS COUNTY CHAMBER OF COMMERCE

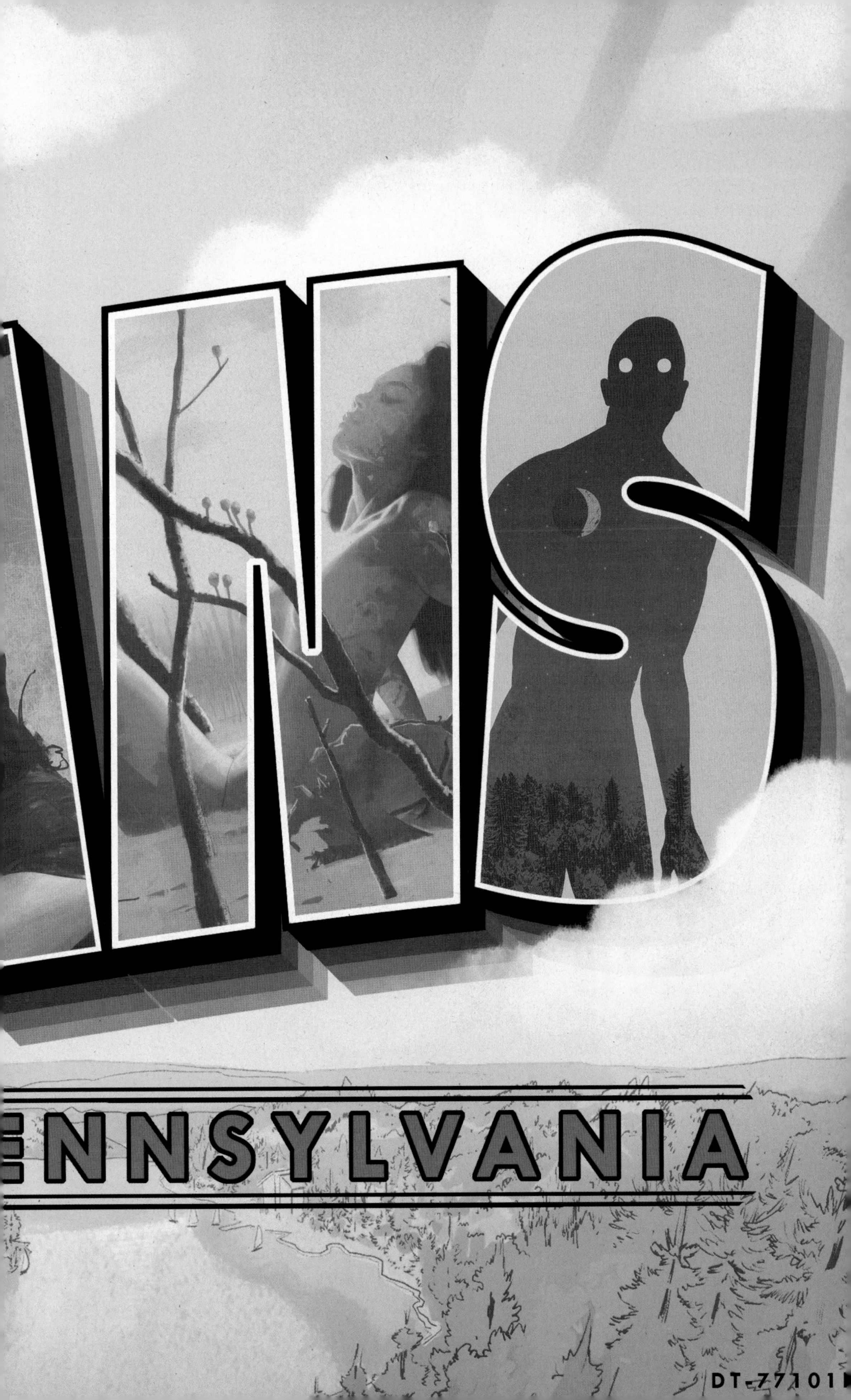
ENNSYLVANIA
DT-77101

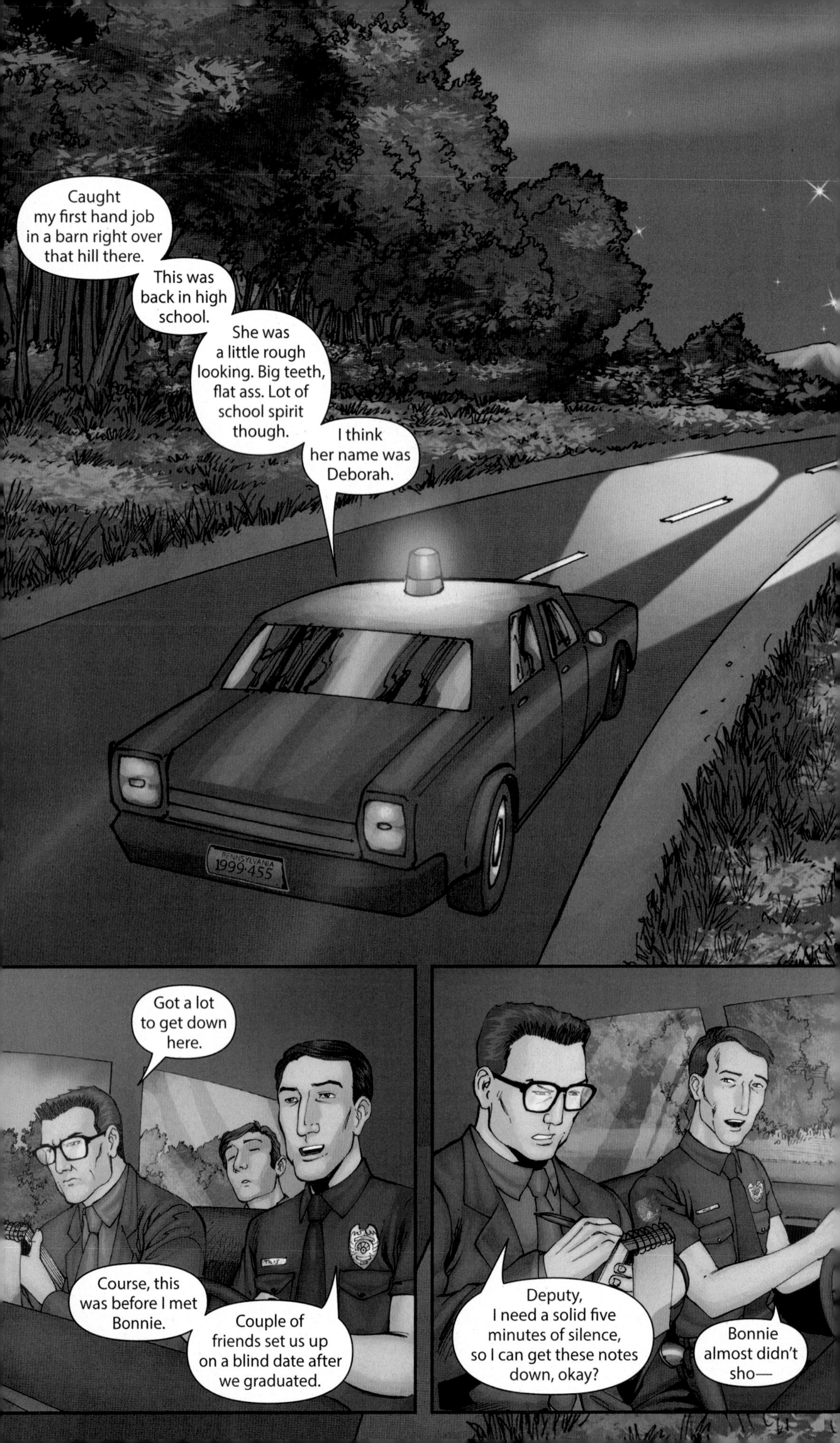
Caught my first hand job in a barn right over that hill there.
This was back in high school.
She was a little rough looking. Big teeth, flat ass. Lot of school spirit though.
I think her name was Deborah.
PENNSYLVANIA 1999·455
Got a lot to get down here.
Course, this was before I met Bonnie.
Couple of friends set us up on a blind date after we graduated.
Deputy, I need a solid five minutes of silence, so I can get these notes down, okay?
Bonnie almost didn't sho—

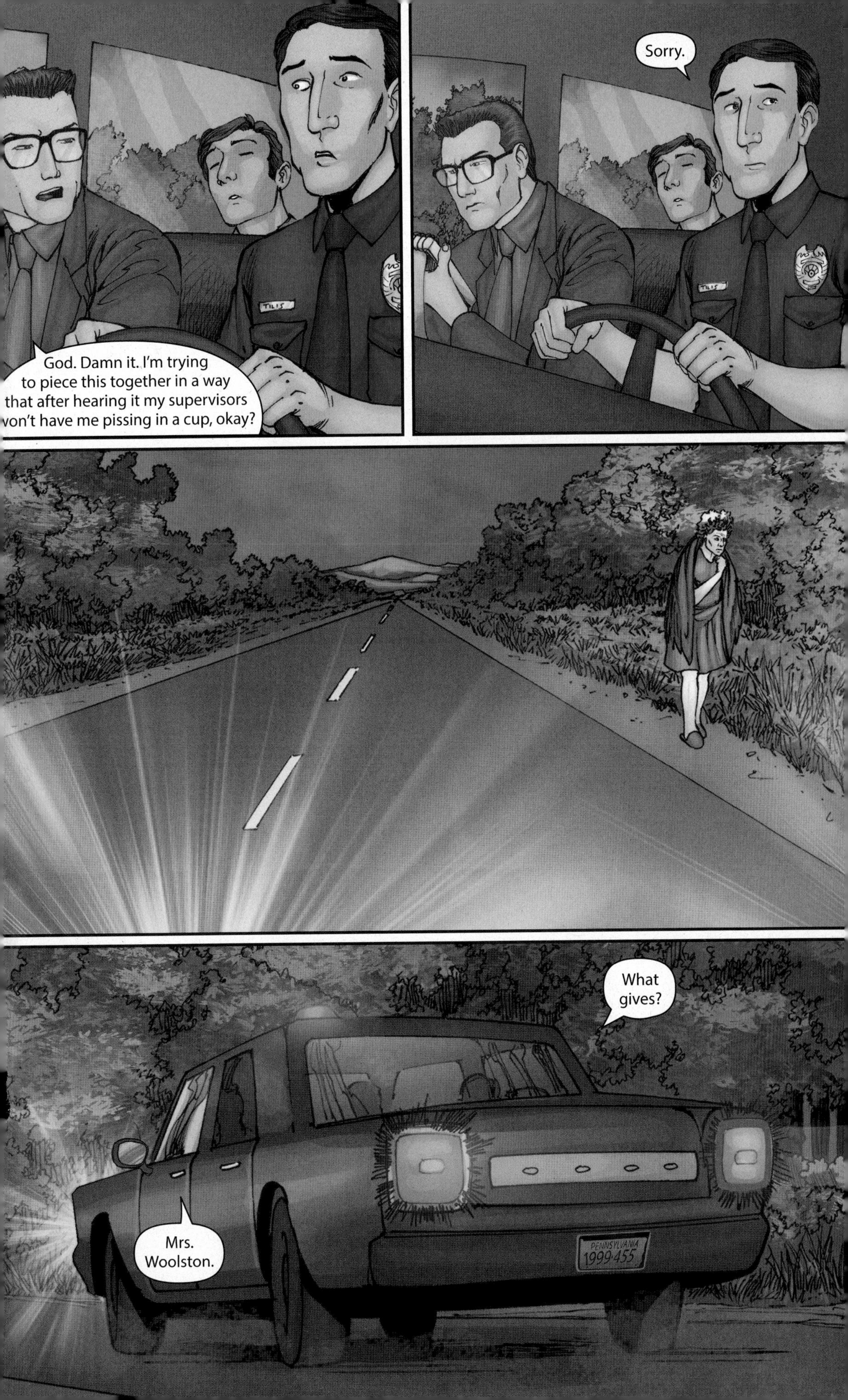
TILIS
God. Damn it. I'm trying to piece this together in a way that after hearing it my supervisors won't have me pissing in a cup, okay?
Sorry.
TILIS
What gives?
Mrs. Woolston.
PENNSYLVANIA
1999-455

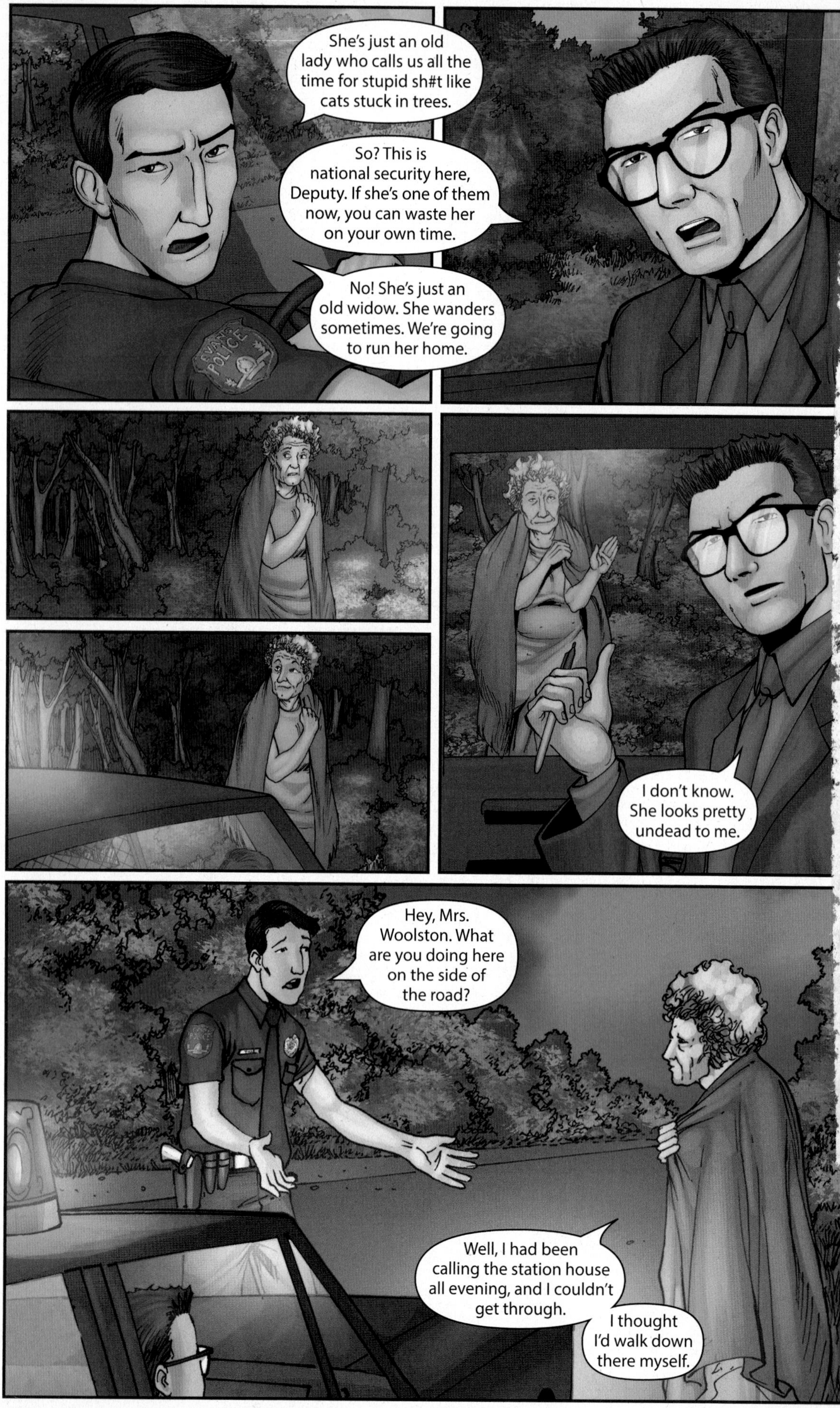
She's just an old lady who calls us all the time for stupid sh#t like cats stuck in trees.
So? This is national security here, Deputy. If she's one of them now, you can waste her on your own time.
No! She's just an old widow. She wanders sometimes. We're going to run her home.
I don't know. She looks pretty undead to me.
Hey, Mrs. Woolston. What are you doing here on the side of the road?
Well, I had been calling the station house all evening, and I couldn't get through.
I thought I'd walk down there myself.

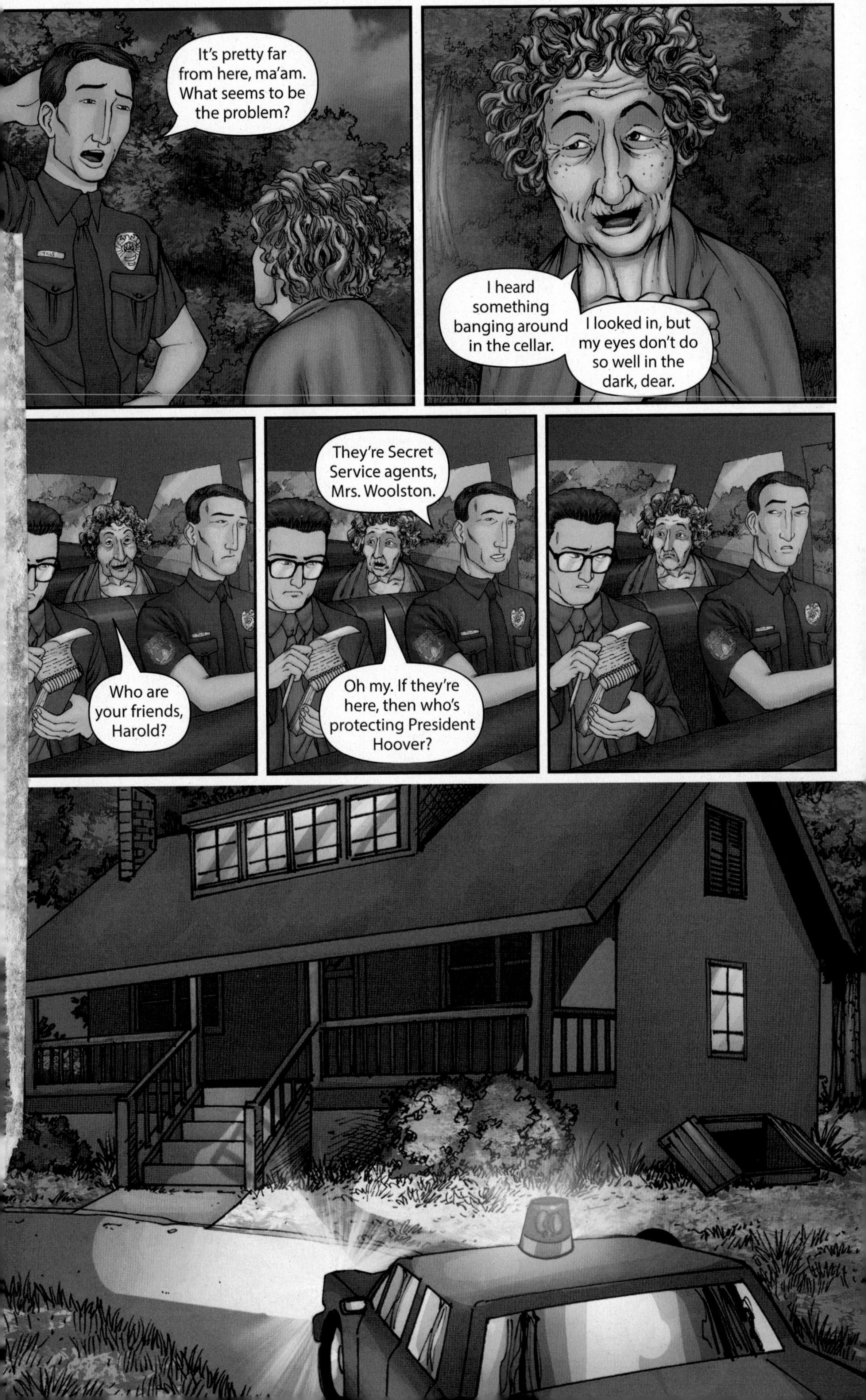
It's pretty far from here, ma'am. What seems to be the problem?
I heard something banging around in the cellar.
I looked in, but my eyes don't do so well in the dark, dear.
Who are your friends, Harold?
They're Secret Service agents, Mrs. Woolston.
Oh my. If they're here, then who's protecting President Hoover?

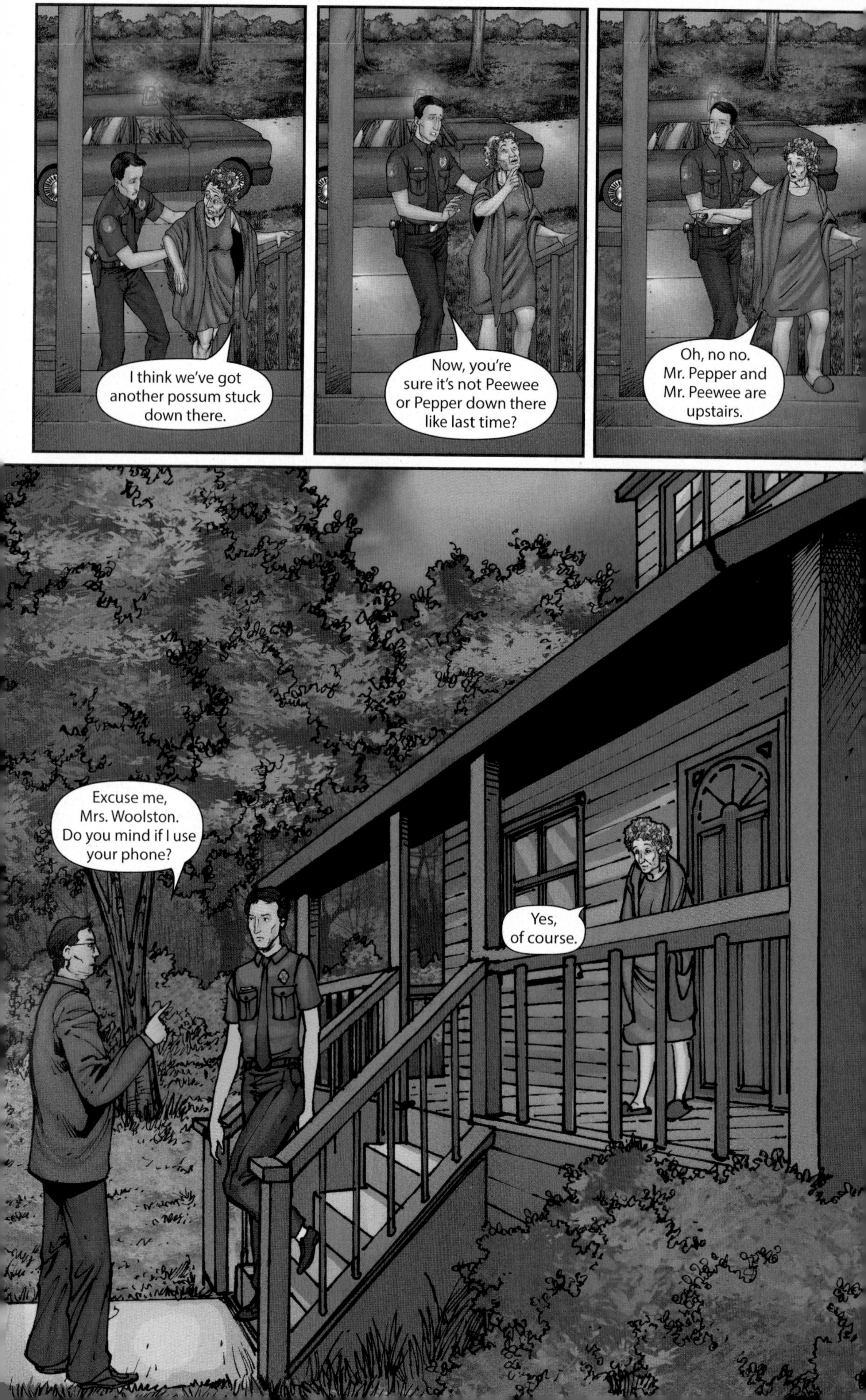
I think we've got another possum stuck down there.
Now, you're sure it's not Peewee or Pepper down there like last time?
Oh, no no. Mr. Pepper and Mr. Peewee are upstairs.
Excuse me, Mrs. Woolston. Do you mind if I use your phone?
Yes, of course.

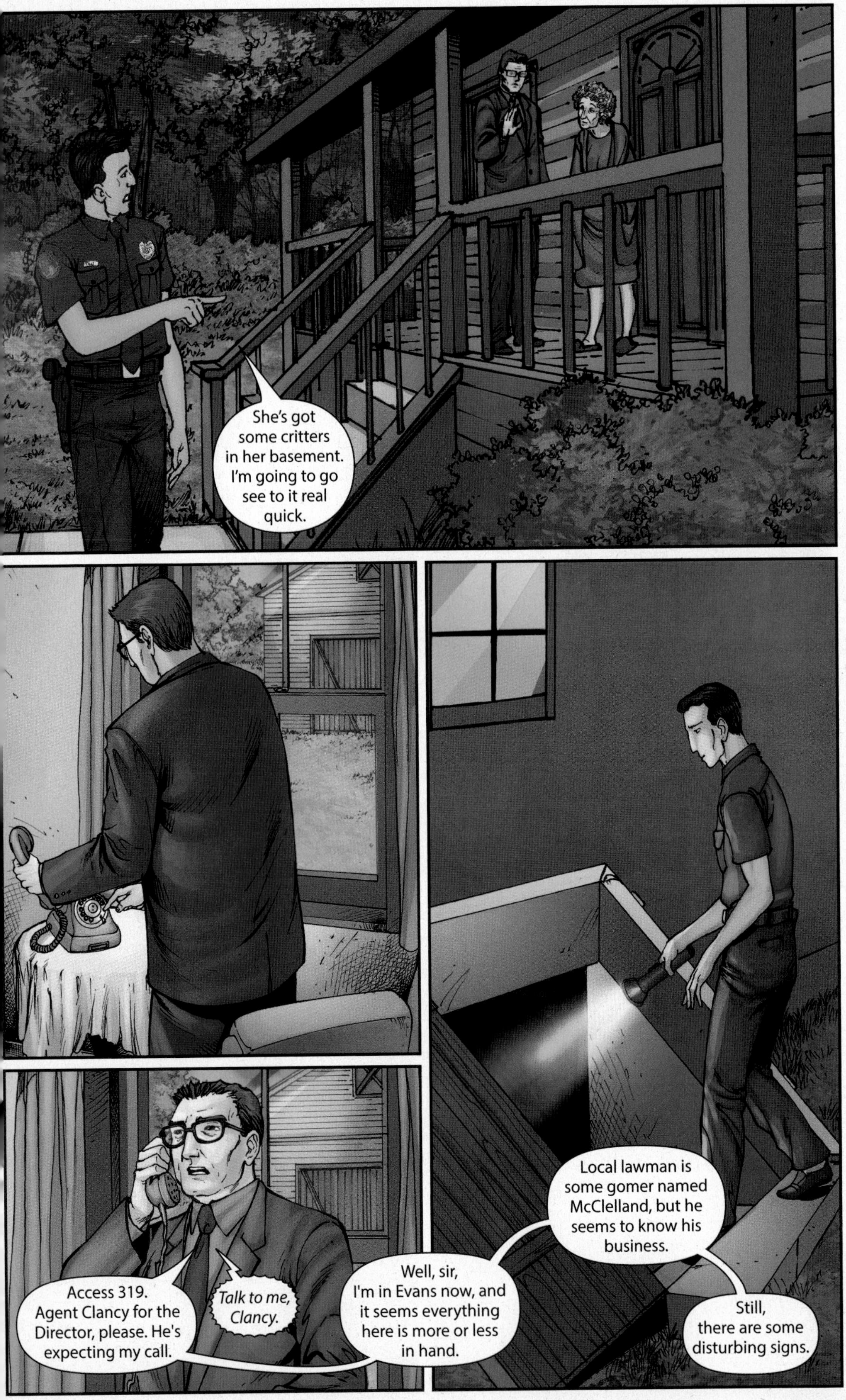
She's got some critters in her basement. I'm going to go see to it real quick.
Access 319. Agent Clancy for the Director, please. He's expecting my call.
Talk to me, Clancy.
Well, sir, I'm in Evans now, and it seems everything here is more or less in hand.
Local lawman is some gomer named McClelland, but he seems to know his business.
Still, there are some disturbing signs.

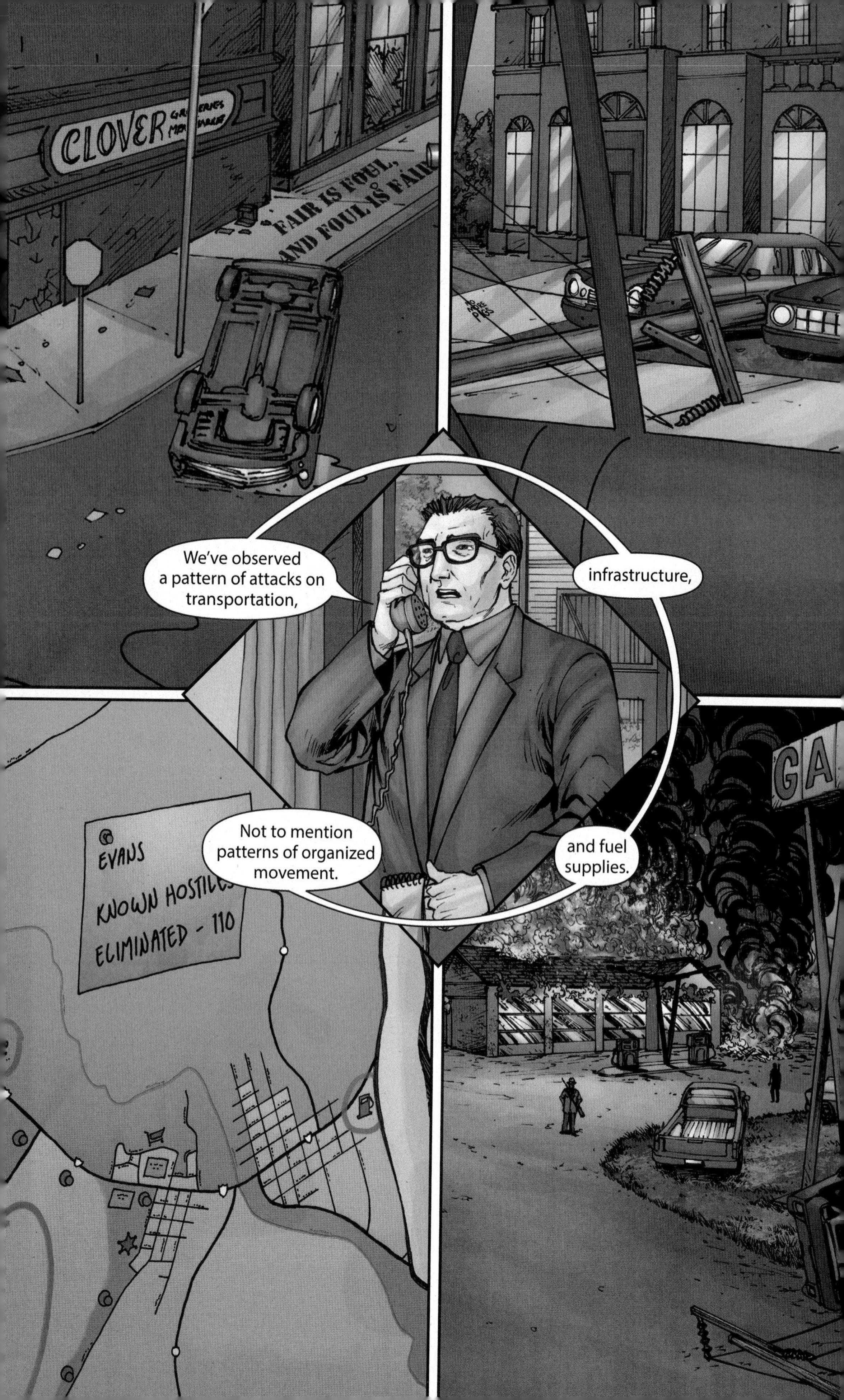
CLOVER
FAIR IS FOUL,
AND FOUL IS FAIR
We've observed a pattern of attacks on transportation,
infrastructure,
and fuel supplies.
Not to mention patterns of organized movement.
EVANS
KNOWN HOSTILES
ELIMINATED - 110
GA

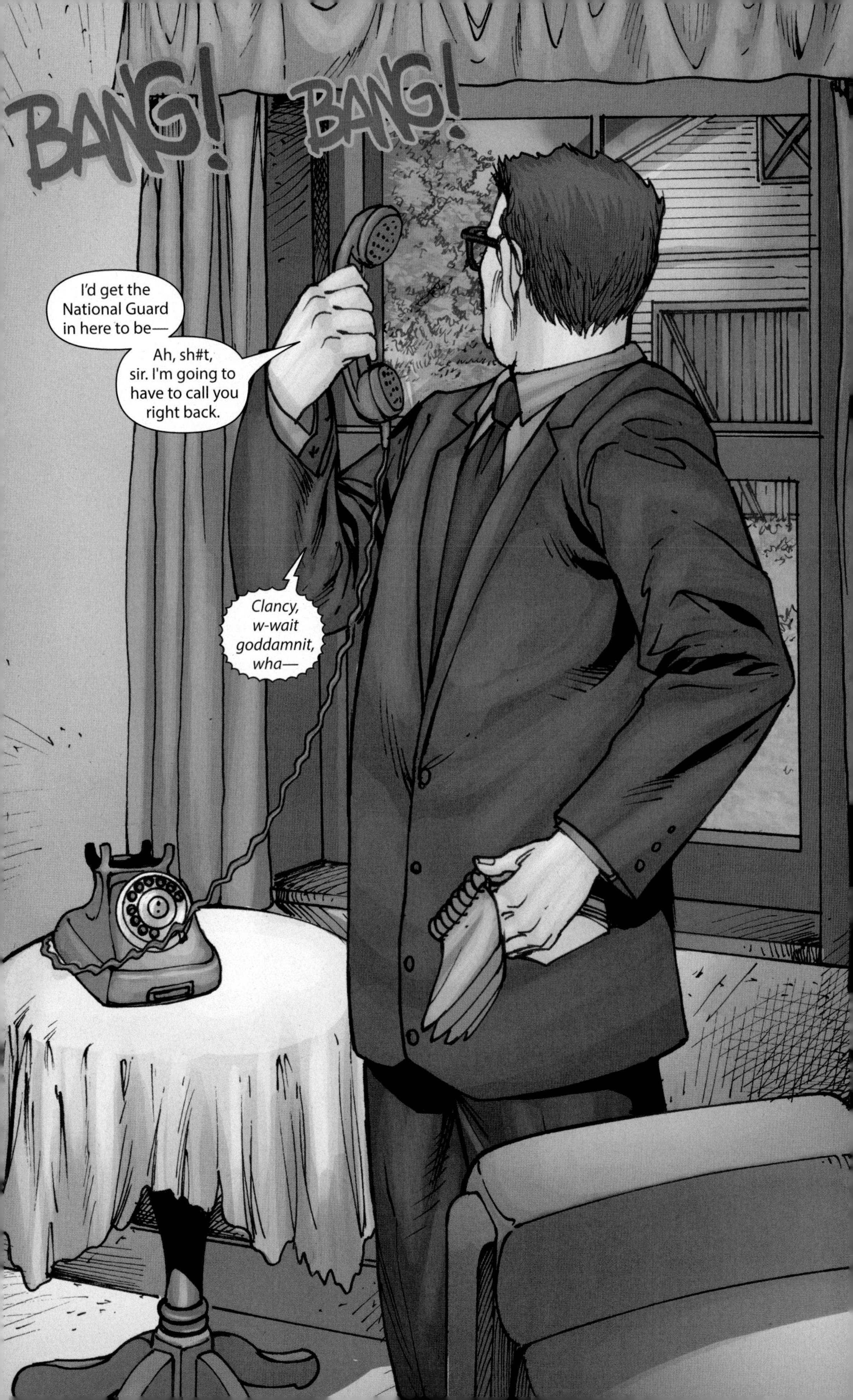
BANG! BANG!
I'd get the National Guard in here to be—
Ah, sh#t, sir. I'm going to have to call you right back.
Clancy, w-wait goddamnit, wha—

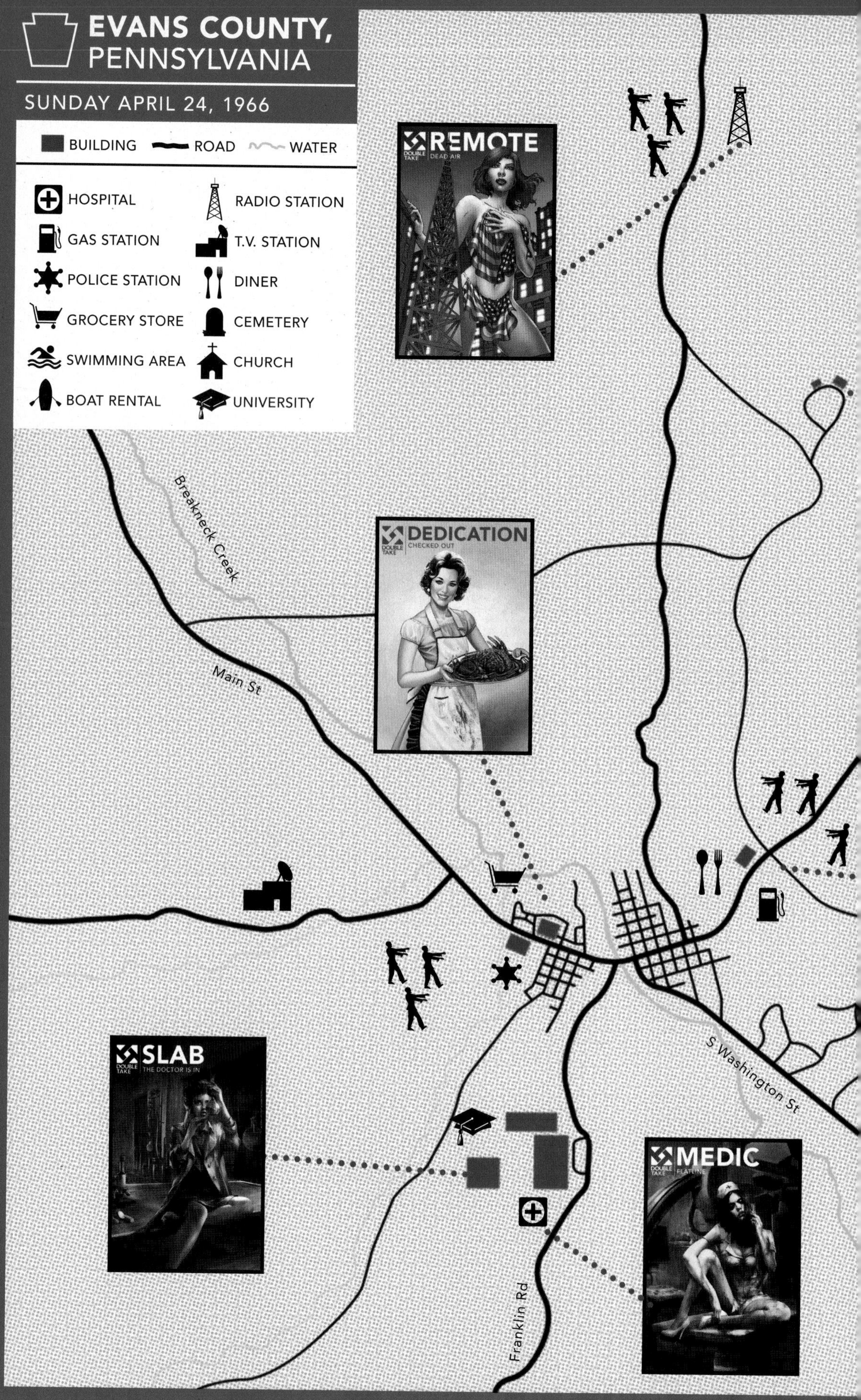
EVANS COUNTY,
PENNSYLVANIA
SUNDAY APRIL 24, 1966
BUILDING
ROAD
WATER
HOSPITAL
RADIO STATION
GAS STATION
T.V. STATION
POLICE STATION
DINER
GROCERY STORE
CEMETERY
SWIMMING AREA
CHURCH
BOAT RENTAL
UNIVERSITY
REMOTE
DOUBLE TAKE
DEAD AIR
DEDICATION
DOUBLE TAKE
CHECKED OUT
Breakneck Creek
Main St
SLAB
DOUBLE TAKE
THE DOCTOR IS IN
S Washington St
MEDIC
DOUBLE TAKE
FLATLINE
Franklin Rd

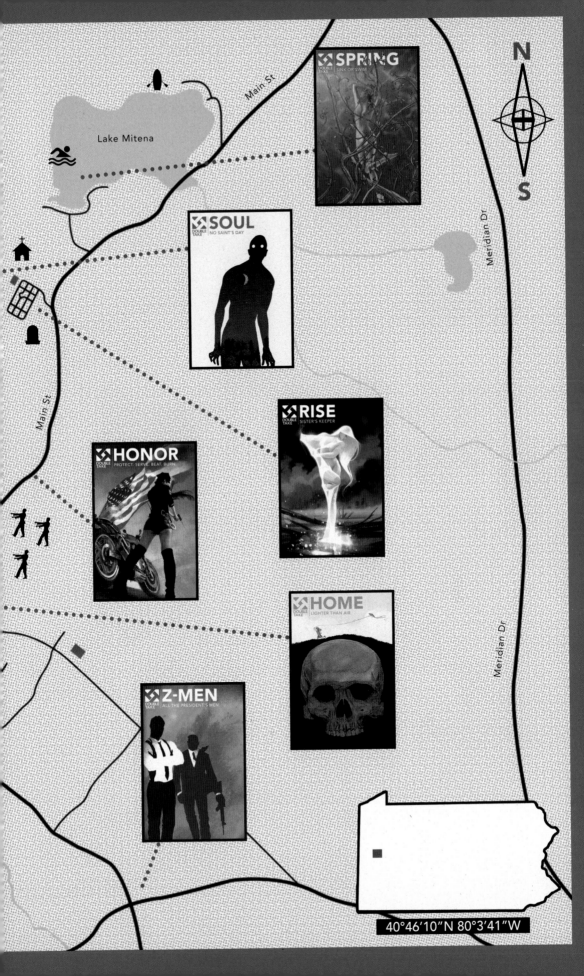

SPRING
DOUBLE TAKE
SINK OR SWIM

SOUL
DOUBLE TAKE
NO SAINT'S DAY

RISE
DOUBLE TAKE
SISTER'S KEEPER

HONOR
DOUBLE TAKE
PROTECT. SERVE. BEAT. BURN.

HOME
DOUBLE TAKE
LIGHTER THAN AIR

Z-MEN
DOUBLE TAKE
ALL THE PRESIDENT'S MEN

Lake Mitena

Main St

Meridian Dr

Meridian Dr

N

S

40°46'10"N 80°3'41"W

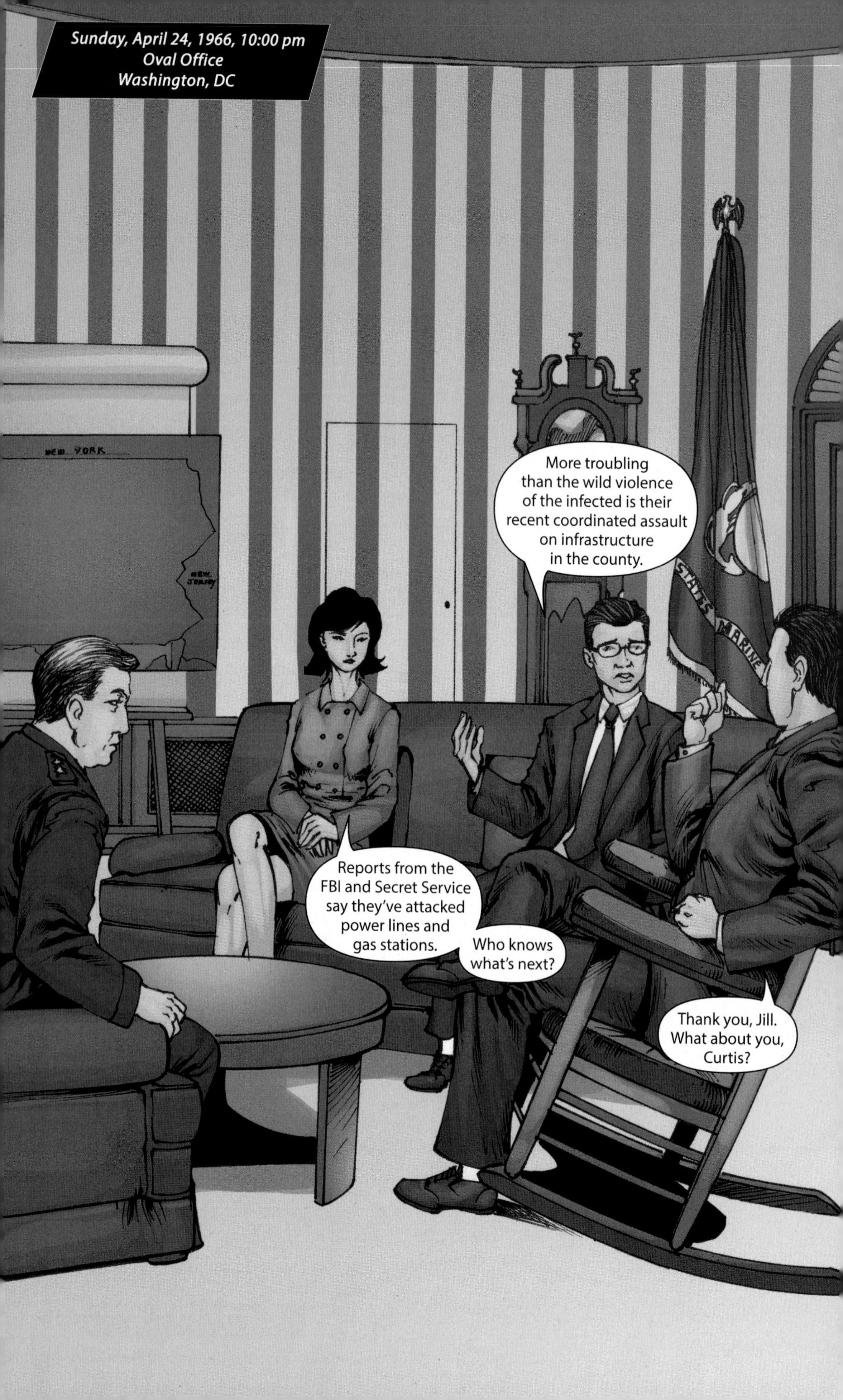
Sunday, April 24, 1966, 10:00 pm
Oval Office
Washington, DC
NEW YORK
NEW JERSEY
More troubling than the wild violence of the infected is their recent coordinated assault on infrastructure in the county.
Reports from the FBI and Secret Service say they've attacked power lines and gas stations.
Who knows what's next?
Thank you, Jill. What about you, Curtis?

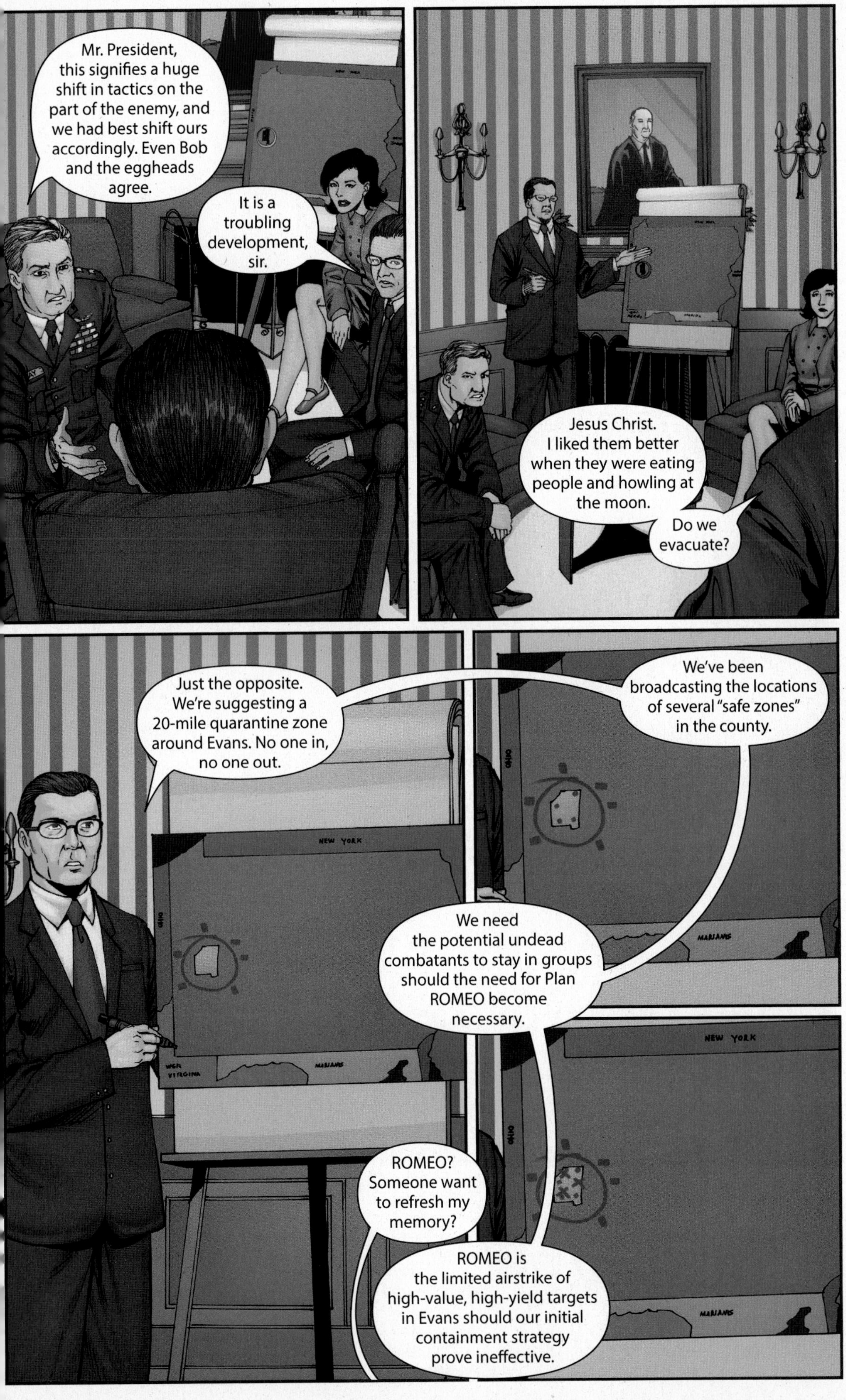

Mr. President, this signifies a huge shift in tactics on the part of the enemy, and we had best shift ours accordingly. Even Bob and the eggheads agree.
It is a troubling development, sir.
Jesus Christ. I liked them better when they were eating people and howling at the moon.
Do we evacuate?
Just the opposite. We're suggesting a 20-mile quarantine zone around Evans. No one in, no one out.
NEW YORK
We've been broadcasting the locations of several "safe zones" in the county.
We need the potential undead combatants to stay in groups should the need for Plan ROMEO become necessary.
NEW YORK
ROMEO? Someone want to refresh my memory?
ROMEO is the limited airstrike of high-value, high-yield targets in Evans should our initial containment strategy prove ineffective.

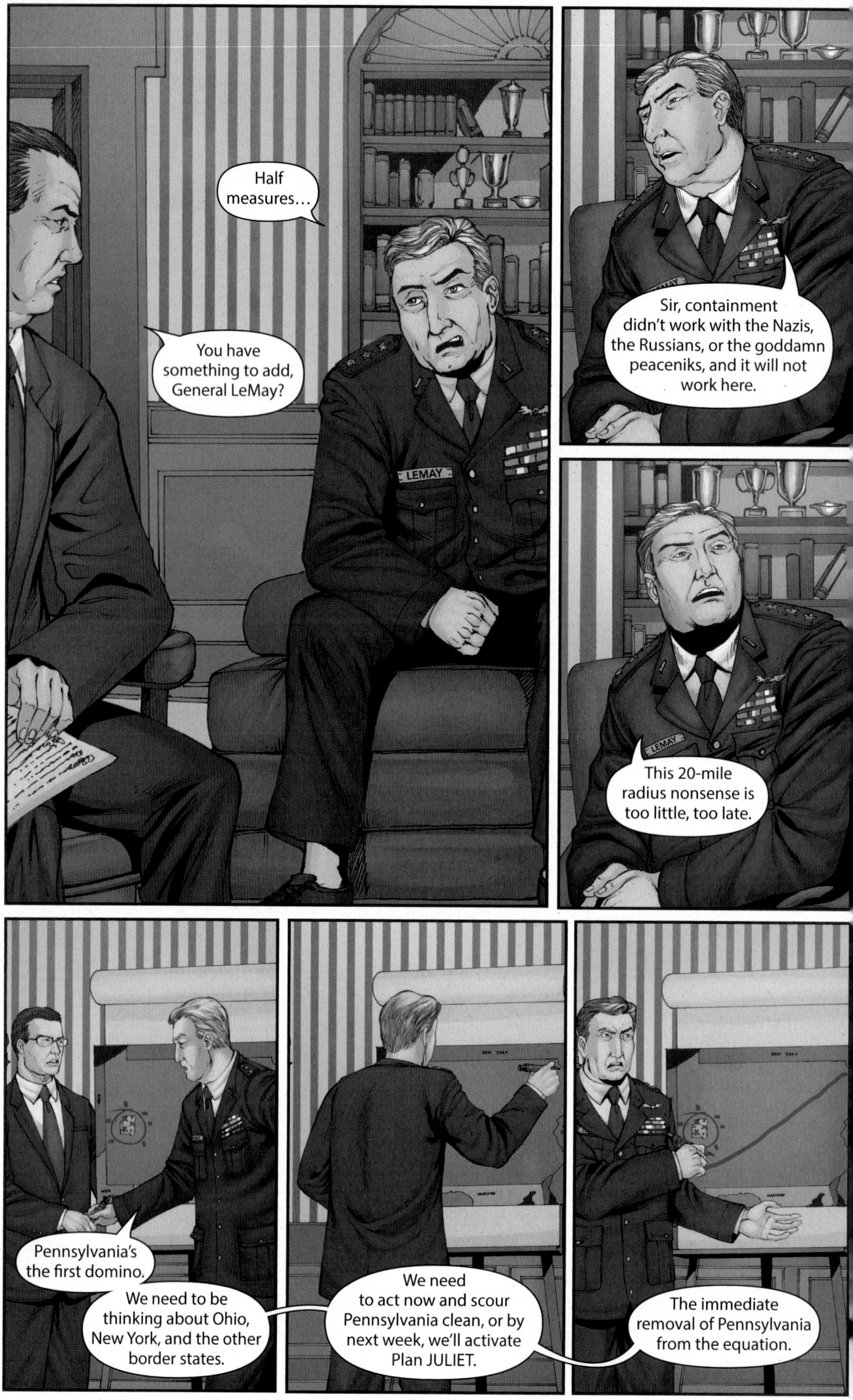
Half measures…
You have something to add, General LeMay?
LEMAY
LEMAY
Sir, containment didn't work with the Nazis, the Russians, or the goddamn peaceniks, and it will not work here.
LEMAY
This 20-mile radius nonsense is too little, too late.
Pennsylvania's the first domino.
We need to be thinking about Ohio, New York, and the other border states.
We need to act now and scour Pennsylvania clean, or by next week, we'll activate Plan JULIET.
The immediate removal of Pennsylvania from the equation.

THE SECRET SERVICE

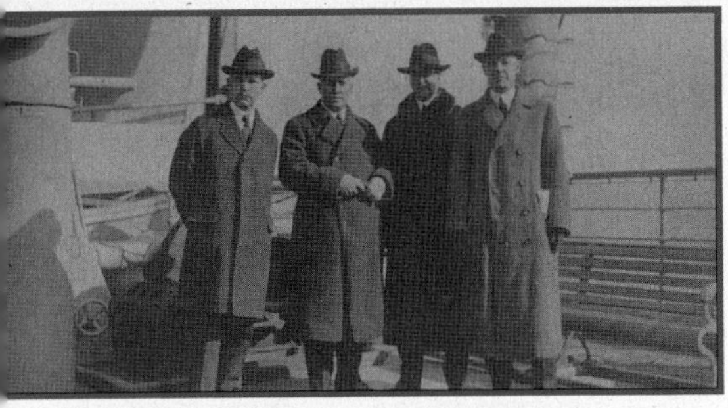

The President's Secret Service men (1900)

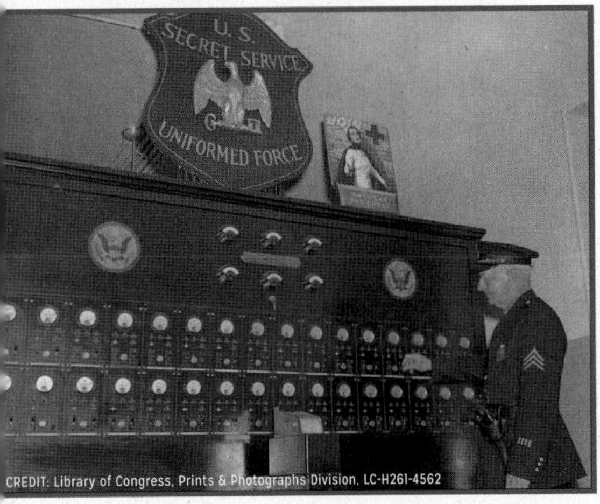
U.S.
SECRET SERVICE
UNIFORMED FORCE

CREDIT: Library of Congress, Prints & Photographs Division, LC-H261-4562

Alarm system of White House Police (1938)

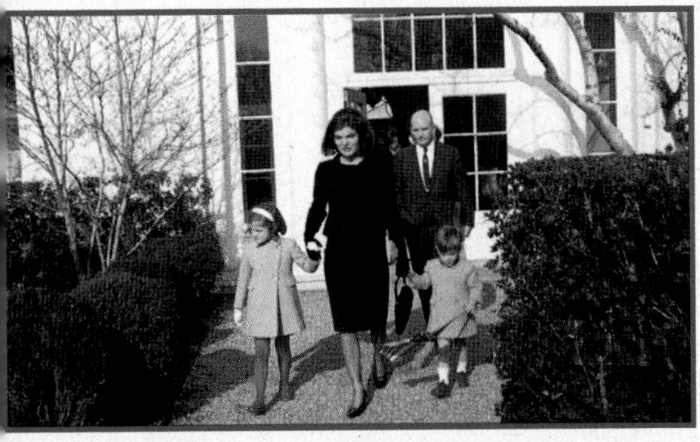

Jackie Kennedy leaving the White House (1963)

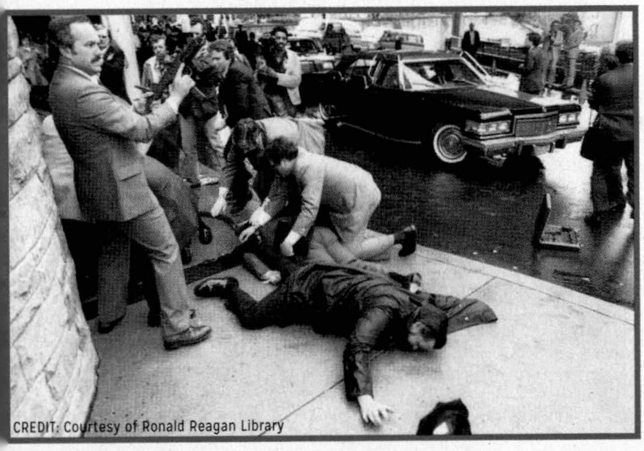

CREDIT: Courtesy of Ronald Reagan Library

Reagan assassination attempt (1981)

On February 25, 1863, President Abraham Lincoln signed the National Banking Act, which, for the first time in American history, established the federal dollar as the sole United States currency.

Prior to the Civil War, private and state banks, not the federal government, issued paper money. Thousands of entities, printing tens of thousands of denominations, created an environment in which counterfeiting ran rampant. As was the case with alcohol prohibition in the 1920s and marijuana prohibition today, rampant crime engendered widespread corruption of law enforcement agencies.

In response, on April 14, 1865, President Lincoln established the Secret Service to combat local counterfeiting with federal agents.

On the same day, President Lincoln was assassinated; protecting the President was not in the Secret Service's charter.

Spring 1894 – Secret Service thwarted a plot to assassinate President Grover Cleveland.

September 14, 1901 – President William McKinley was assassinated.

January 1902 – Secret Service assumed full-time responsibility for protection of the President; only two men were assigned to full-time White House Detail.

November 22, 1963 – The Secret Service failed to prevent the assassination of President John F. Kennedy.

March 30, 1981 – The Secret Service prevented President Reagan's assassination.

April 11, 2012 – Eight agents were fired following allegations that they had solicited prostitutes while on duty in Colombia.

March 18, 2015 – Agents foiled an Aryan supremacist plot to assassinate President Barack Obama.

April 13, 2015 – For the second time in eight months, a toddler breached the White House perimeter.

AN EXPERIMENTAL SUBSCRIPTION TO THE **2T BOOK-OF-THE-DECADE CLUB** WILL DEMONSTRATE HOW DEVOT
MEMBERSHIP IS THE BEST INSURANCE AGAINST MISSING OUT ON THE BEST BOOKS FROM BYGONE DECADES.

YOUR CHOICE OF ANY 3 FOR ONLY $1

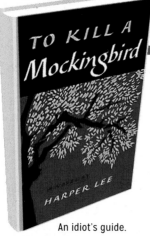

TO KILL A
Mockingbird
HARPER LEE

An idiot's guide.

Cat's Cradle
a novel by KURT VONNEGUT, JR.

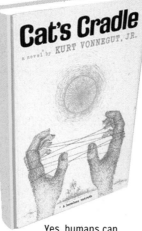

Yes, humans can cause climate change.

The Godfather
A NOVEL
by
Mario Puzo

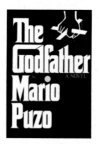

Guaranteed to include zero references to *The Godfather III*.

SLAUGHTERHOUSE-FIVE
OR
The Children's Crusade
A NEW NOVEL BY
KURT VONNEGUT, JR.

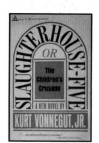

The most hilarious book about firebombing that you'll ever read.

The Giving Tree

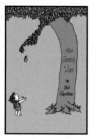

An illustrated guide to conquering nature.

Tom Wolfe
The Electric Kool-Aid Acid Test

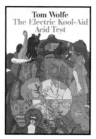

Makes for great reading on any trip.

THE AGONY AND THE ECSTASY
the biographical novel of MICHELANGELO
IRVING STONE

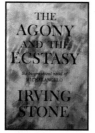

50 shades of marble.

Please enroll me as a member. I am to receive for $1 the three books I've selected below. I will pay $300 for each book-of-the-decade I buy after. I agree to purchase at least 6 books-of the-decade from 2T each year I am a member. I may cancel the subscription only if I pay 2T $1 million and give 2T the soul of my firstborn child.

SELECT THREE BOOKS ☐ ☐ ☐

NAME ____________________
Please do not actually

ADDRESS ____________________
fill this out and send it in.

CITY ________ POSTAL ZONE No. ________ STATE ________

Valley of the Dolls
A NOVEL BY
Jacqueline Susann

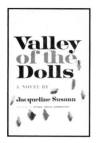

Downers are a girl's best friend.

Portnoy's Complaint
Philip Roth

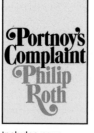

Includes new liver recipe.

JAMES AND THE GIANT PEACH
by ROALD DAHL

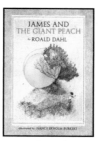

Story of the first GMO.

MAIL TO:
2T BOOK-OF-THE-DECADE CLUB
38 W. 39TH STREET 2ND FLOOR,
NEW YORK, NY 10018

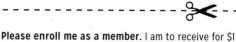

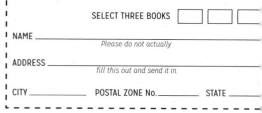

Signing and mailing the coupon enrolls you into the 2T Book of the Decade Club ("2T Club") for life. You start with three books of your choice for $1 but thereafter are obligated to purchase at least six books-of-the-decade for $300 each within a twelve-month period after you enroll. You do not have the right to cancel your membership at any point until you have given us $1 million and the soul of your firstborn child, plus postage, handling, and any other expenses 2T feels like tacking onto your bill. We understand money can be tight so we accept payment plans. Any payment plans will be subject to a 15 percent interest to account for inflation and the ever depreciating value of your child's soul as your child ages. Please note, under no circumstances will 2T actually send you any books.

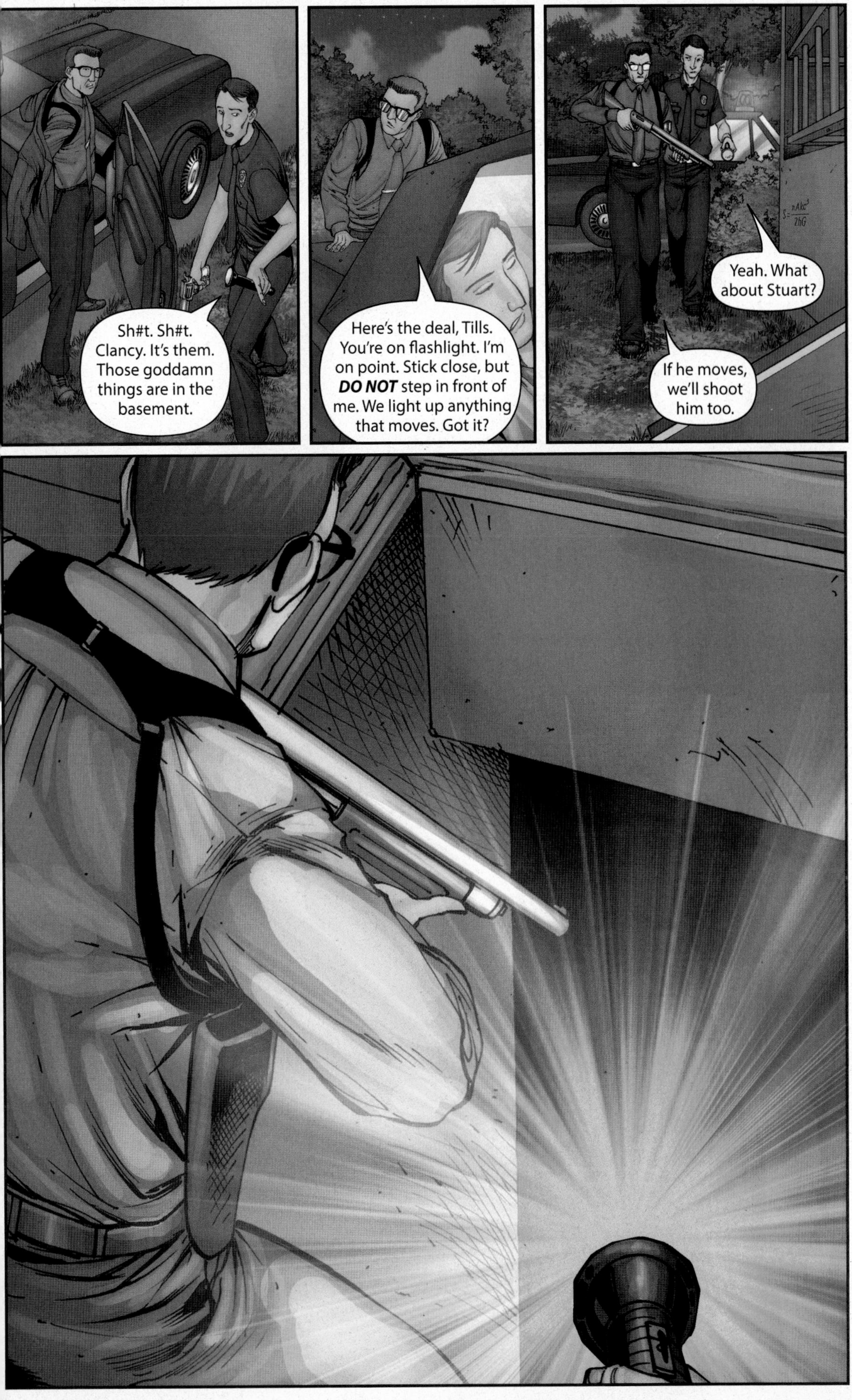
Sh#t. Sh#t. Clancy. It's them. Those goddamn things are in the basement.
Here's the deal, Tills. You're on flashlight. I'm on point. Stick close, but ***DO NOT*** step in front of me. We light up anything that moves. Got it?
Yeah. What about Stuart?
If he moves, we'll shoot him too.

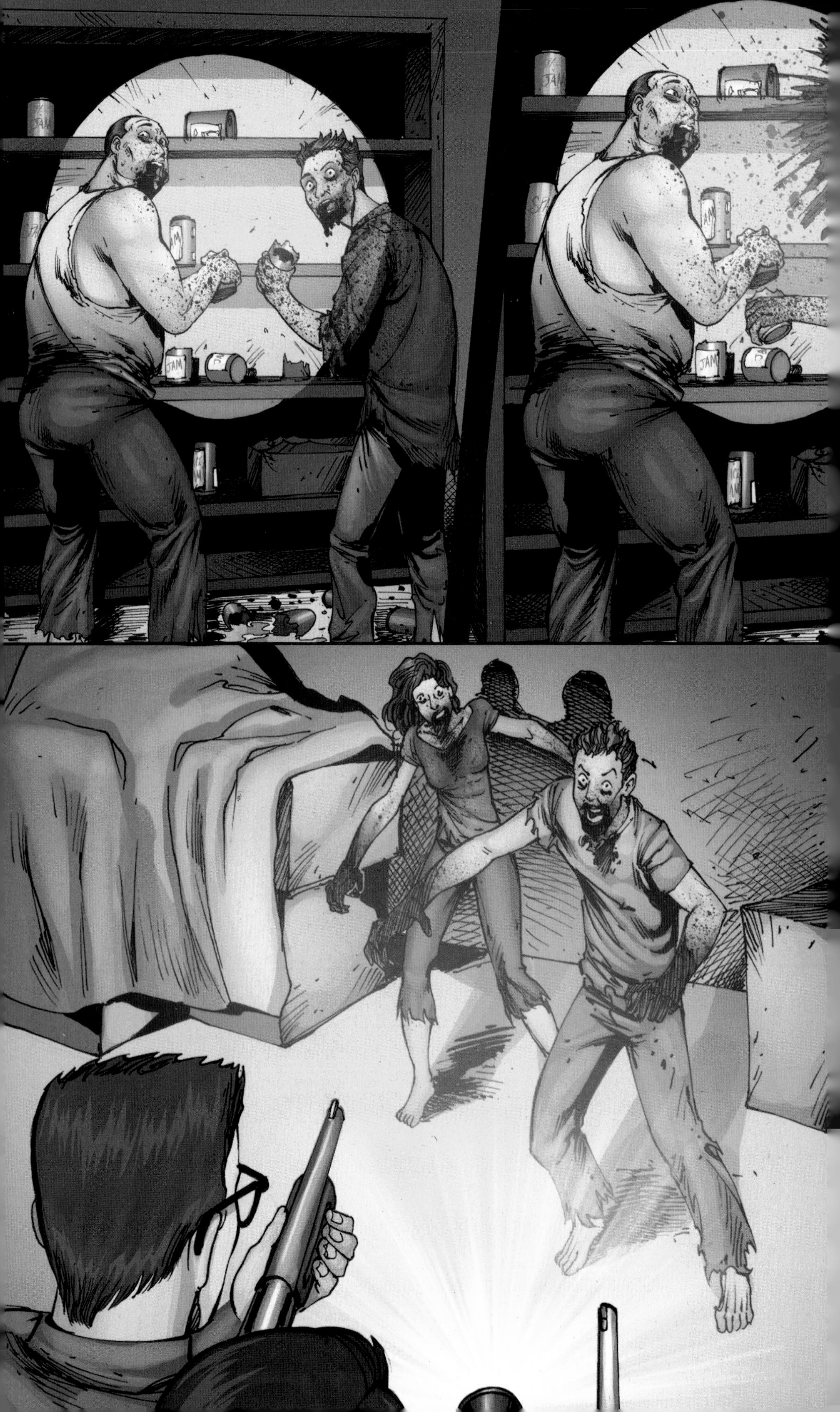
JAM

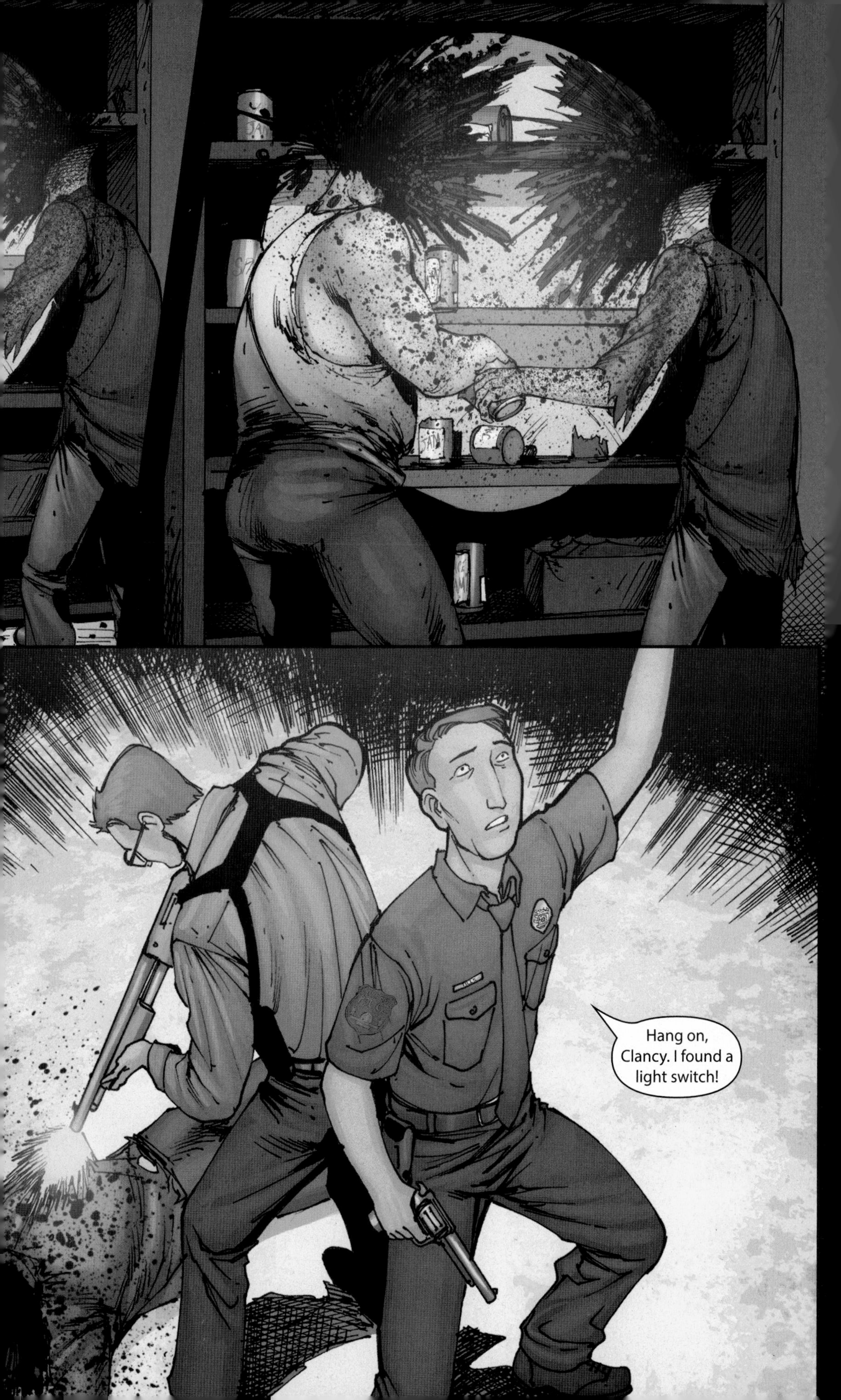
Hang on, Clancy. I found a light switch!

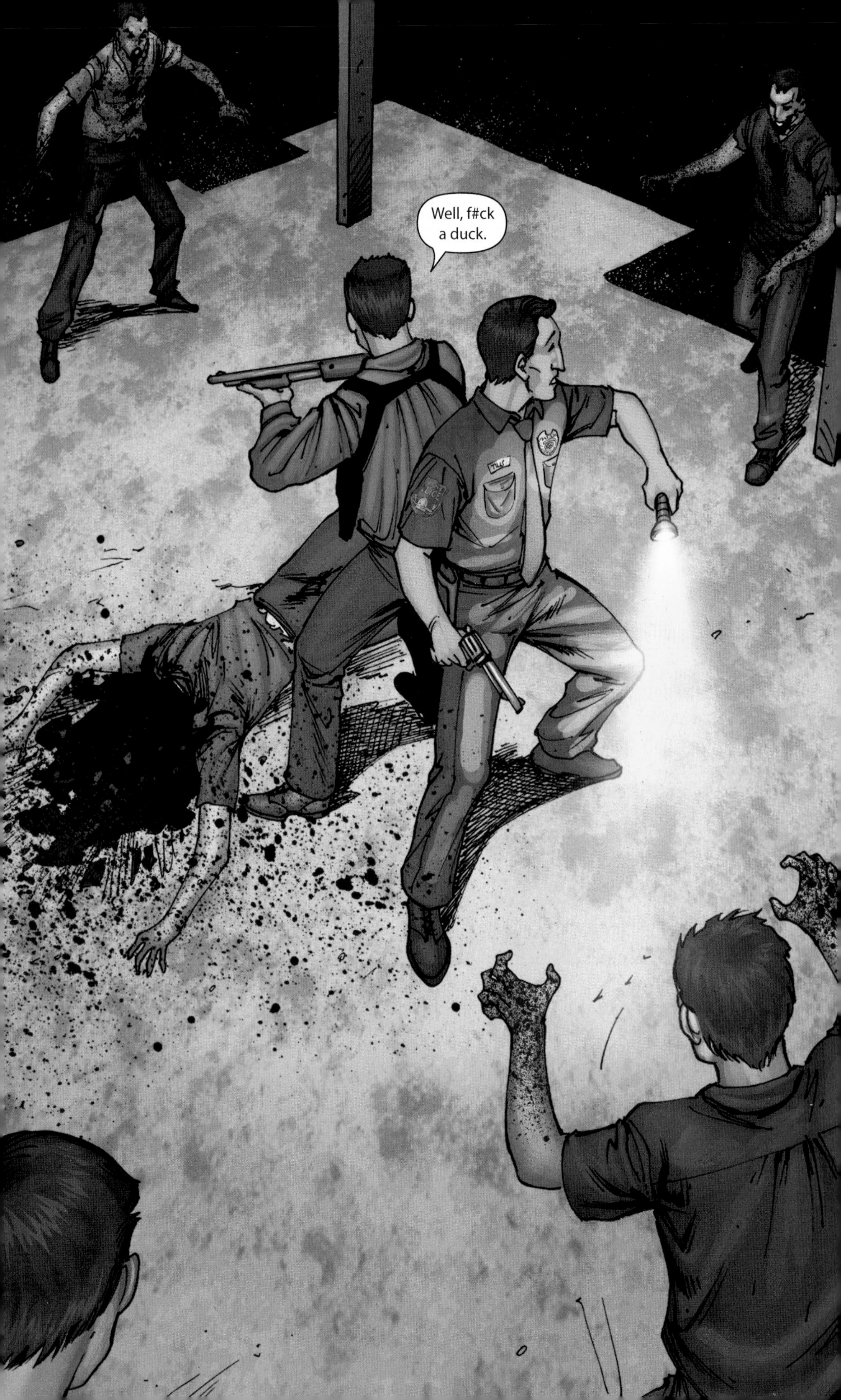
Well, f#ck a duck.

3

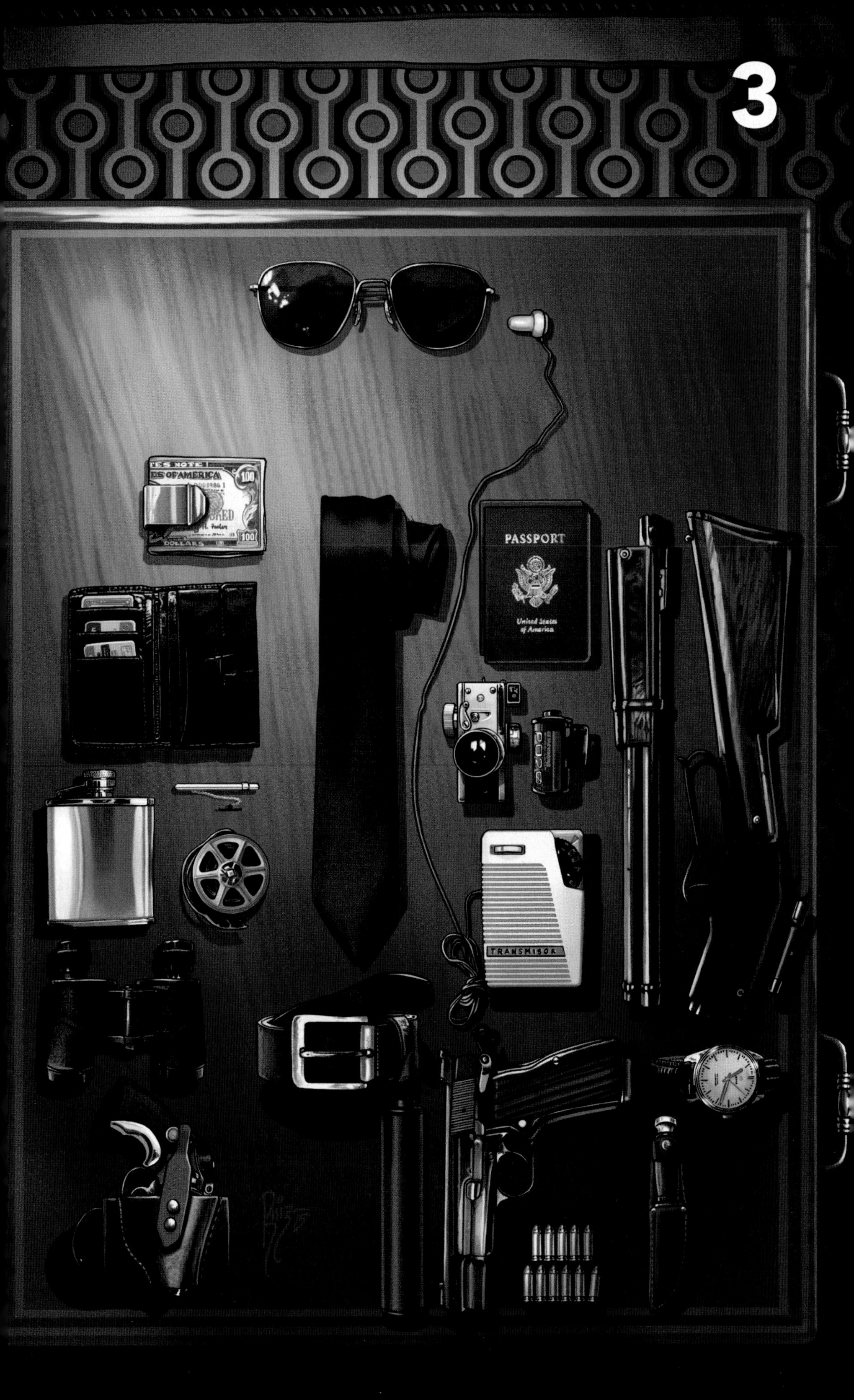
PASSPORT
United States of America
TRANSMISOR
100
DOLLARS

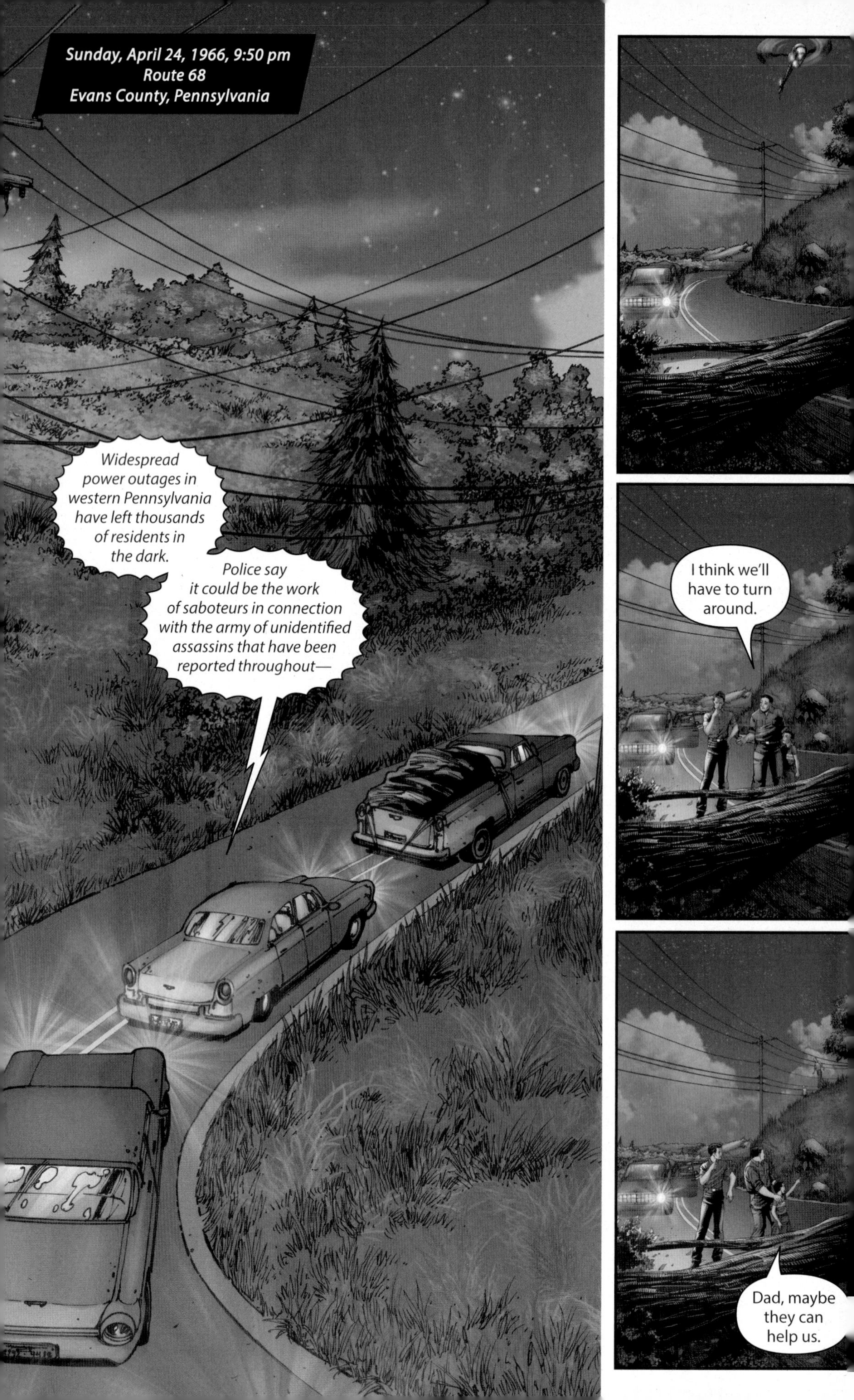
Sunday, April 24, 1966, 9:50 pm
Route 68
Evans County, Pennsylvania
Widespread power outages in western Pennsylvania have left thousands of residents in the dark.
Police say it could be the work of saboteurs in connection with the army of unidentified assassins that have been reported throughout—
I think we'll have to turn around.
Dad, maybe they can help us.

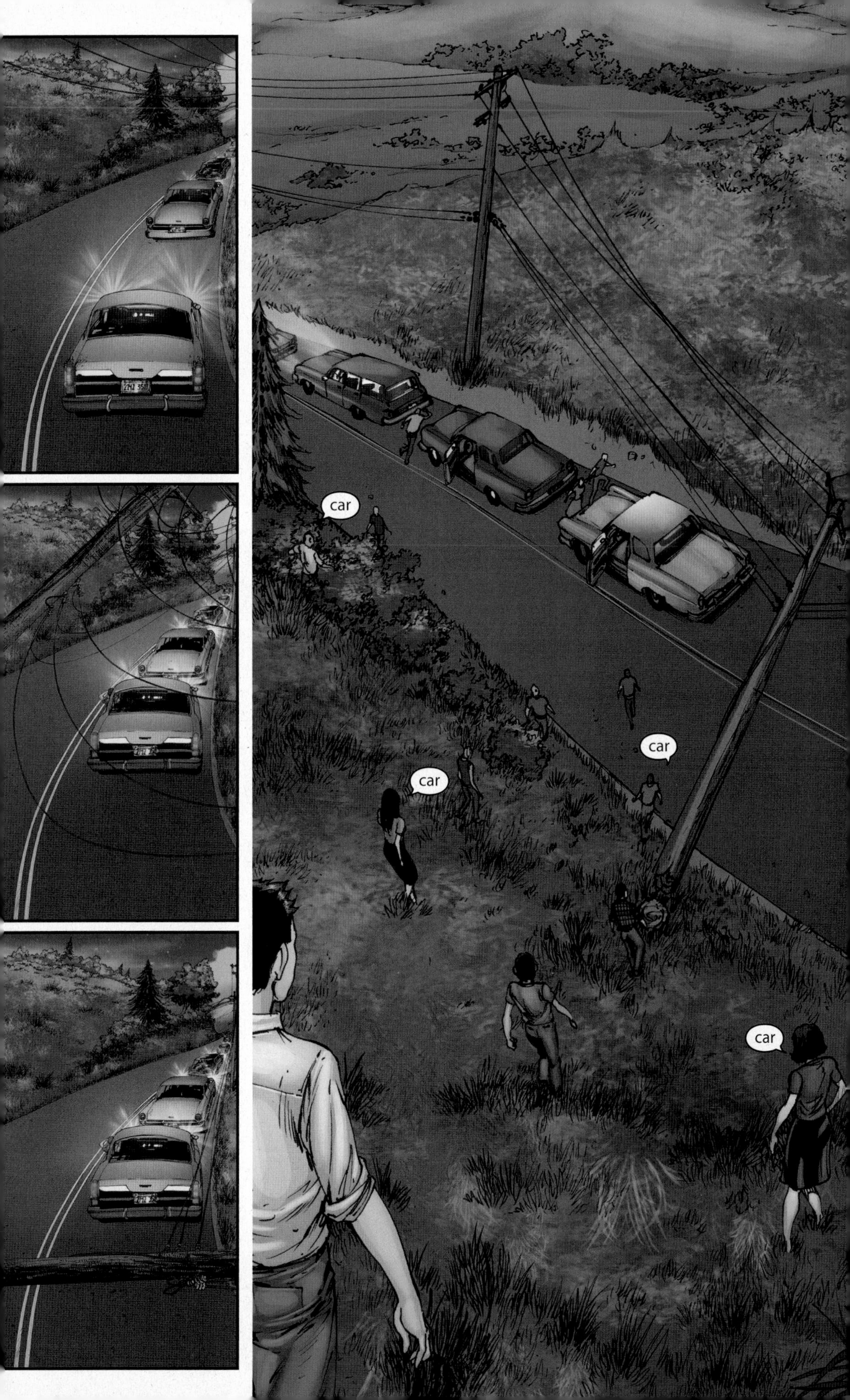
car
car
car
car

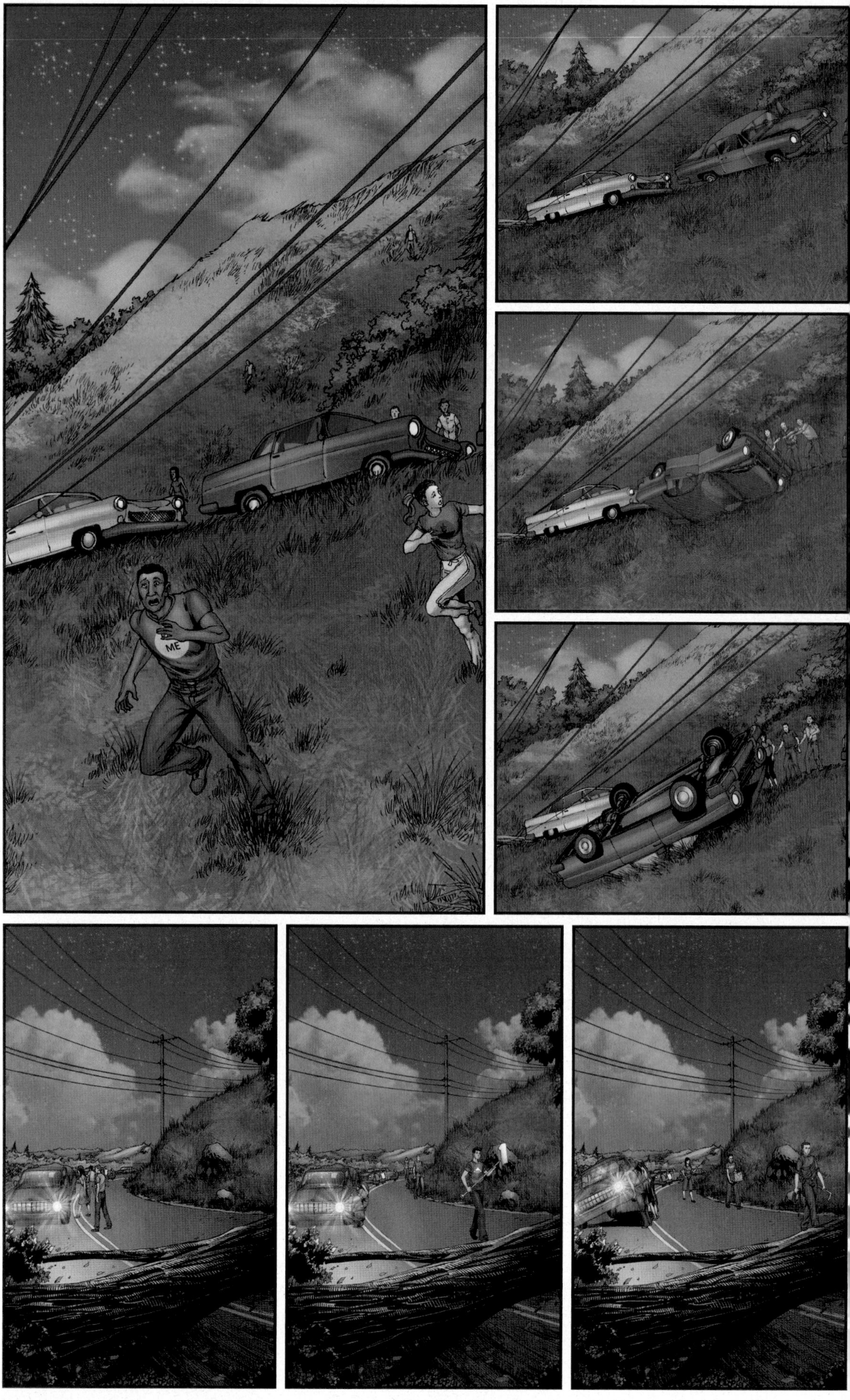
ME

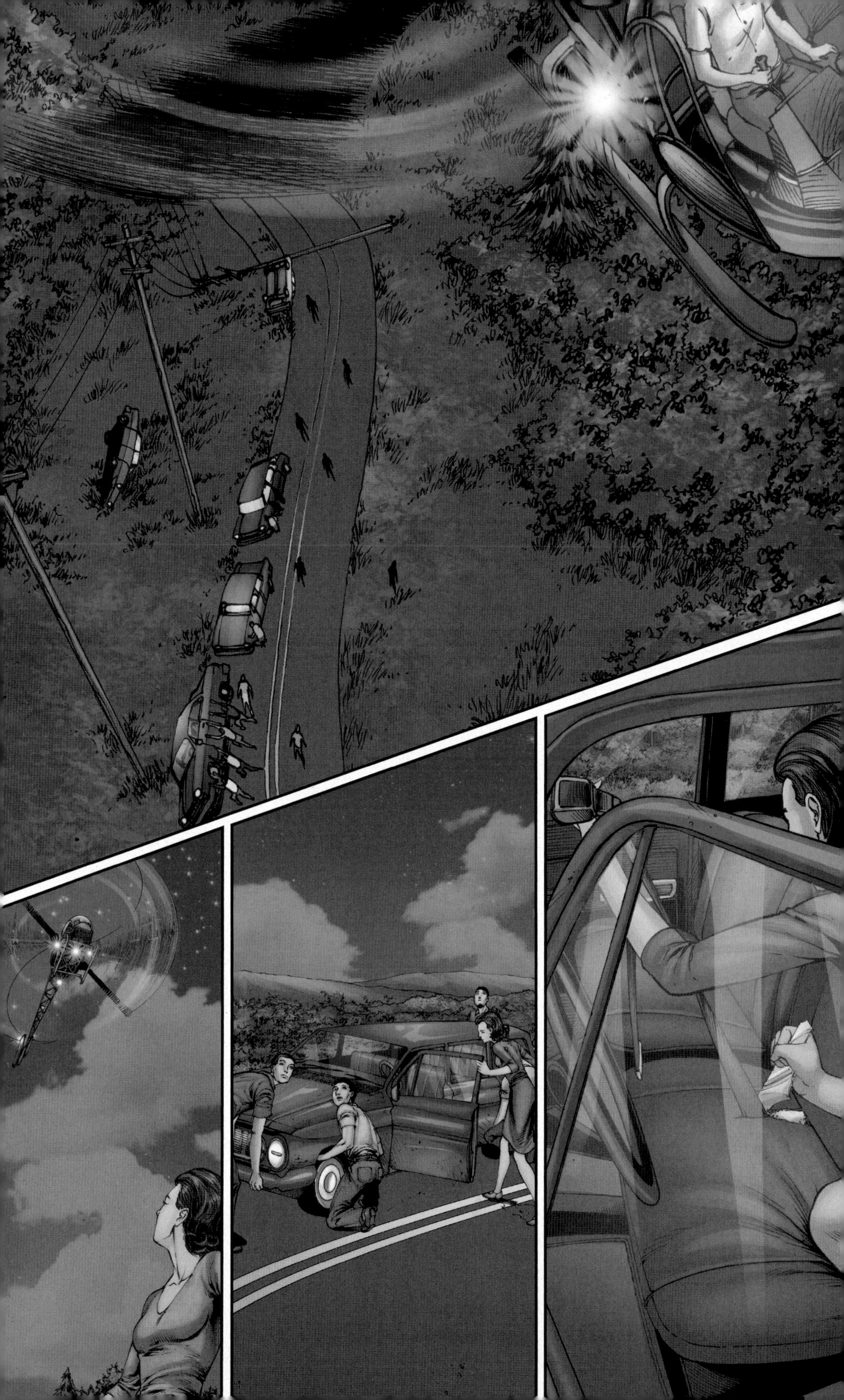

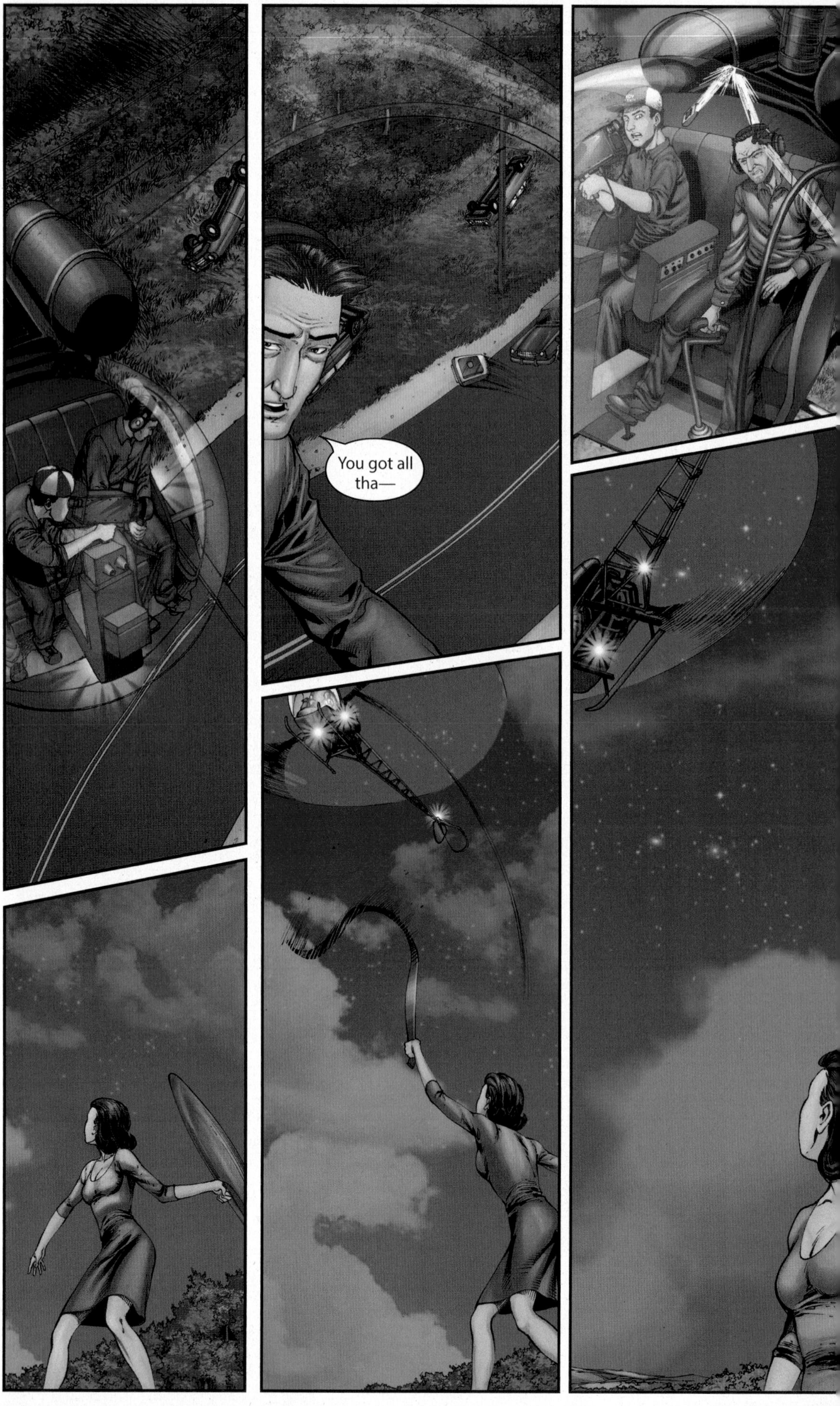
You got all tha—

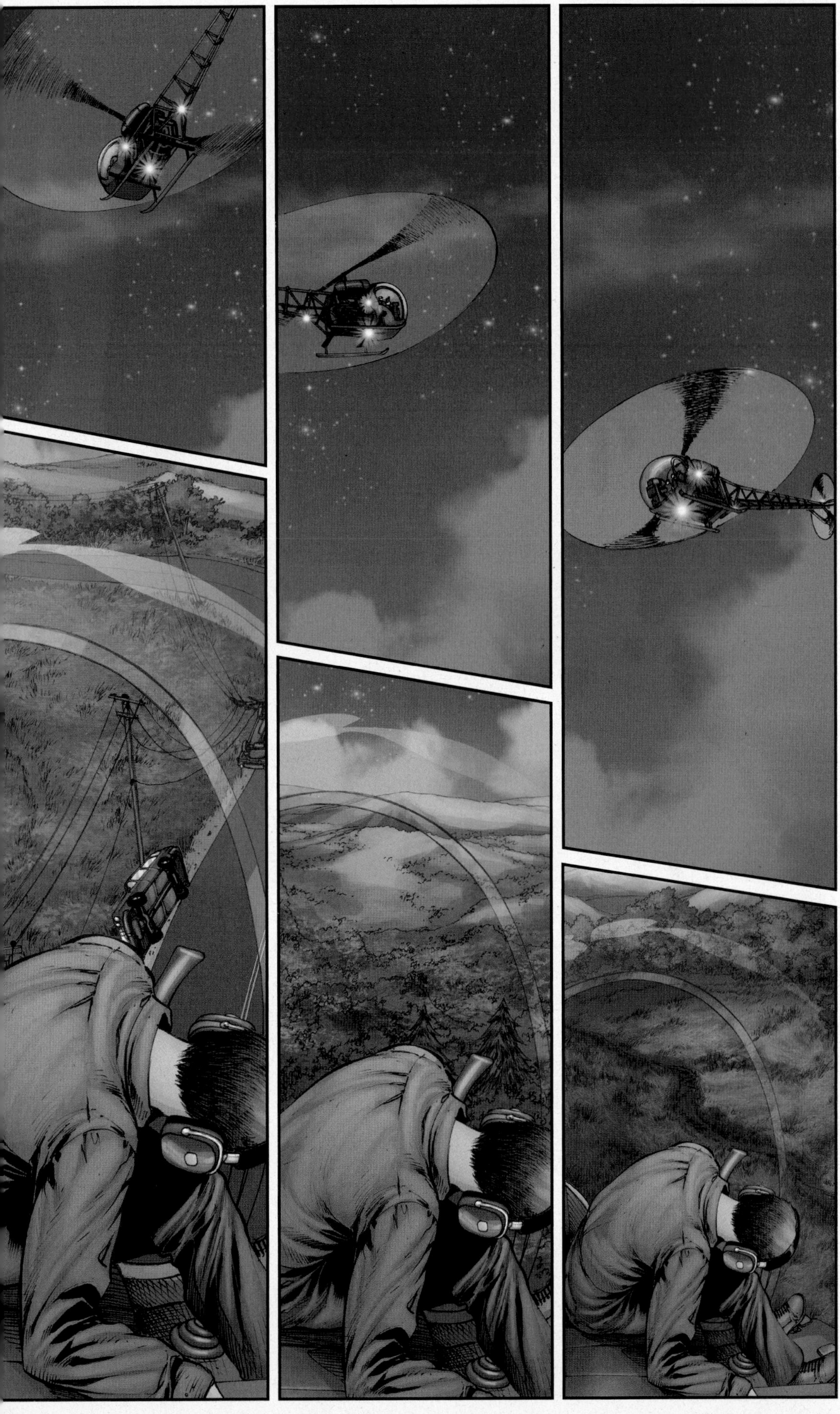

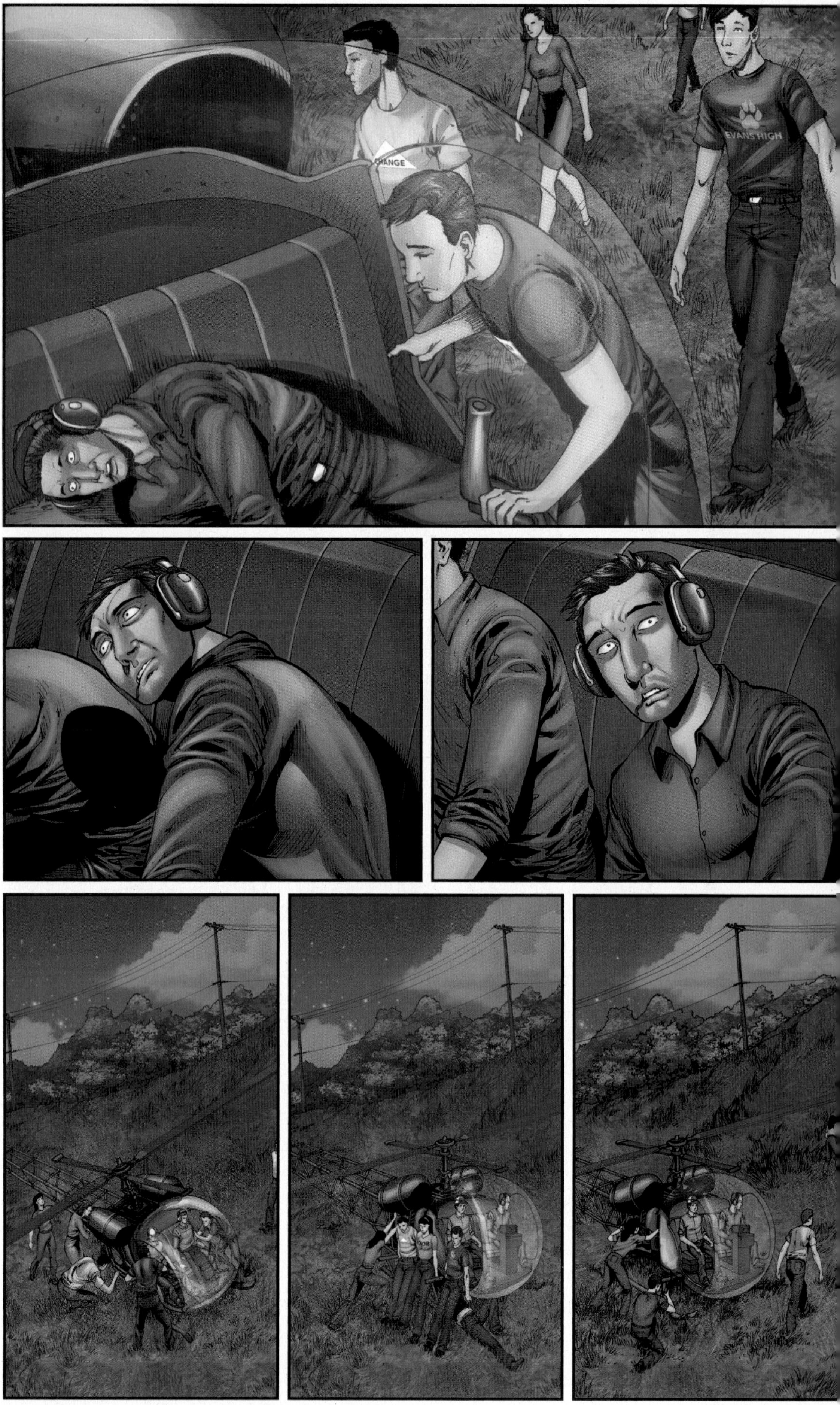
CHANGE
EVANS HIGH

DOUBLE TAKE RECORD HOUSE

SUMMER SELECTION

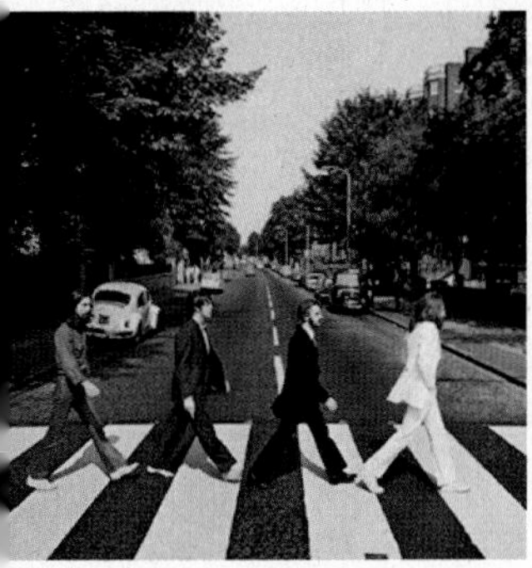

inally you'll be able to understand
ll those album cover parodies!

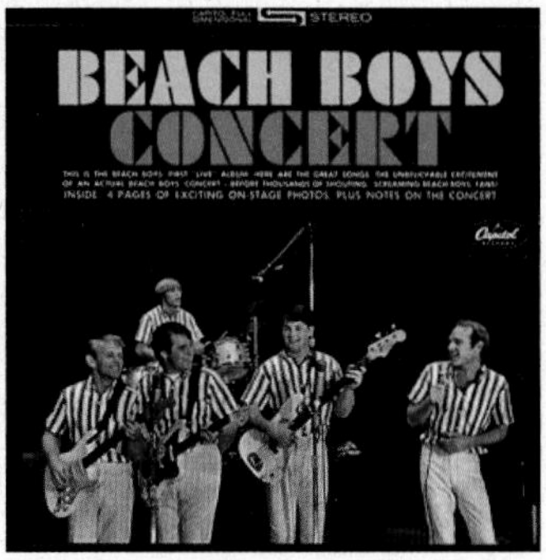
STEREO
BEACH BOYS CONCERT

Sunburn for the soul!

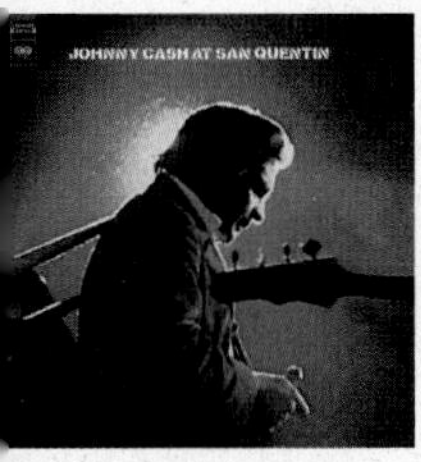
JOHNNY CASH AT SAN QUENTIN

erfectly captures the
eeling of being in
rison!

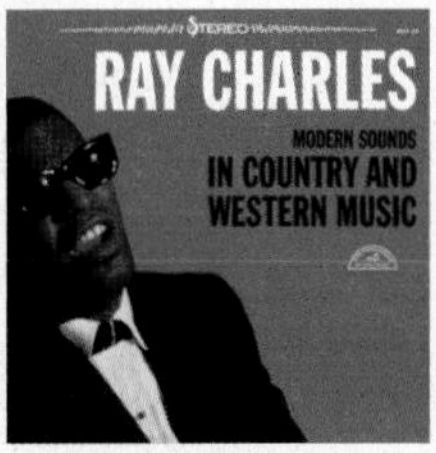
RAY CHARLES
MODERN SOUNDS
IN COUNTRY AND
WESTERN MUSIC

Maybe it will remind you how much you like Jamie Foxx!

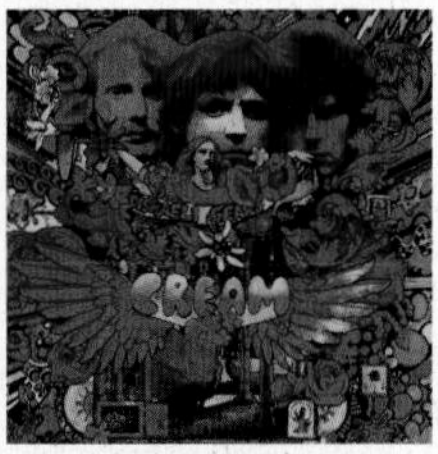

Consider it an Eric Clapton prequel!

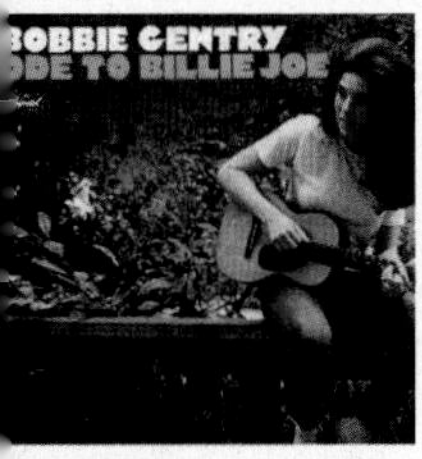
OBBIE GENTRY
DE TO BILLIE JOE

eally close to being
Billy Joel!'

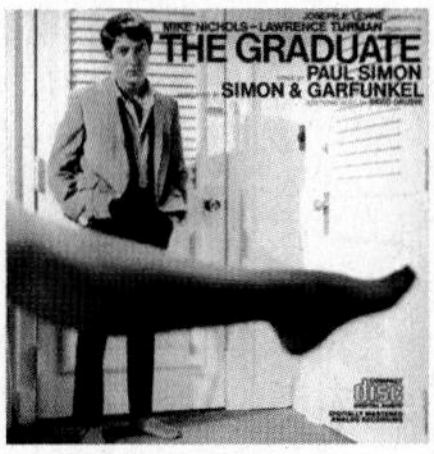
THE GRADUATE
PAUL SIMON
SIMON & GARFUNKEL

Why bother seeing the movie? Use this musical Cliff Notes!

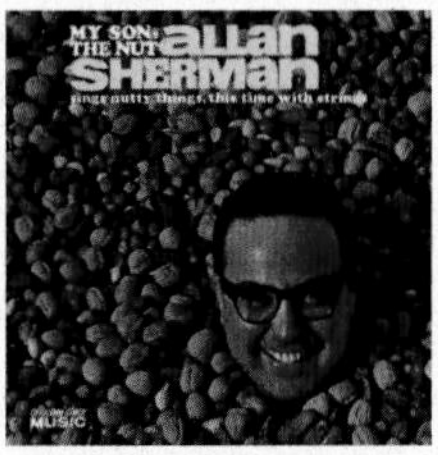
MY SON, THE NUT
allan SHERMAN

Like Weird Al without the fun!

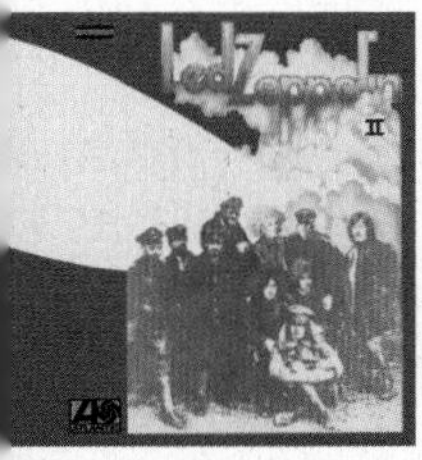

n case your local
lassic rock station isn't
lready playing Zeppelin
wice an hour!

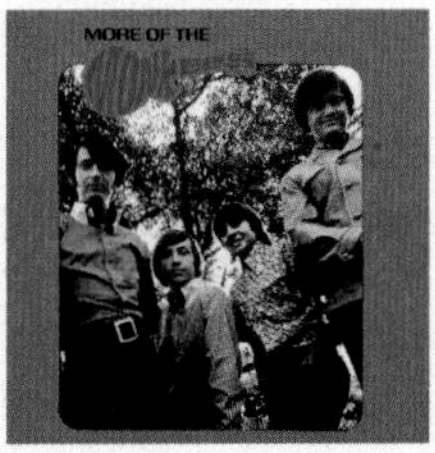
MORE OF THE

12 tracks, 19 credited songwriters - Now that's value!

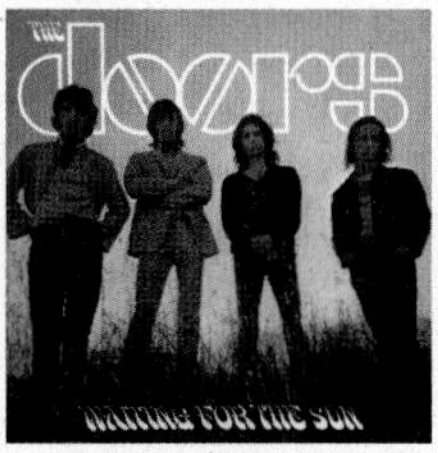
the doors

Even the worst poets can find success in this world!

ANY 3 RECORDS FOR ONLY $5.95

A LIFETIME PURCHASE! You may have any three of the best-selling records shown here—for ONLY $5.95! That's the fantastic bargain the Double Take Record House is offering new members who join and commit to purchasing as few as four additional records from our Buying Guide in the next year.

FREE SUBSCRIPTION TO THE RECORD BUYING GUIDE! You'll have no problem selecting four more records with our quarterly Buying Guide, which you'll get for free. With all the movie and musical soundtracks your heart desires, you'll only struggle with your choices!

YOUR OWN CHARGE ACCOUNT! Upon enrollment, the Double Take Record House will open a charge account in your name (or your husband's name, ladies). You pay for your records only after you've received them. They will be mailed and billed to you at the regular service price of $66.95.*

YOU GET FREE RECORDS! Once you've signed on, you'll groove on with a FREE record of your choice for every two records purchased! That's a 33 1/3% discount for your lifetime and post-mortem membership!

Please note under no circumstances will Double Take Record House send you any records.

SEND NO MONEY NOW!

Just fill in and mail the coupon to:

DOUBLE TAKE RECORD HOUSE
38 W. 39th Street, 2nd Floor
New York, New York 10018

Please enroll me as a member of the Double Take Record House. I've indicated here the 3 records I wish to receive for $5.95, plus postage and handling, etc. I agree to purchase four more selections in the next 12 months at the regular service price of $66.95,* and I may try to cancel my membership any time thereafter.** If I continue, I am to receive a FREE record of my choice for every two additional records purchased.

SELECT THREE RECORDS ☐ ☐ ☐

NAME ____________________
Please do not actually

ADDRESS ____________________
fill this out and send it in.

CITY ________ POSTAL ZONE No. ________ STATE ________

*Additional charges include a penalizing upcharge for buying British albums, plus postage, handling, and other charges Double Take Record House will tack on your charge account. **Good luck. Even death won't cancel your membership.

THE AMERICAN STUDENT
DEBT CRISIS

	1960s*	2010s	DIFFERENCE
Median Family Income	$45,700	$51,939	14%
Total Annual Student Loans	$891.4 million	$260 billion	29,068%
Federal	$891.4 million	$178 billion	19,869%
Non-federal	$0	$81 billion	0%
Average Public College Tuition	$7,432	$14,500	103%
Average Private College Tuition	$15,348	$34,000	130%
Average Income for Male Grad	$91,100	$36,000	-61%
Average Income for Female Grad	$25,000	$36,000	44%
Bachelor Degrees Conferred	5,200,000	19,000,000	265%
Public Law School Tuition	$3,664	$42,000	1,046%
Private Law School Tuition	$1,661	$24,000	1,345%

As of late 2014, federal-owned student loans totaled $850 billion, jumping up 750% from $100 billion in the mid-1990s; student loans now make up almost half of the federal portfolio (not including assets owned by the Federal reserve and land).

*IN 2016 DOLLARS

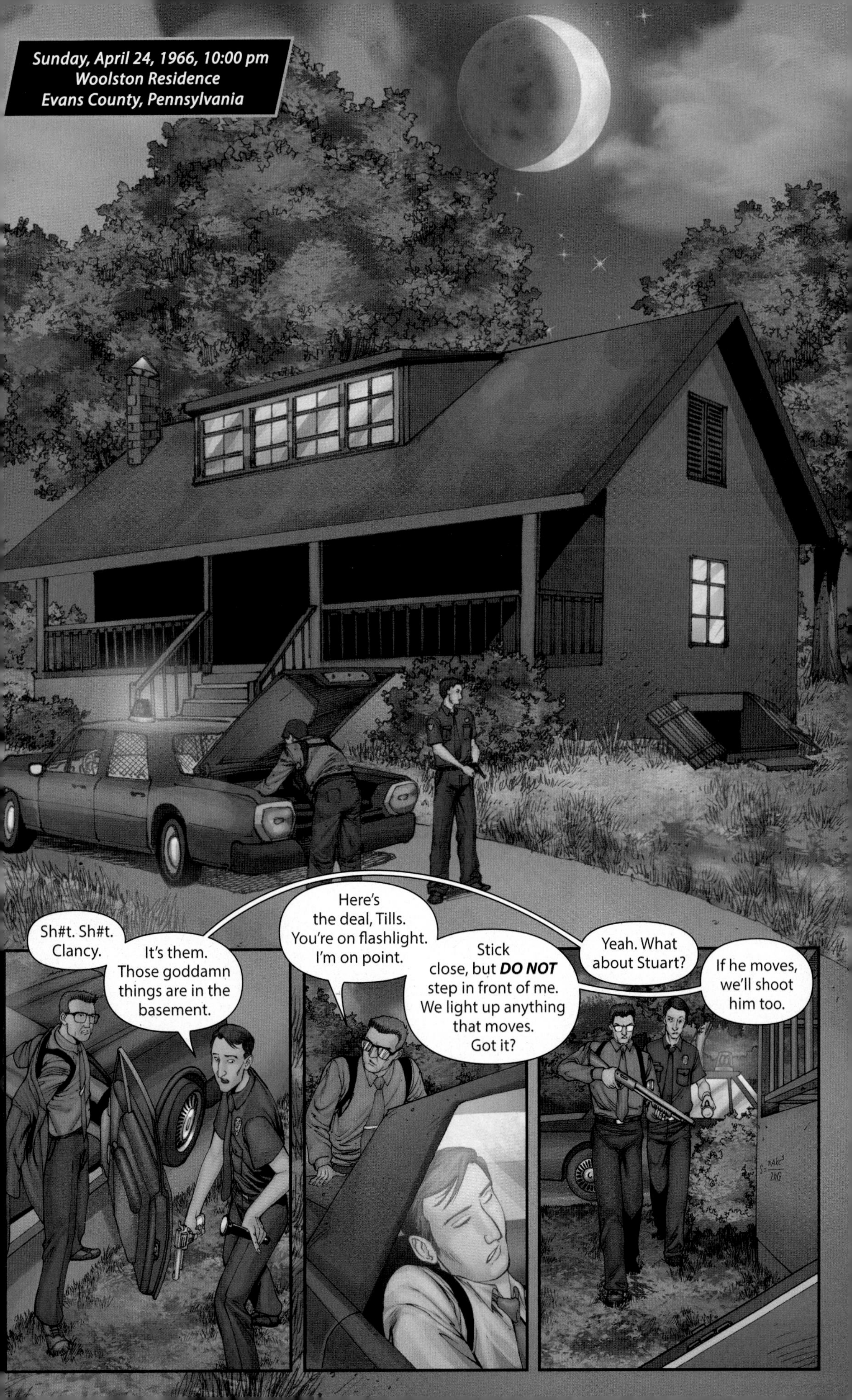
Sunday, April 24, 1966, 10:00 pm
Woolston Residence
Evans County, Pennsylvania
Sh#t. Sh#t. Clancy.
It's them. Those goddamn things are in the basement.
Here's the deal, Tills. You're on flashlight. I'm on point.
Stick close, but **DO NOT** step in front of me. We light up anything that moves. Got it?
Yeah. What about Stuart?
If he moves, we'll shoot him too.

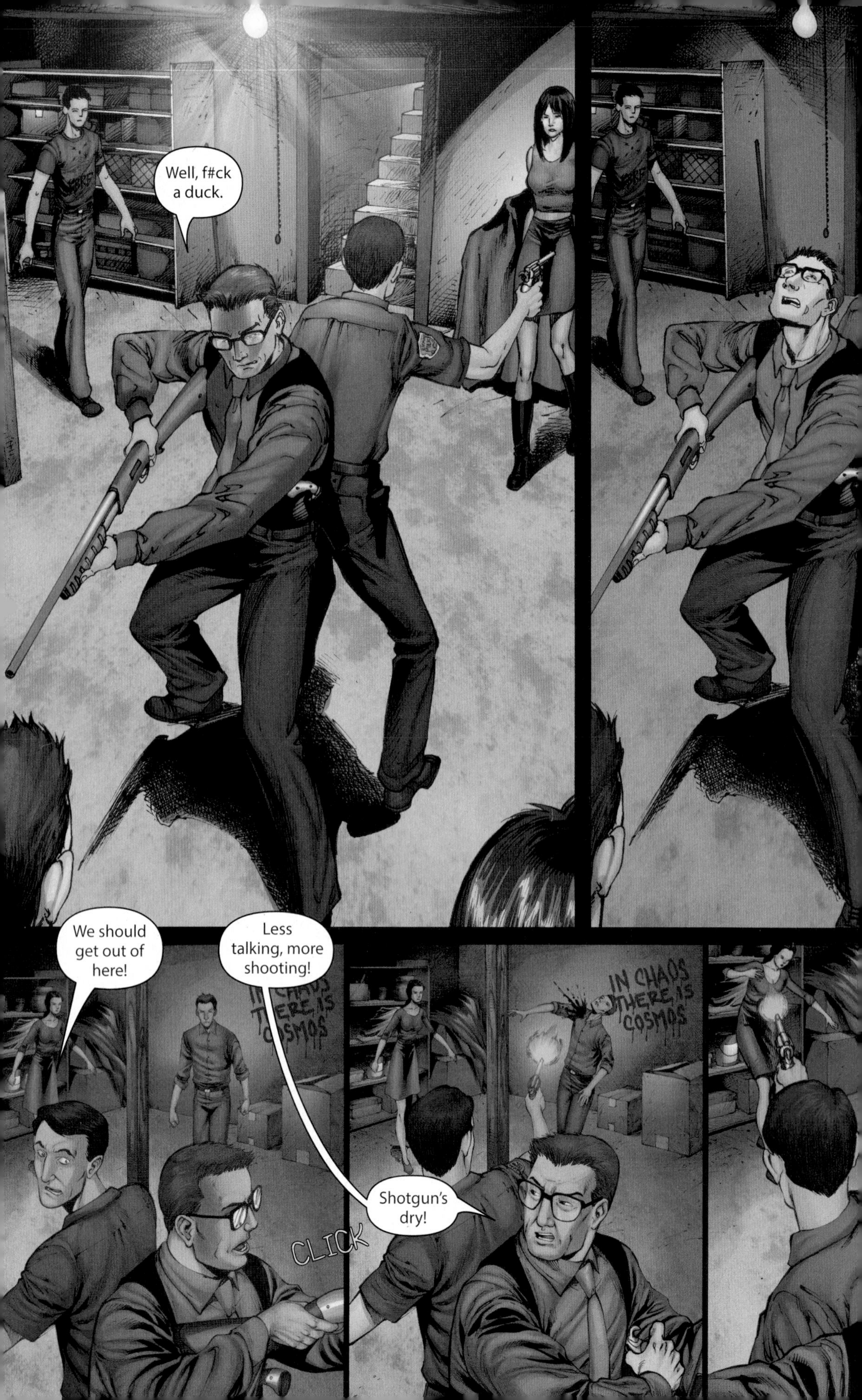
Well, f#ck a duck.
We should get out of here!
Less talking, more shooting!
IN CHAOS THERE IS COSMOS
CLICK
Shotgun's dry!
IN CHAOS THERE IS COSMOS

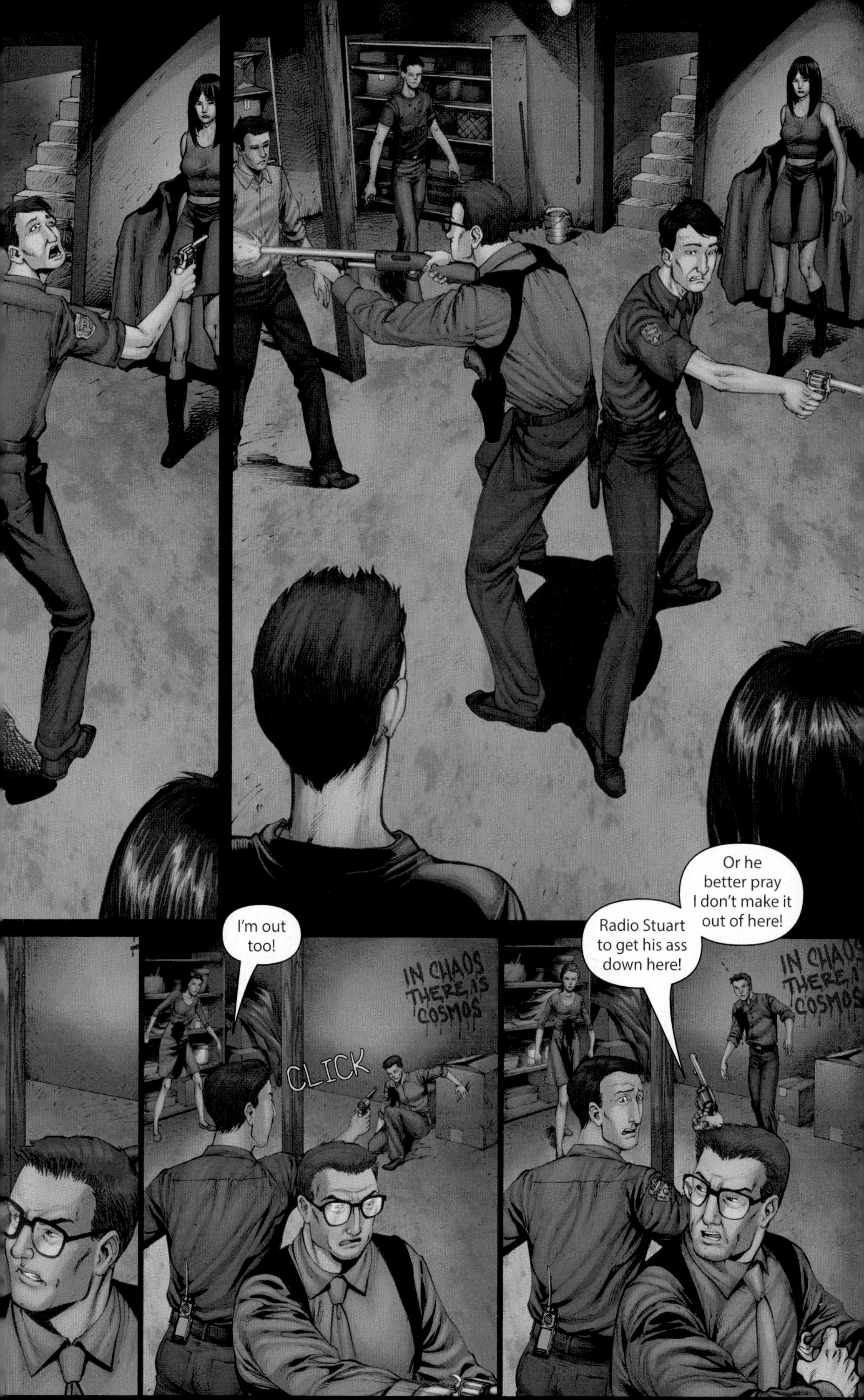
I'm out too!
CLICK
IN CHAOS THERE IS COSMOS
Radio Stuart to get his ass down here!
Or he better pray I don't make it out of here!
IN CHAOS THERE IS COSMOS

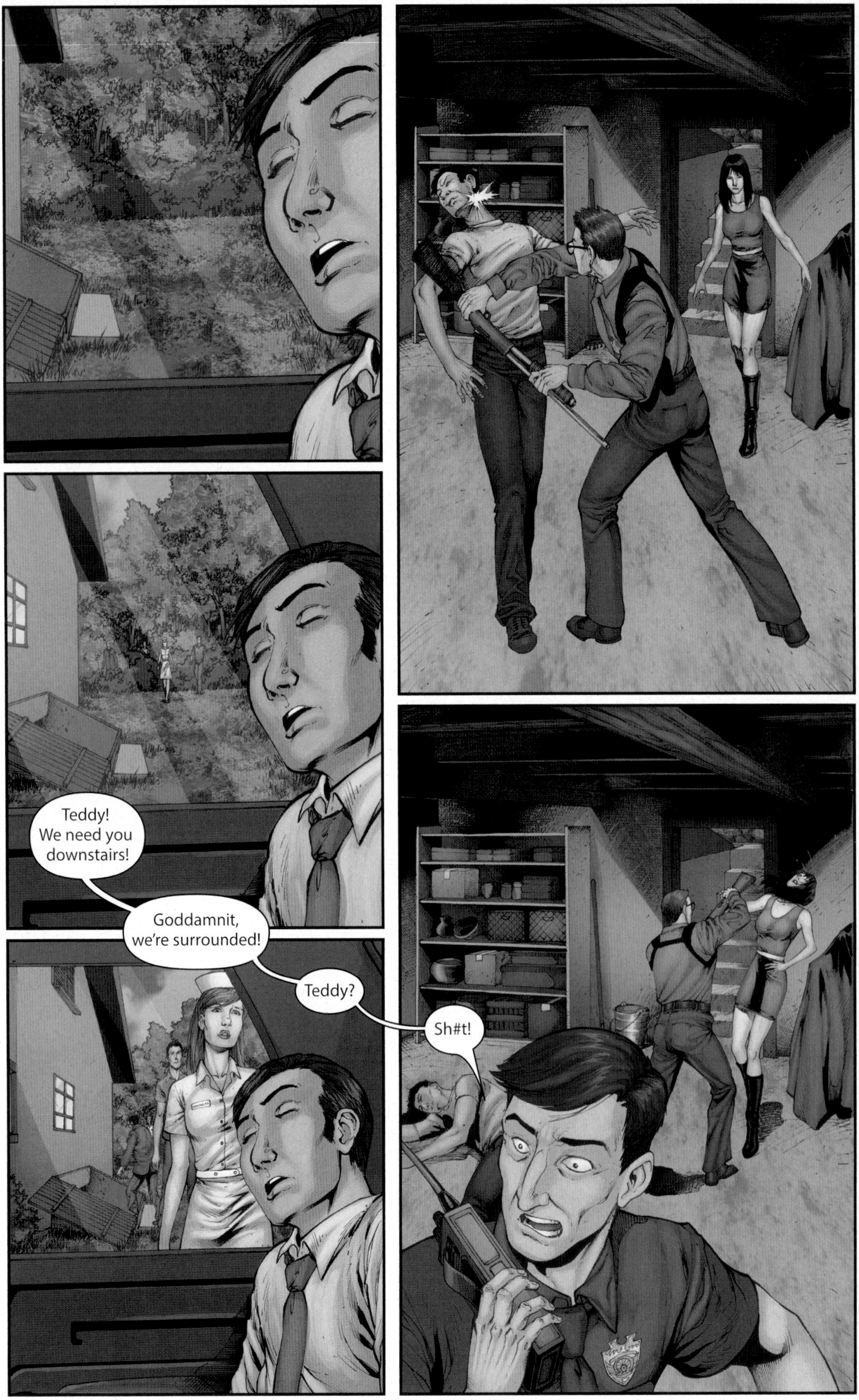
Teddy! We need you downstairs!
Goddamnit, we're surrounded!
Teddy?
Sh#t!

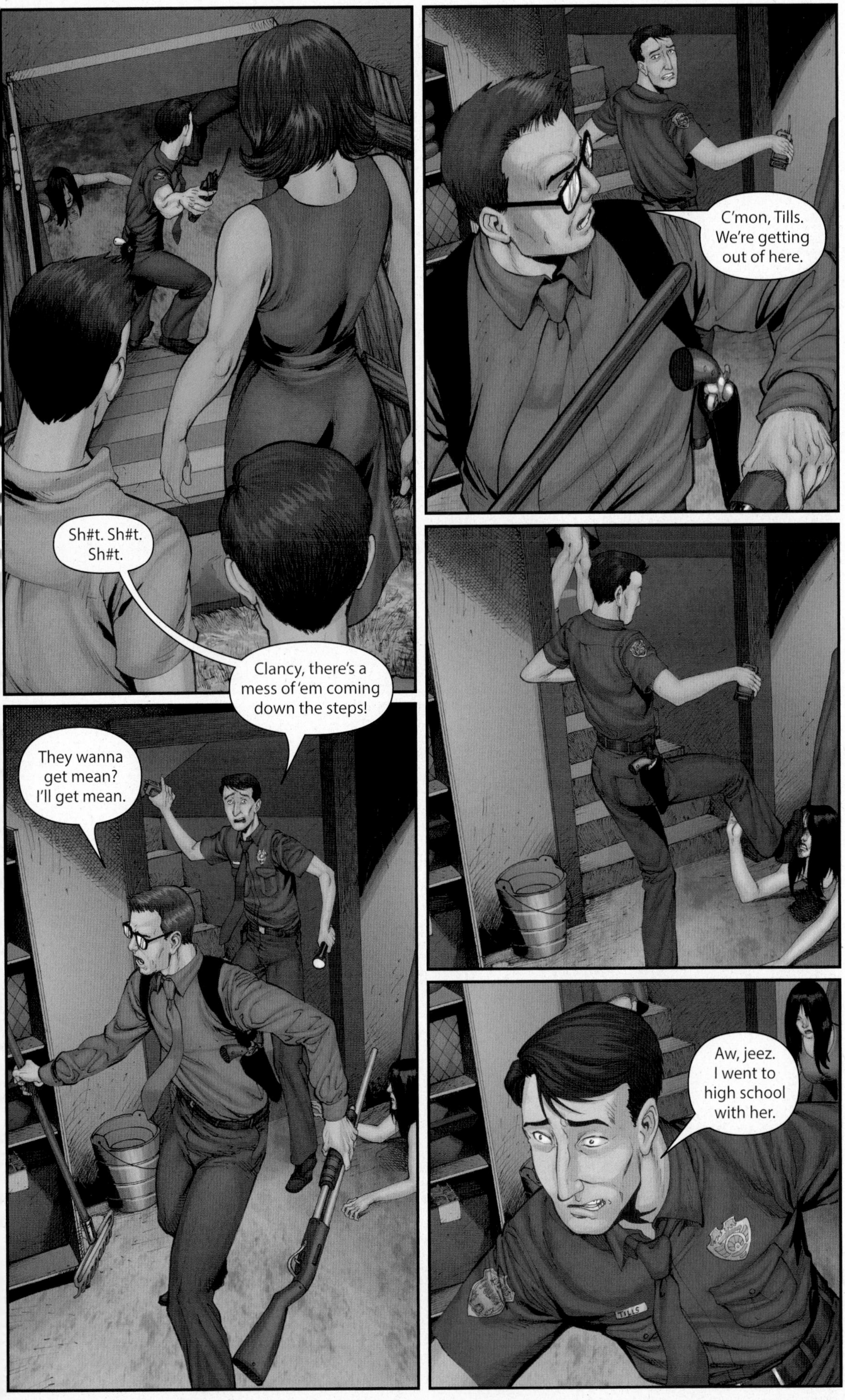
Sh#t. Sh#t. Sh#t.
C'mon, Tills. We're getting out of here.
Clancy, there's a mess of 'em coming down the steps!
They wanna get mean? I'll get mean.
Aw, jeez. I went to high school with her.

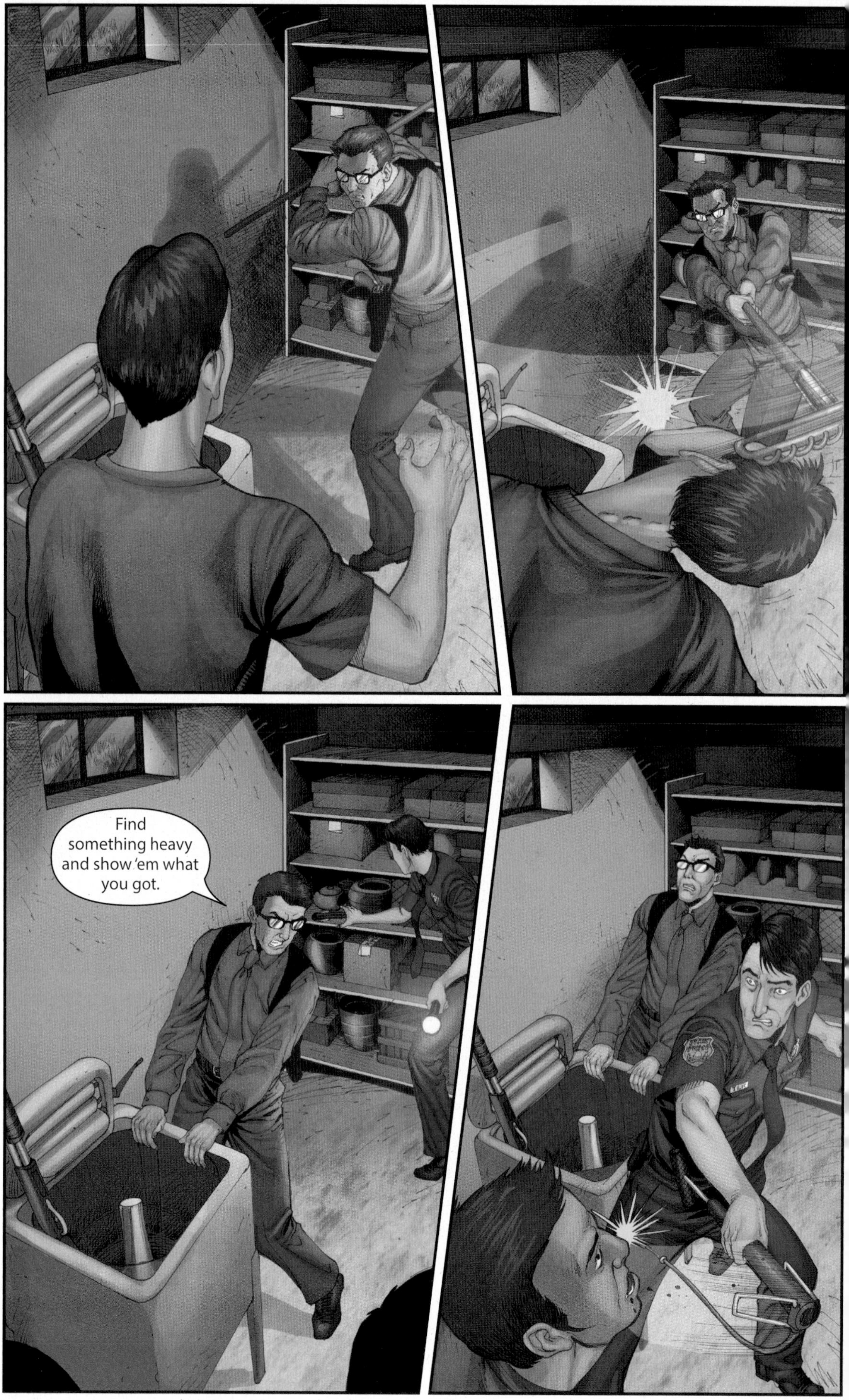
Find something heavy and show 'em what you got.

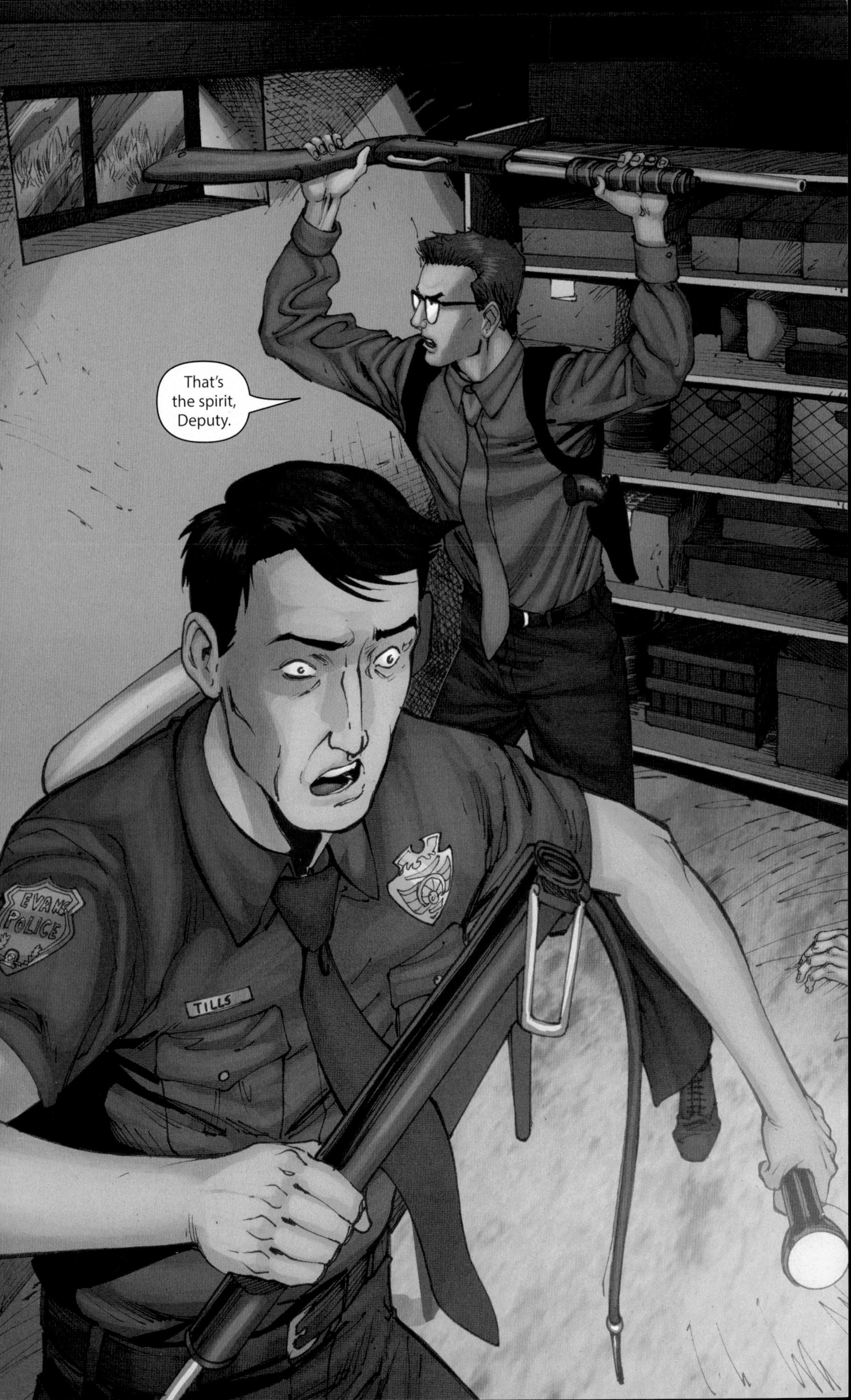
That's the spirit, Deputy.
EVANS POLICE
TILLS

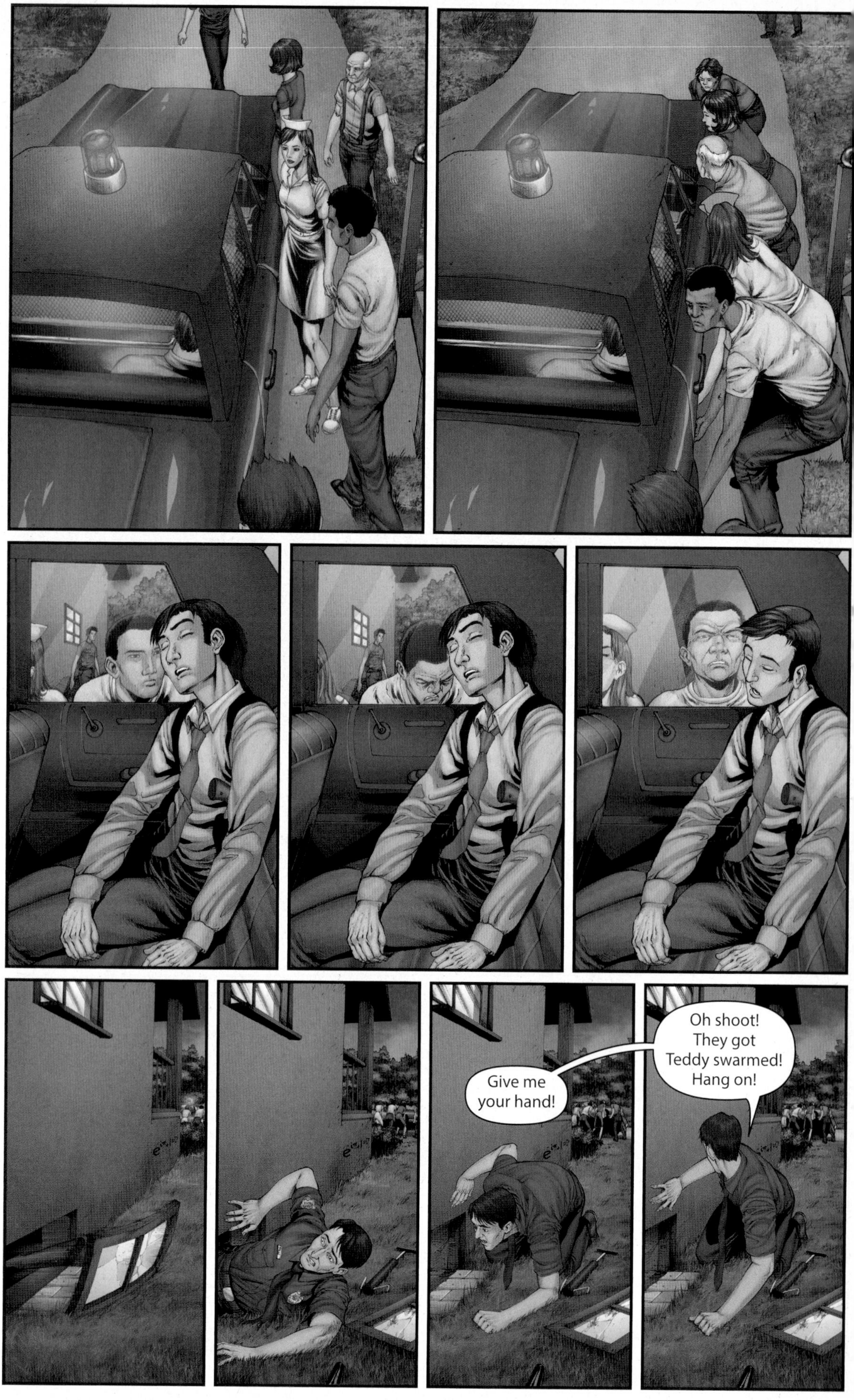
Give me your hand!
Oh shoot! They got Teddy swarmed! Hang on!

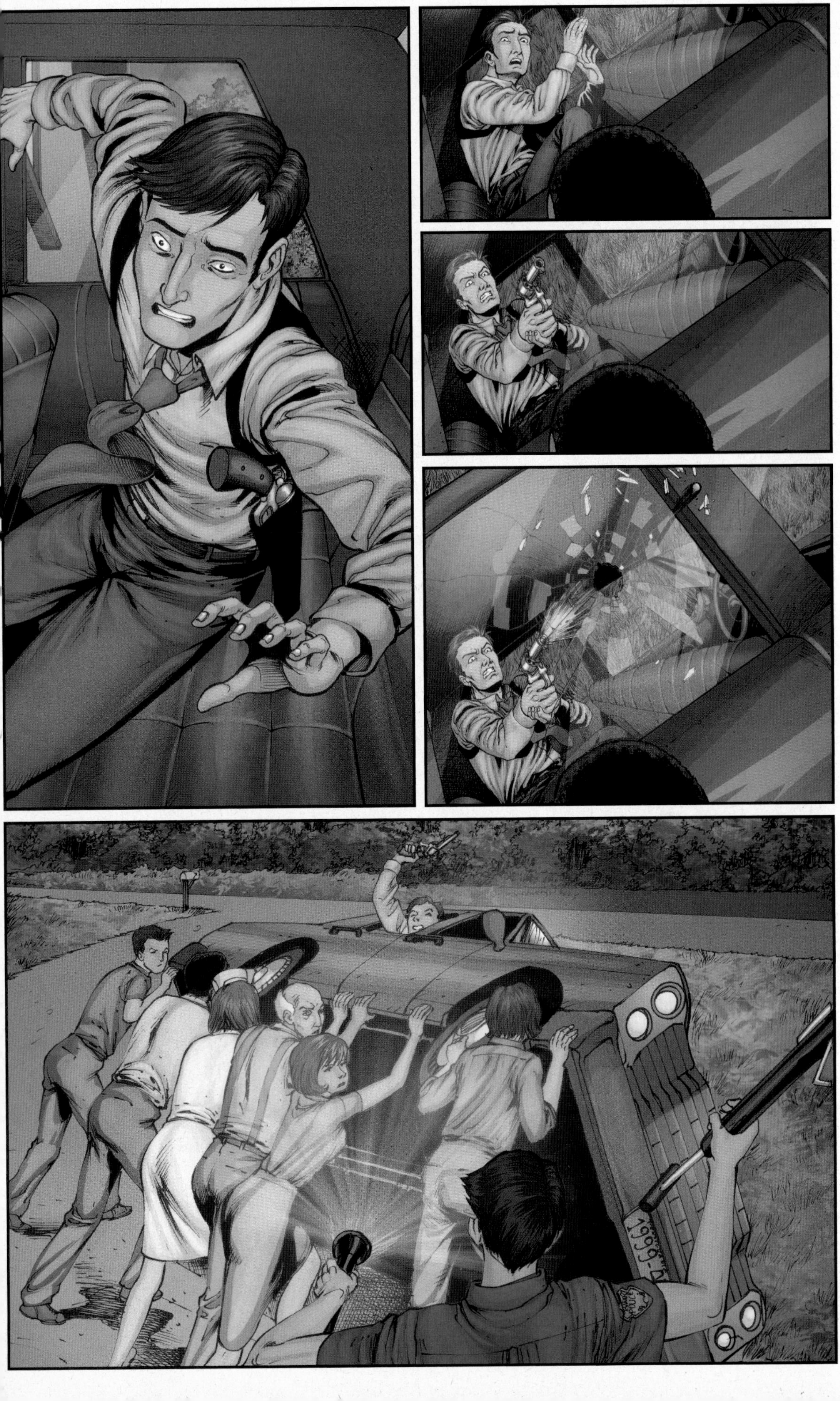

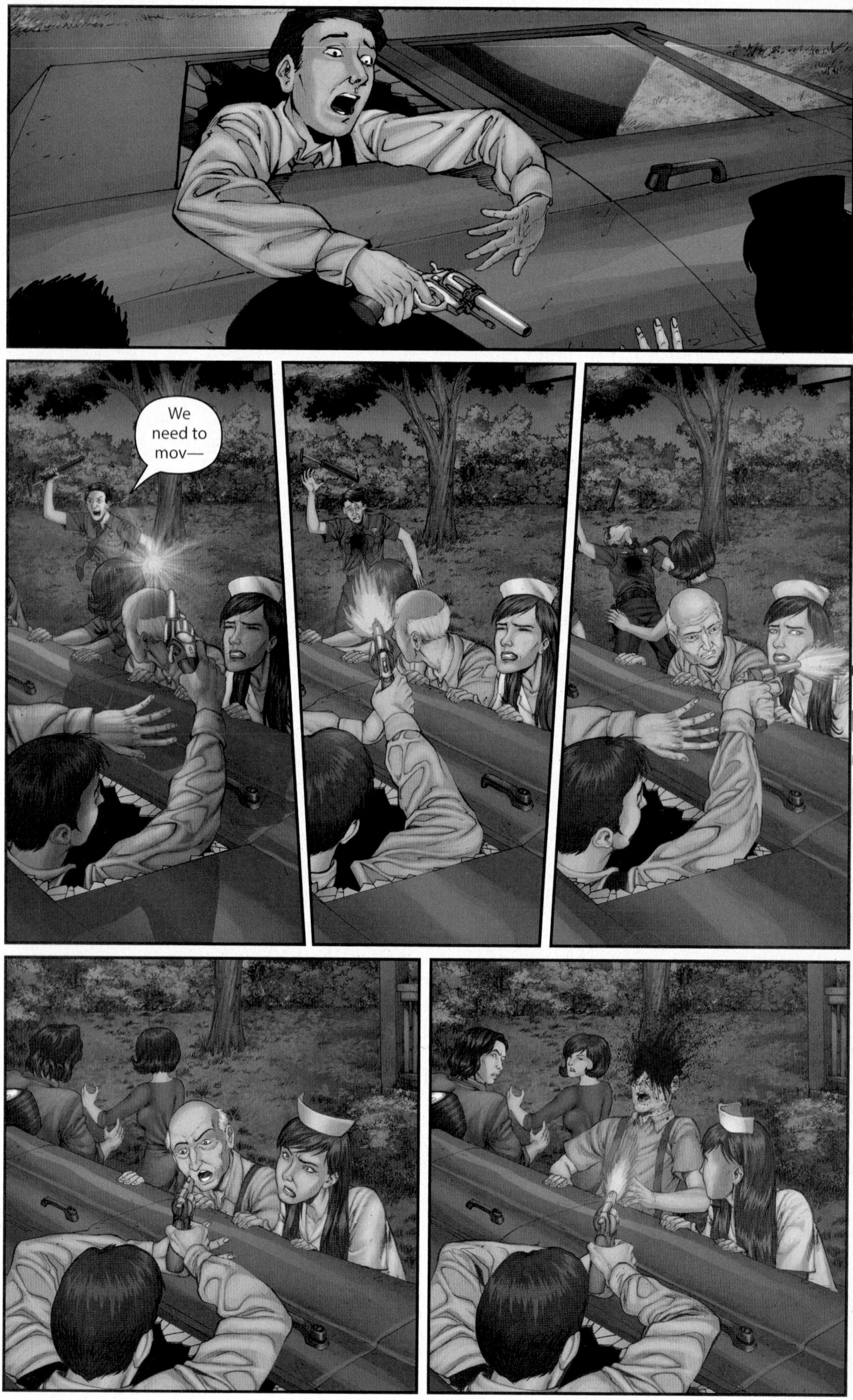
We need to mov—

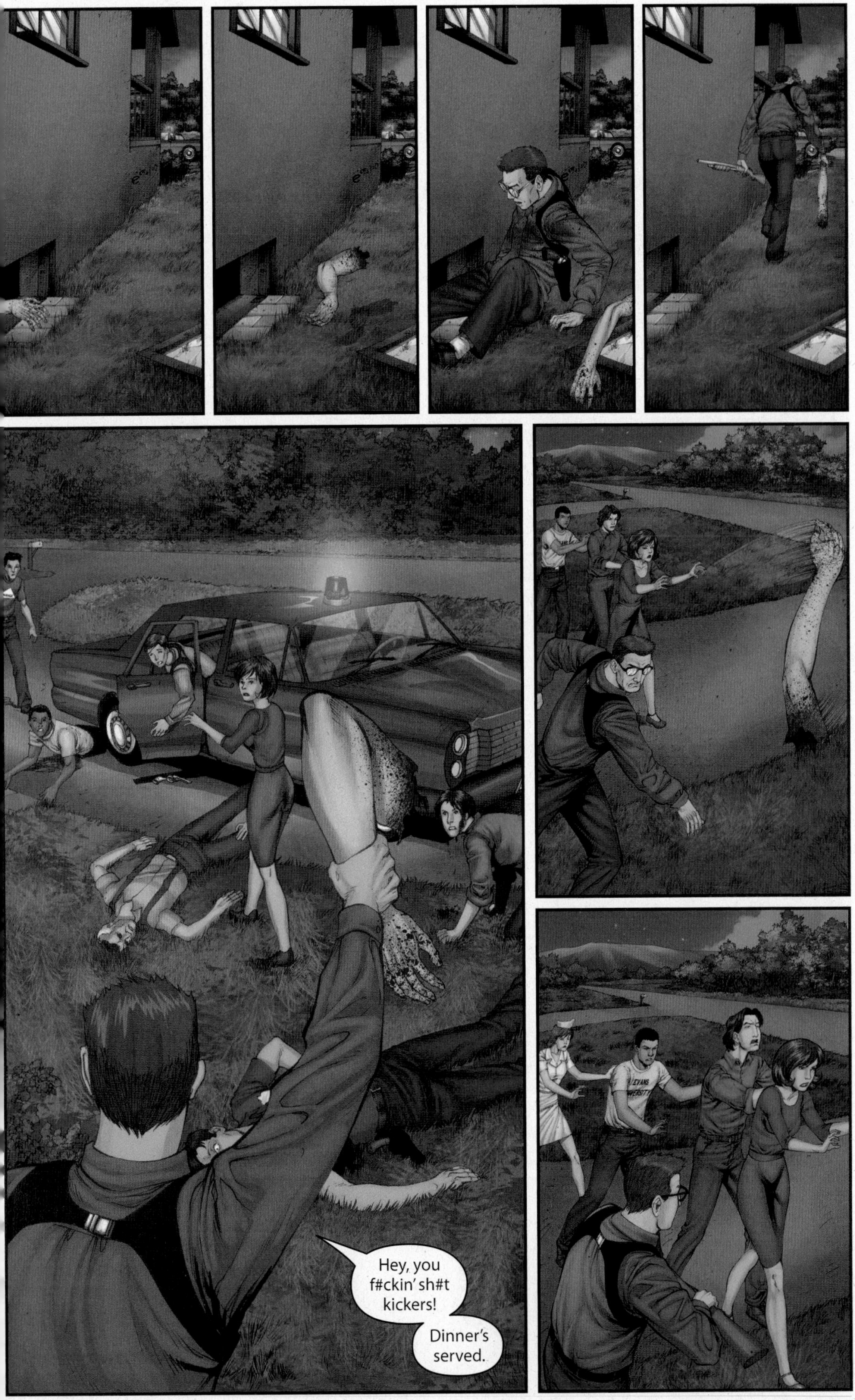
Hey, you
f#ckin' sh#t
kickers!
Dinner's
served.

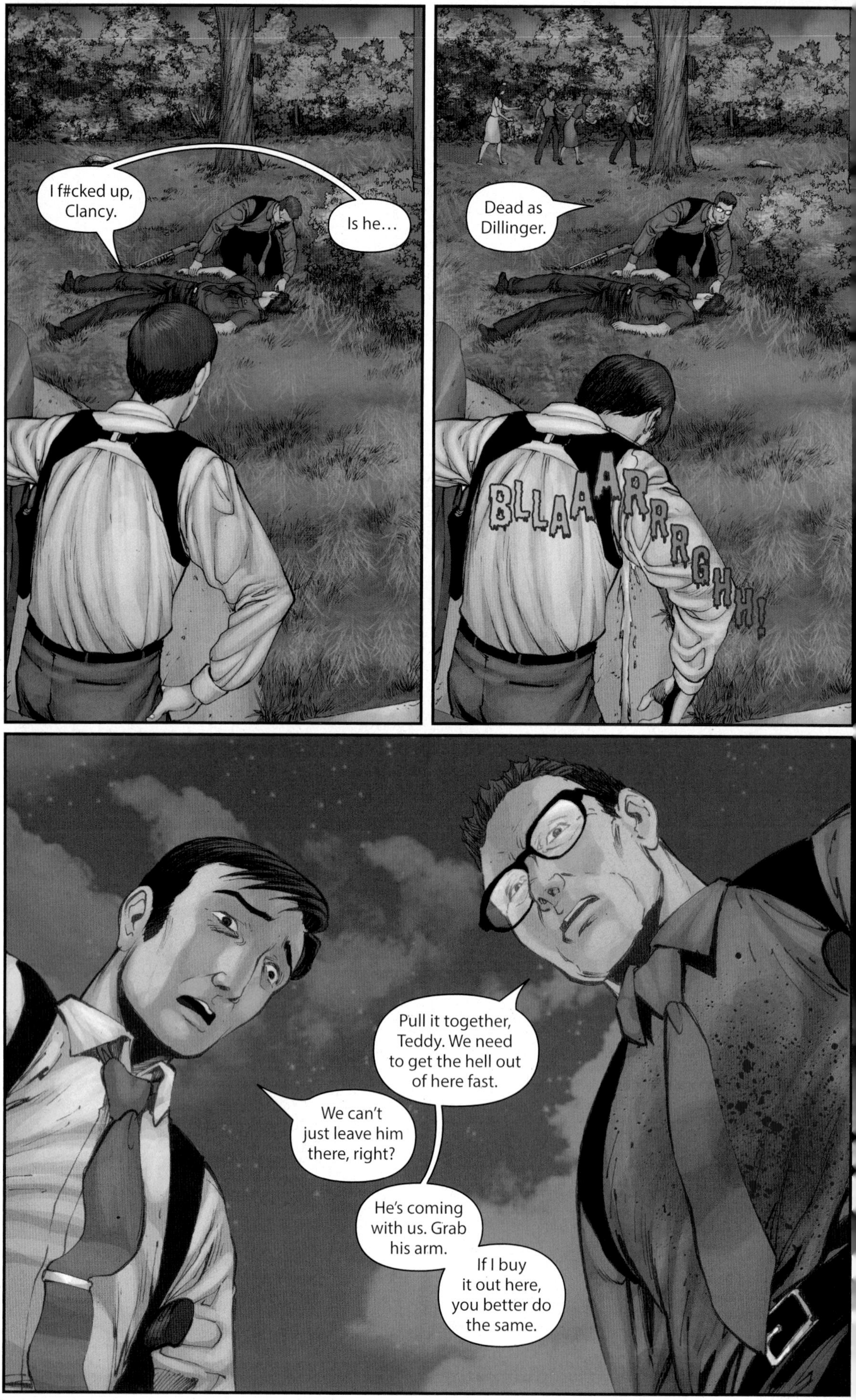
I f#cked up, Clancy.
Is he…
Dead as Dillinger.
BLLAAARRRGHH!
Pull it together, Teddy. We need to get the hell out of here fast.
We can't just leave him there, right?
He's coming with us. Grab his arm.
If I buy it out here, you better do the same.

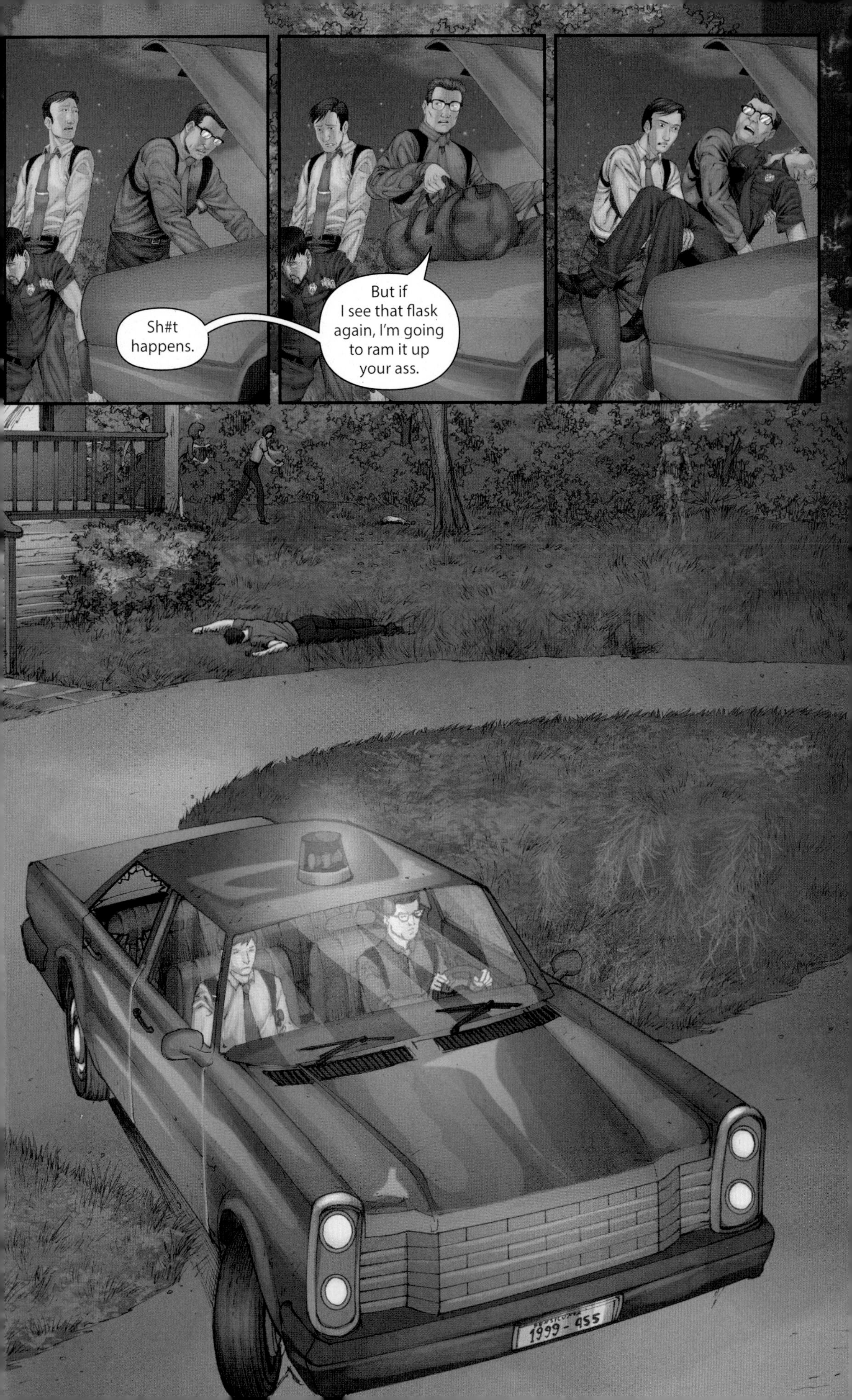
Sh#t happens.
But if I see that flask again, I'm going to ram it up your ass.
1999 - 455

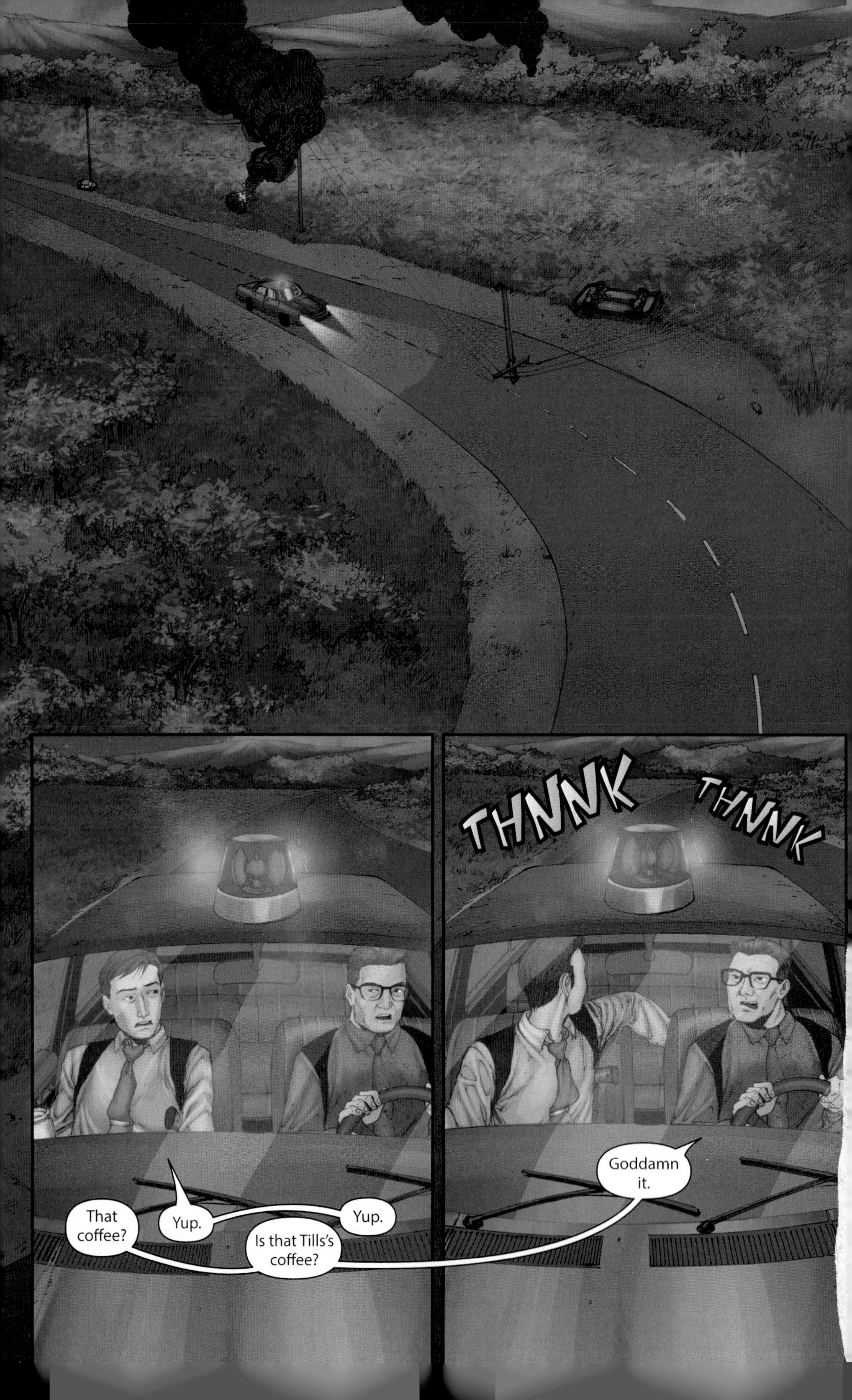
That coffee?
Yup.
Is that Tills's coffee?
Yup.
THNNK
THNNK
Goddamn it.

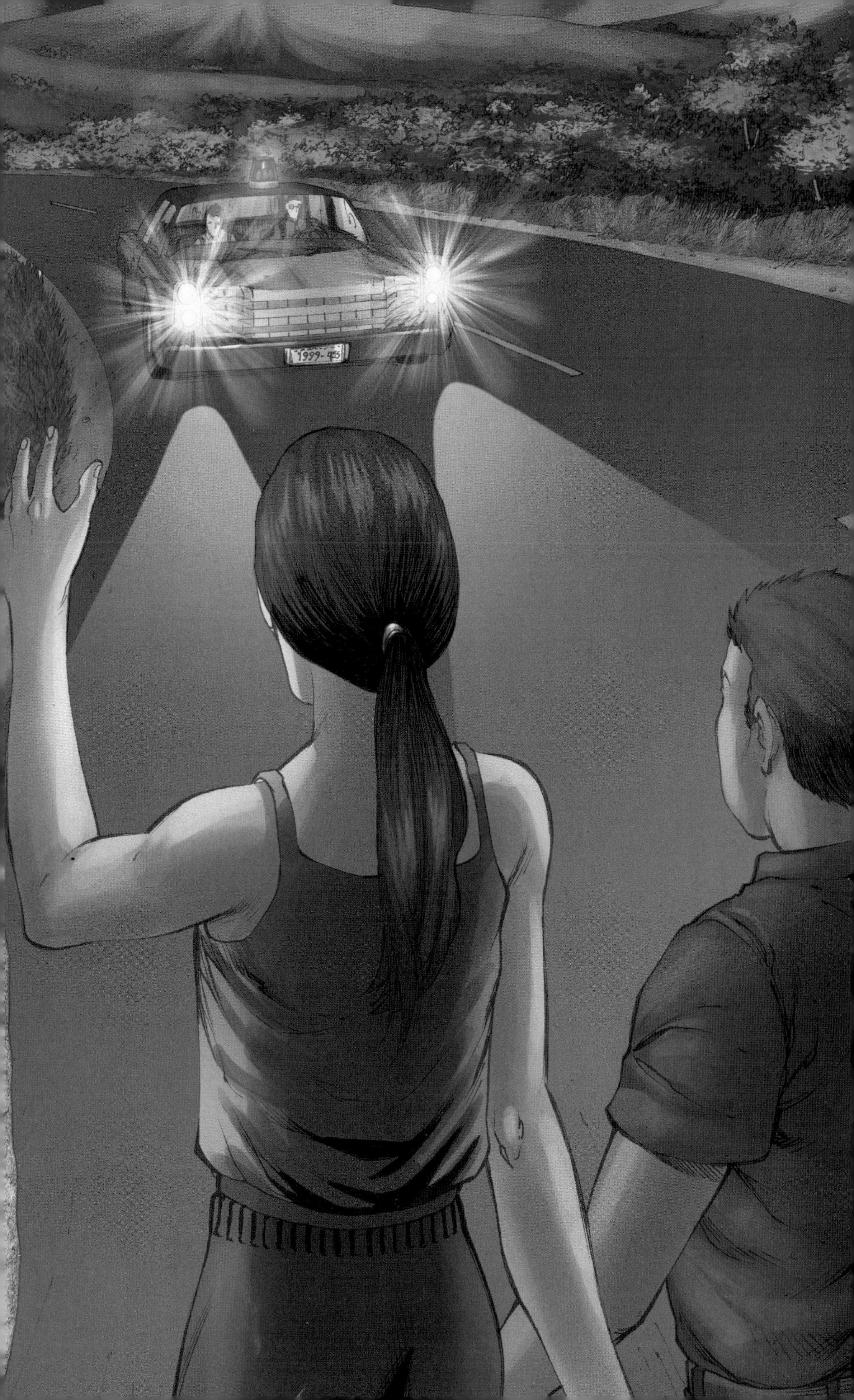
1999-

DOUBLE TAKE MANUAL OF STYLE

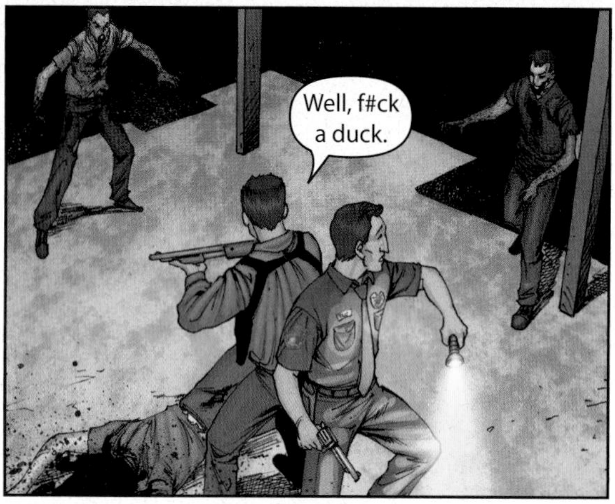
Well, f#ck
a duck.

F#ck a Duck

First use: In Henry Miller's *Tropic of Cancer* (1934): the narrator saw another author's title that he wished he'd come up with and exclaimed, "Well, f#ck a duck! I congratulate him just the same."

Etymology: The original inspiration may have been "duckf#cker," which refers to a person aboard a transatlantic ship who is responsible for keeping the domestic animals alive (and not pleasuring them in exotic ways).

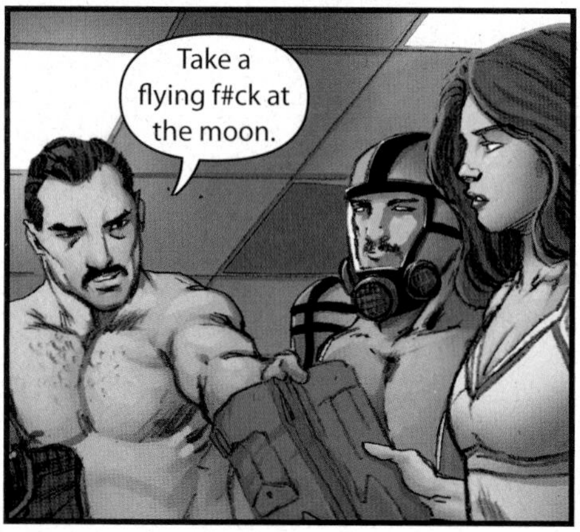
Take a
flying f#ck at
the moon.

Take a flying f#ck at a rolling donut

First use: Kurt Vonnegut used the phrase verbatim in *Slaughterhouse-Five* (1969) and again in *Slapstick* (1976): "Go take a flying f#ck at a rolling doughnut.... Go take a flying f#ck at the moon."

Etymology: Variations of the phrase date back to 1926: American author and US Army Colonel L.H. Nason used the phrase in *Chevrons*, a novel about life in the Field Artillery during WWI ("Me, I'd tell'em to take a flyin' fling at the moon."). "Flying f#ck" originally meant "sex had on horseback." The phrase appeared in 1800 in a broadside ballad called "New Feats of Horsemanship":

Well mounted on a mettled steed
Famed for his strength as well as speed
Corinna and her favorite buck
Are pleas'd to have a flying f#ck.

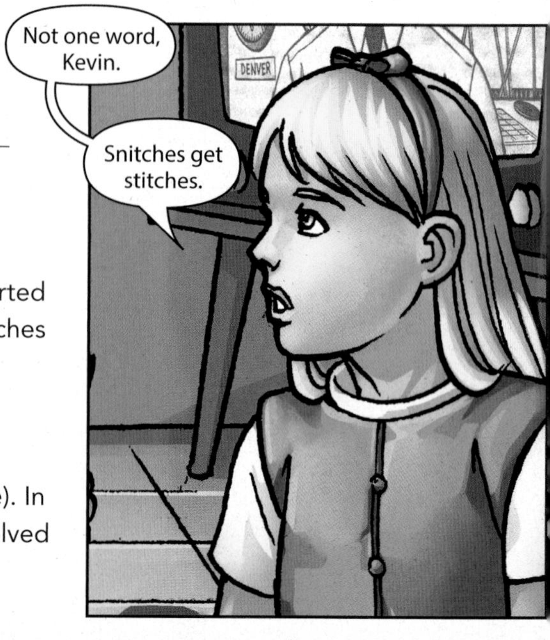
Not one word,
Kevin.
Snitches get
stitches.
DENVER

Snitches get stitches

First use: Possibly in the streets of late 1980s New York City; around this time, newspapers in NYC started using this phrase in articles. Other phrasings: "Snitches get stitches and end up in ditches."

Etymology: "Snitch" as slang for "informer" dates back to 1785. In the late 1600s, "snitch" originally meant a "fillip on the nose" (i.e., a flick on the nose). In the early 18th century, the meaning of "snitch" evolved to mean "nose," a symbol of intrusion into others' business ("nosy").

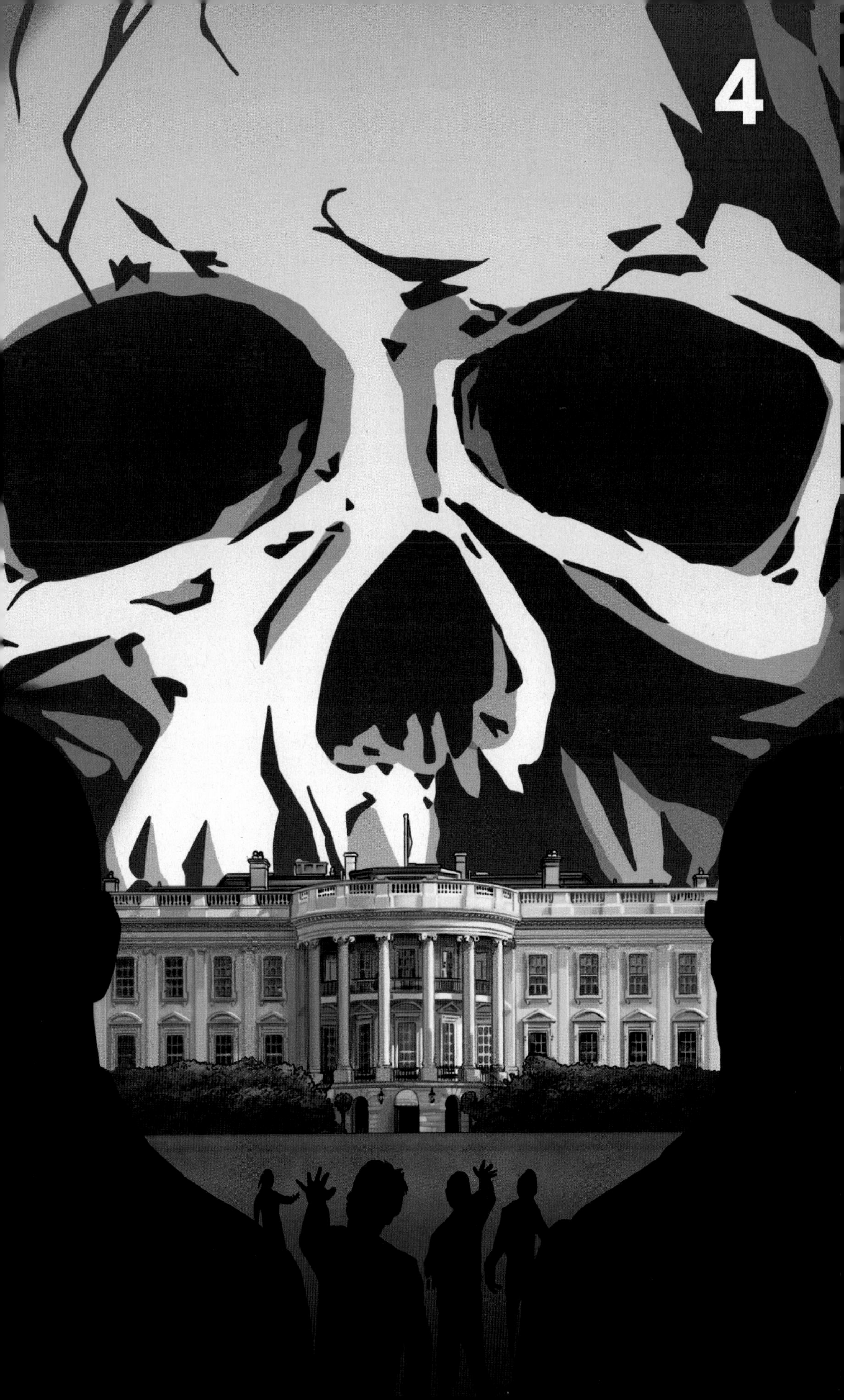
4

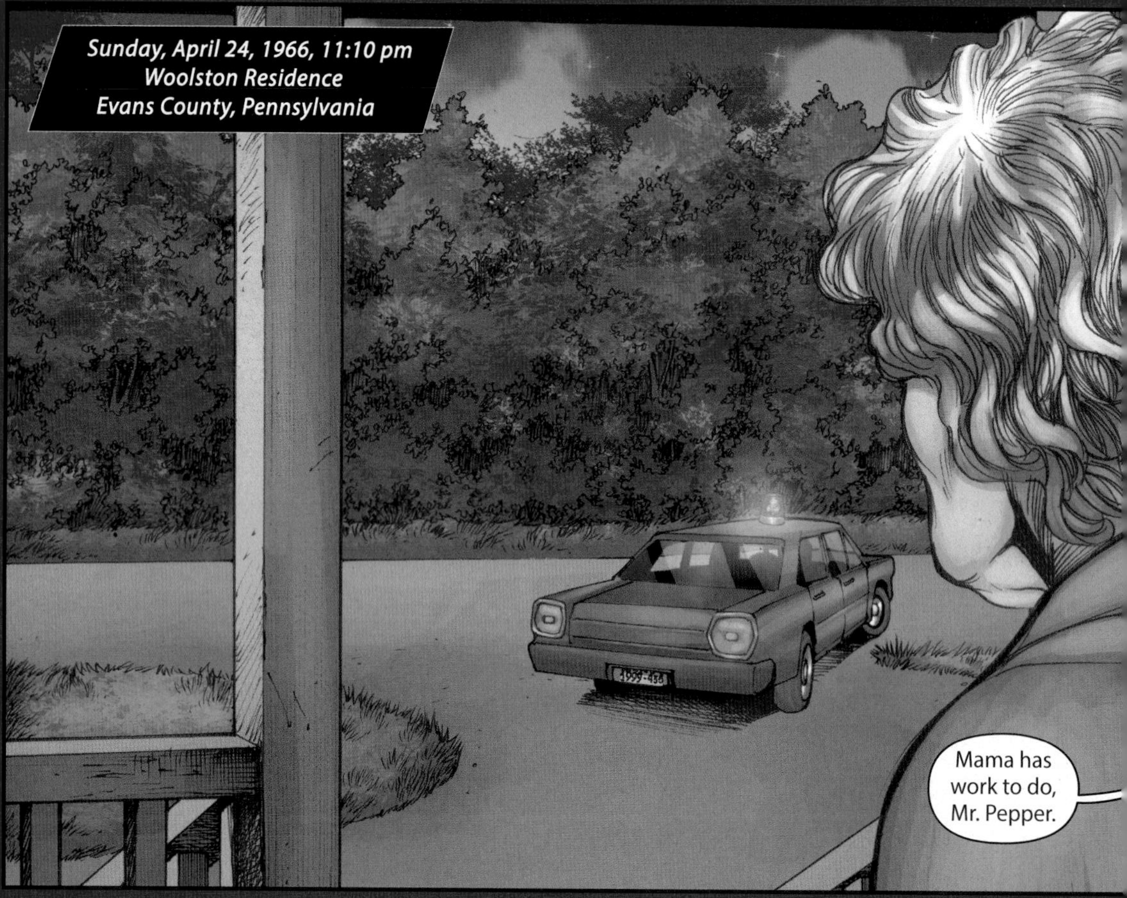
Sunday, April 24, 1966, 11:10 pm
Woolston Residence
Evans County, Pennsylvania
Mama has work to do, Mr. Pepper.

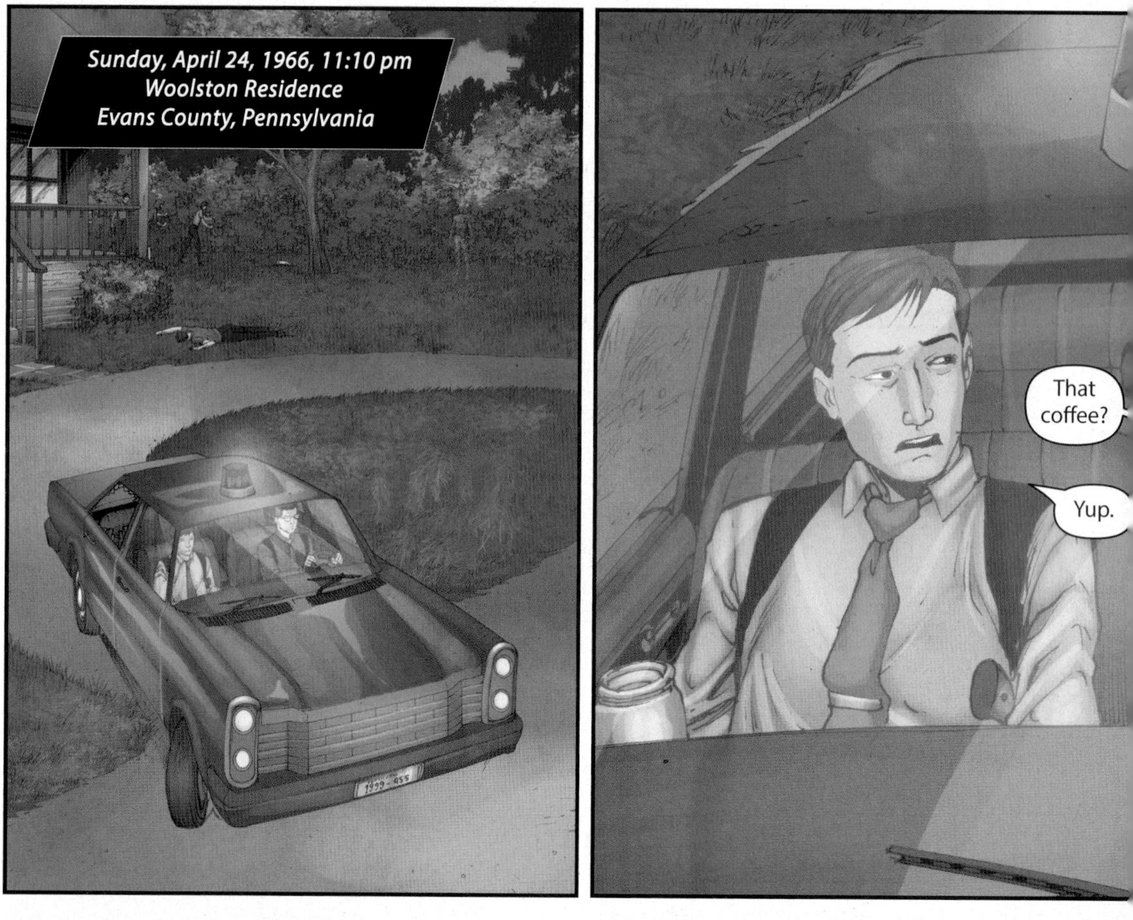
Sunday, April 24, 1966, 11:10 pm
Woolston Residence
Evans County, Pennsylvania
That coffee?
Yup.

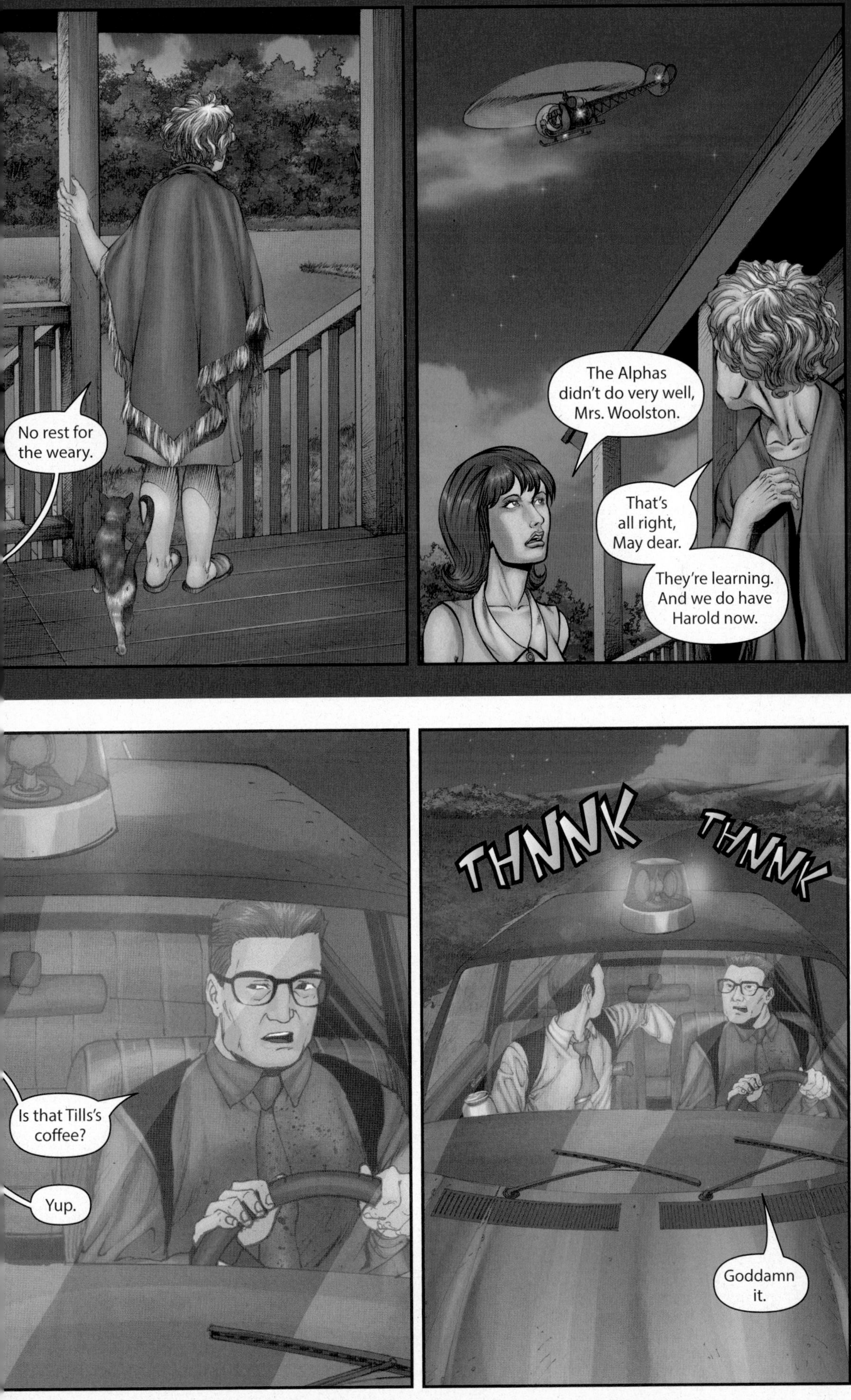
No rest for the weary.
The Alphas didn't do very well, Mrs. Woolston.
That's all right, May dear.
They're learning. And we do have Harold now.
Is that Tills's coffee?
Yup.
THNNK
THNNK
Goddamn it.

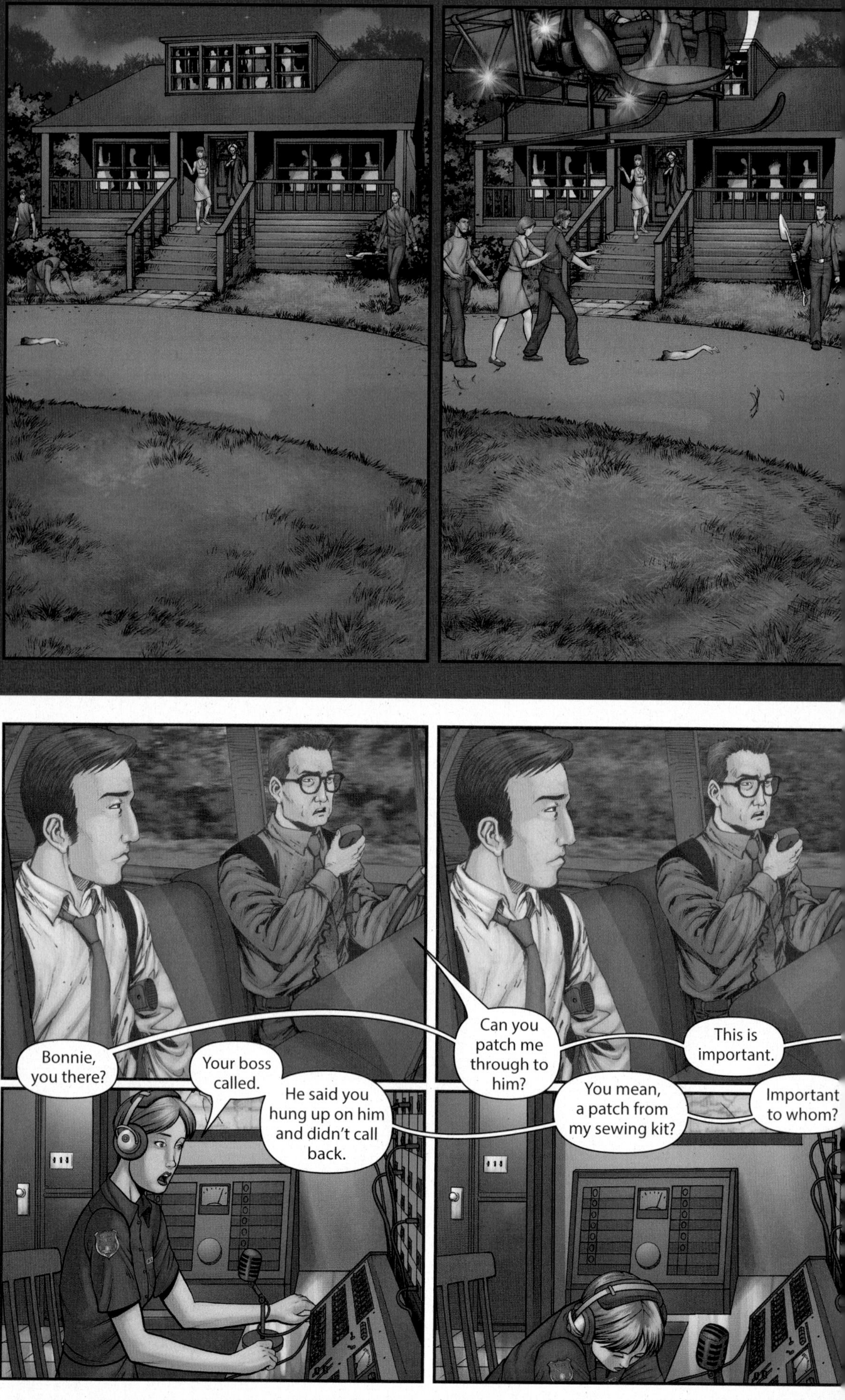
Bonnie, you there?
Your boss called.
He said you hung up on him and didn't call back.
Can you patch me through to him?
You mean, a patch from my sewing kit?
This is important.
Important to whom?

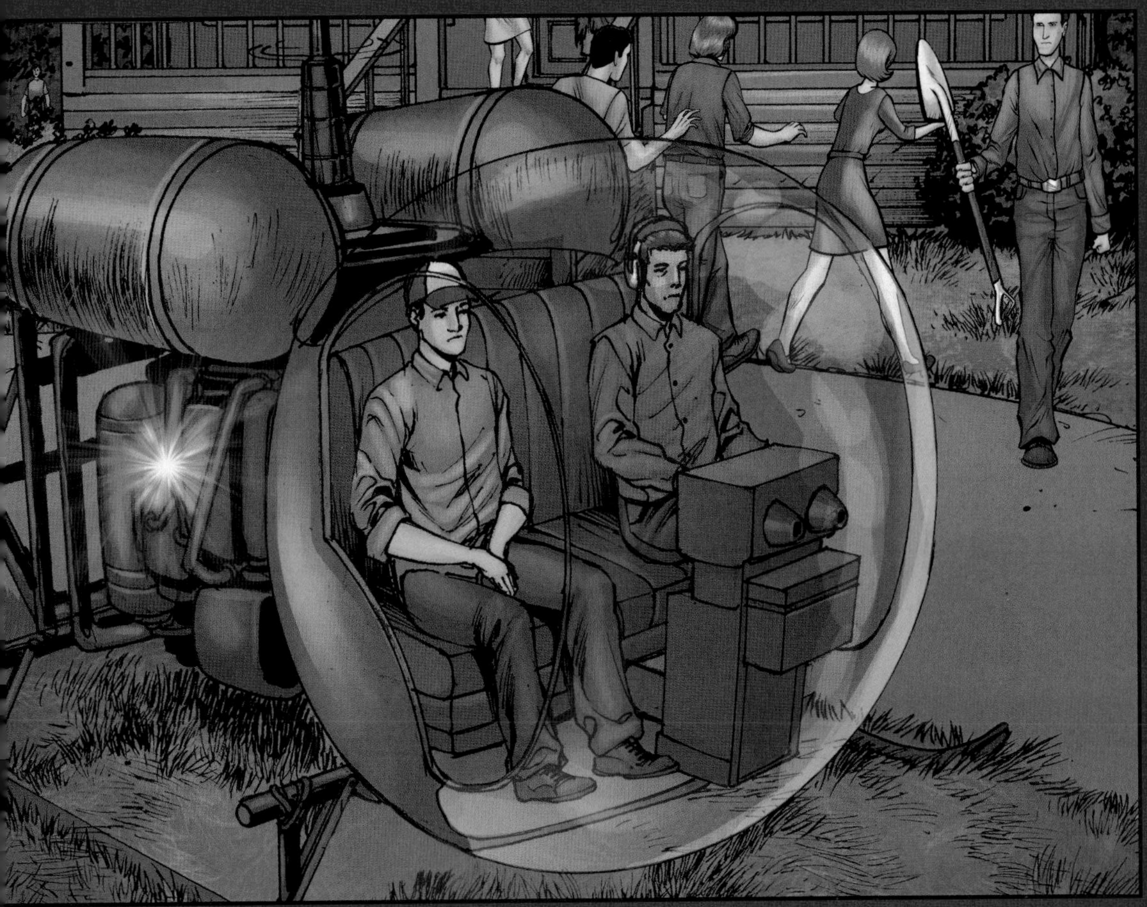

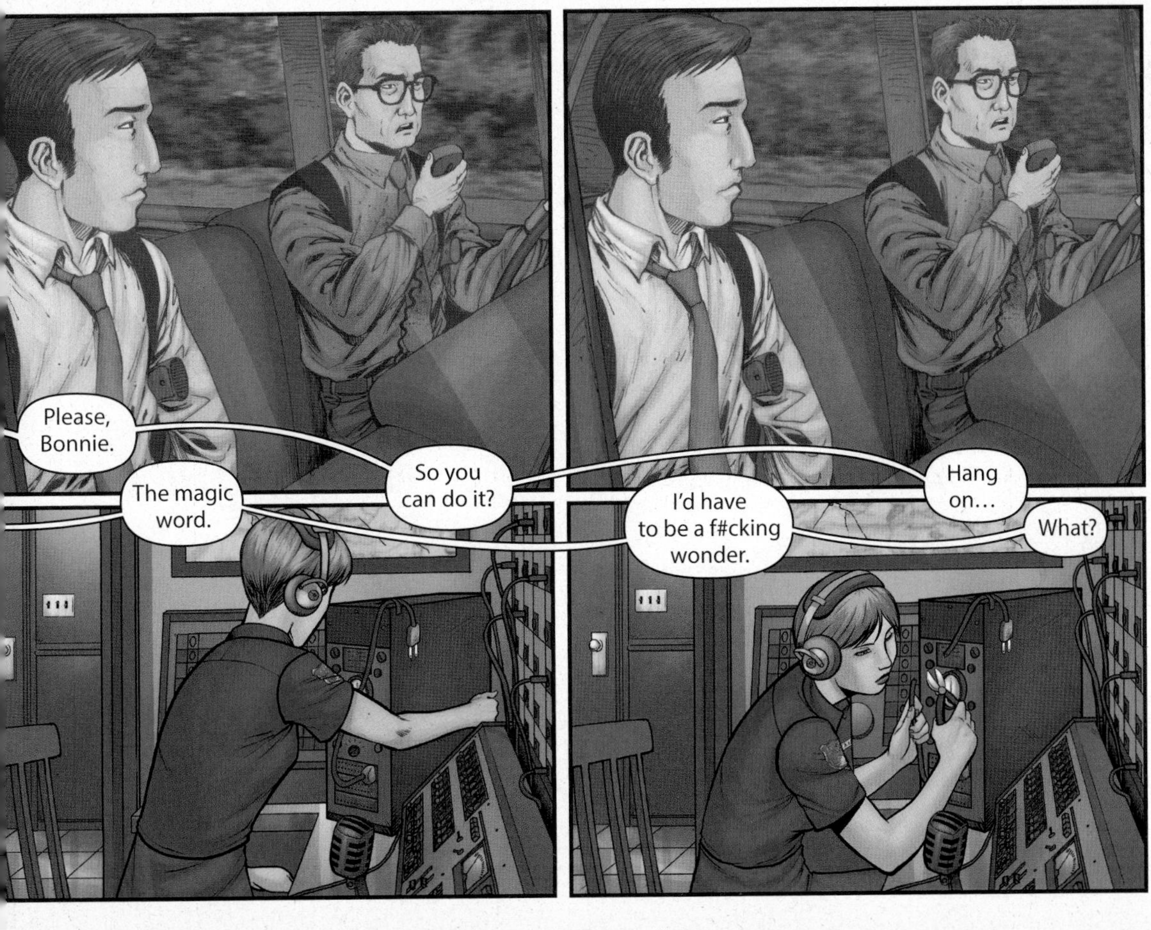

Please, Bonnie.
The magic word.
So you can do it?
I'd have to be a f#cking wonder.
Hang on…
What?

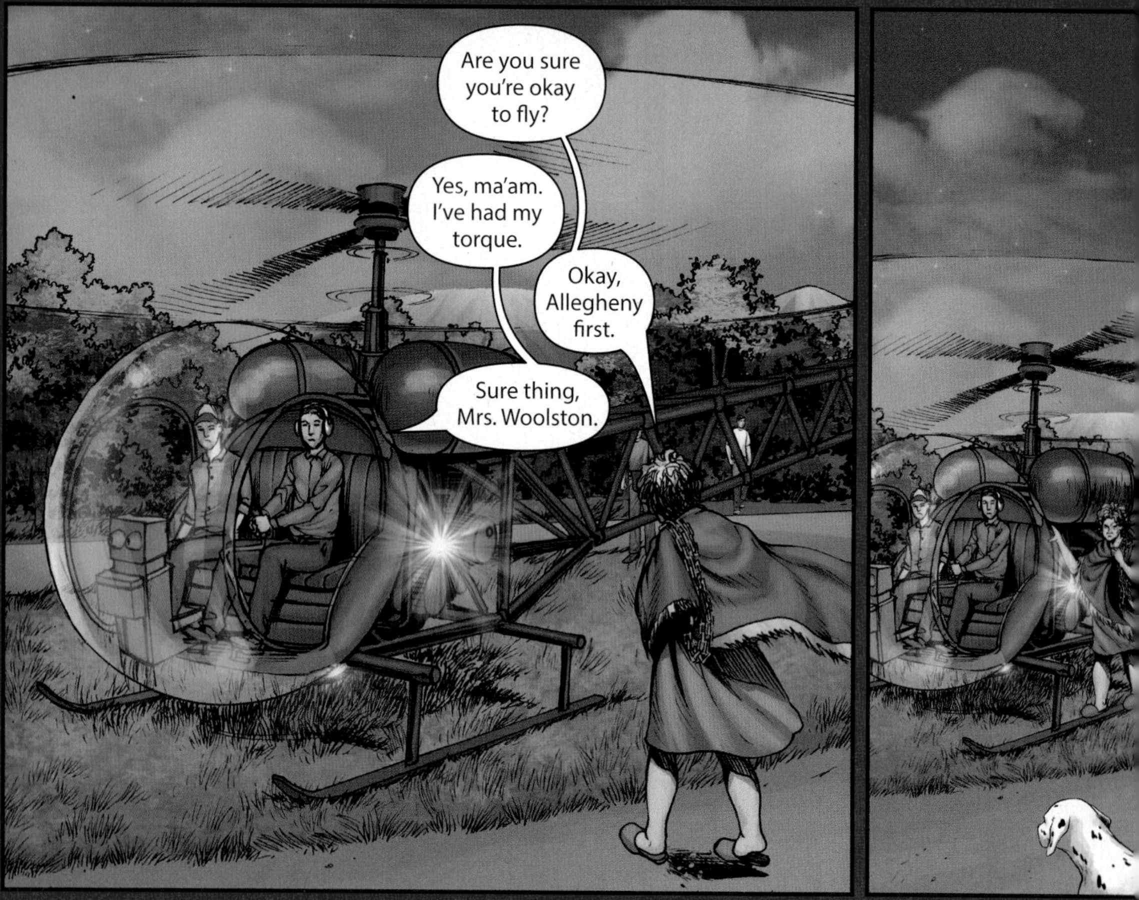
Are you sure you're okay to fly?
Yes, ma'am. I've had my torque.
Okay, Allegheny first.
Sure thing, Mrs. Woolston.

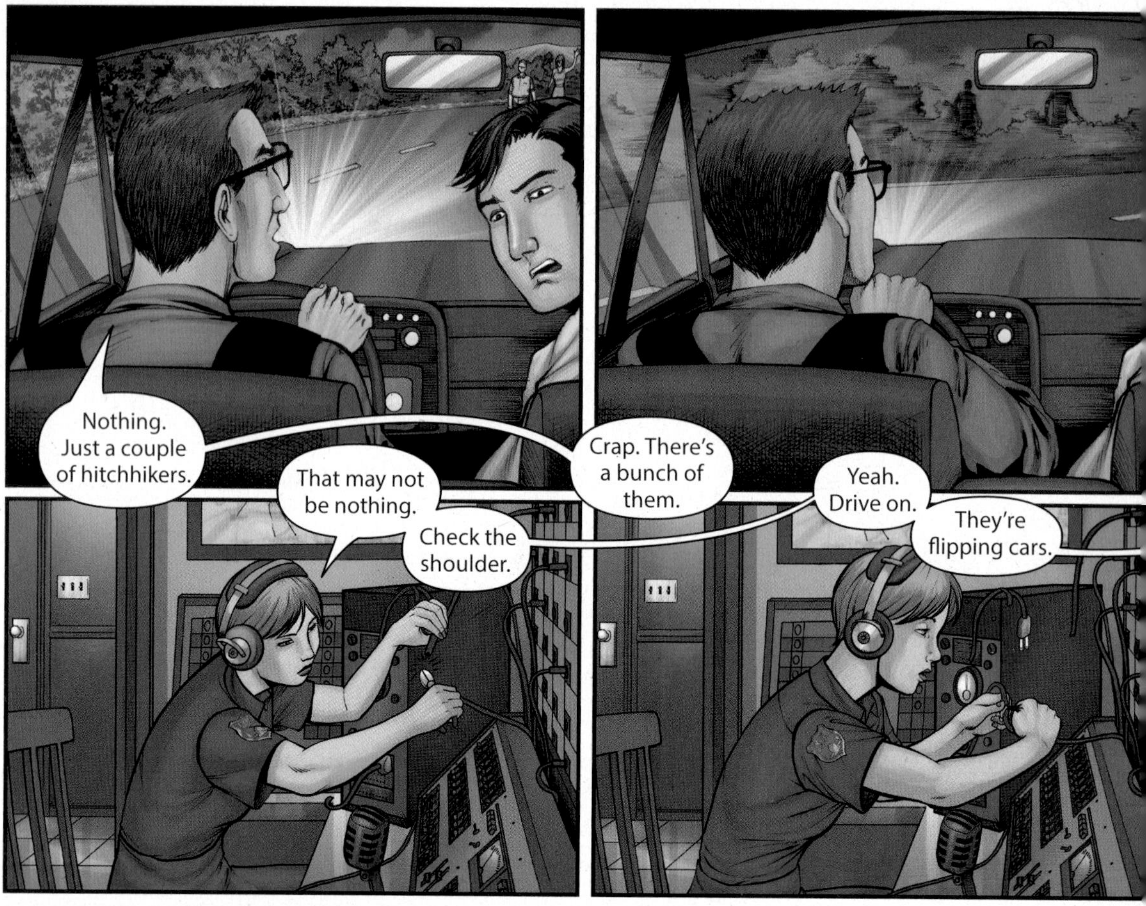
Nothing. Just a couple of hitchhikers.
That may not be nothing.
Check the shoulder.
Crap. There's a bunch of them.
Yeah. Drive on.
They're flipping cars.

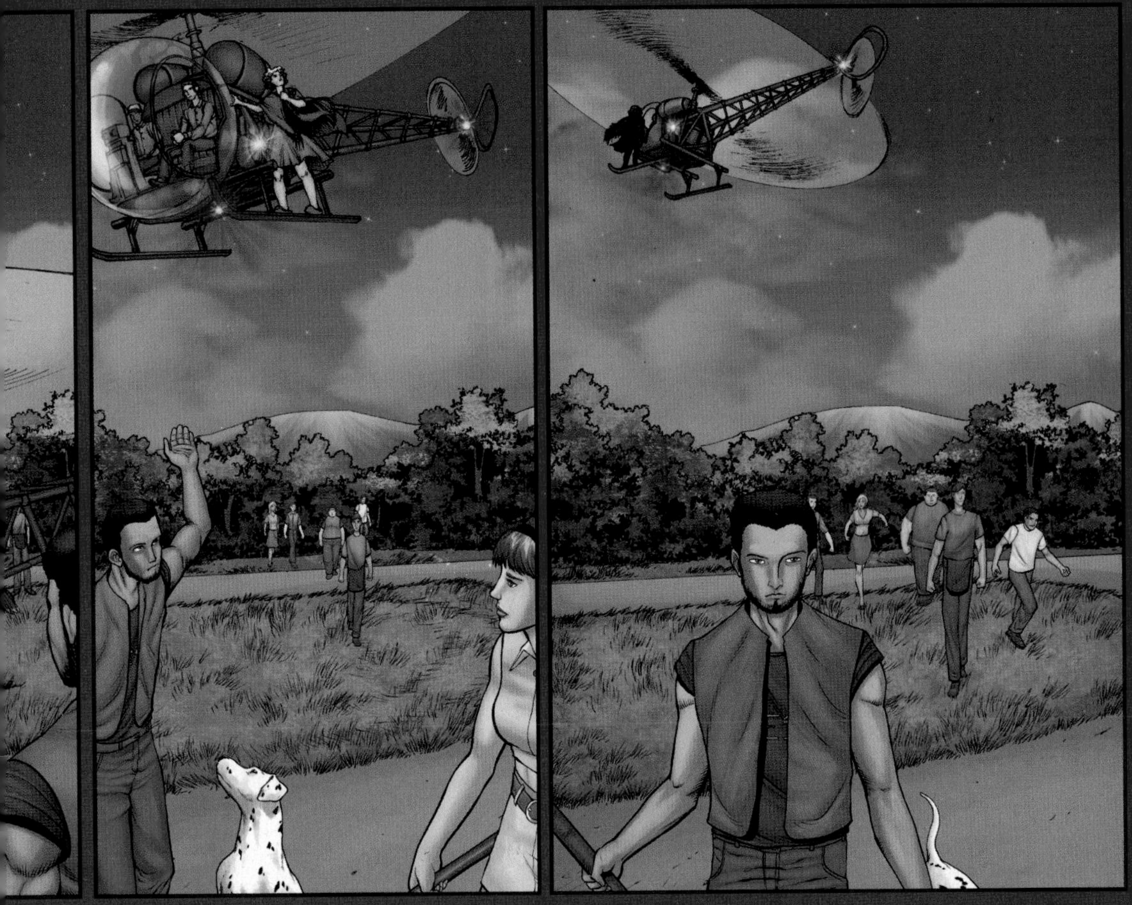

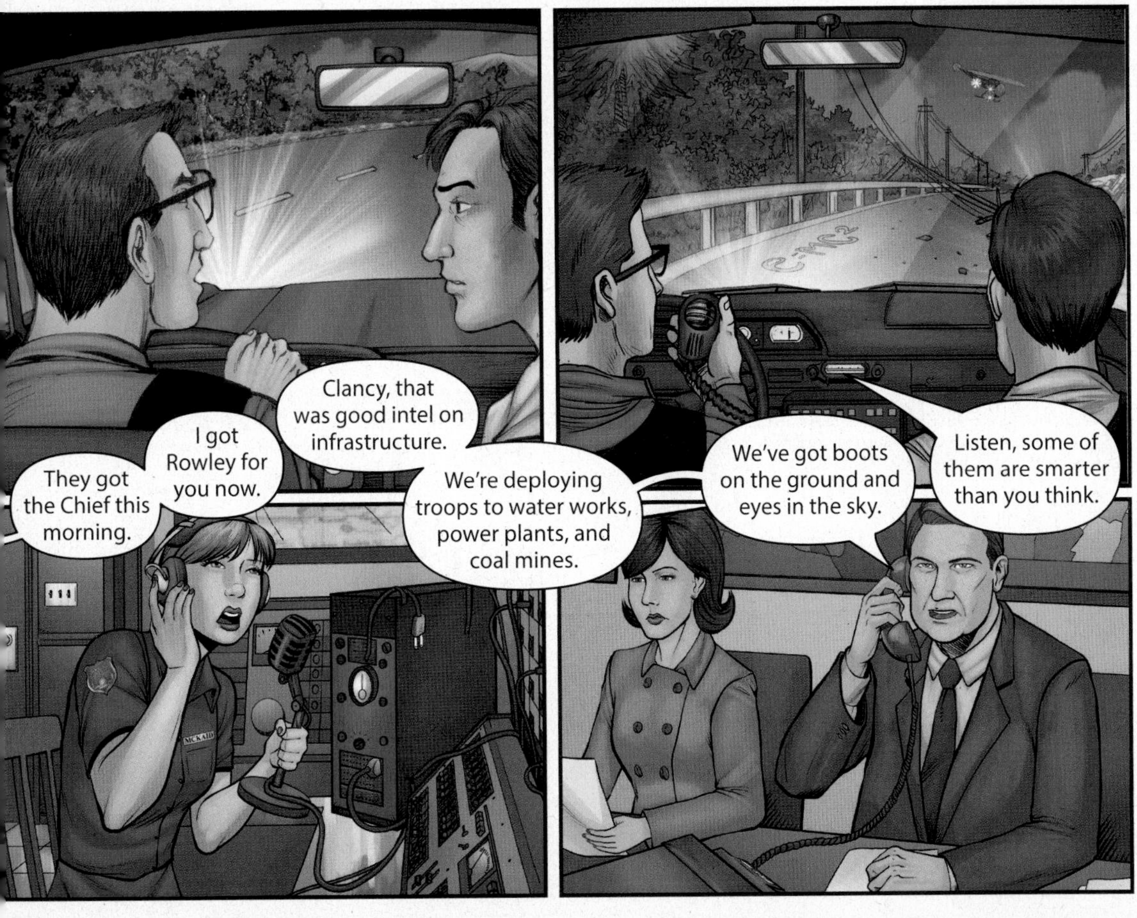
They got the Chief this morning.
I got Rowley for you now.
Clancy, that was good intel on infrastructure.
We're deploying troops to water works, power plants, and coal mines.
We've got boots on the ground and eyes in the sky.
Listen, some of them are smarter than you think.

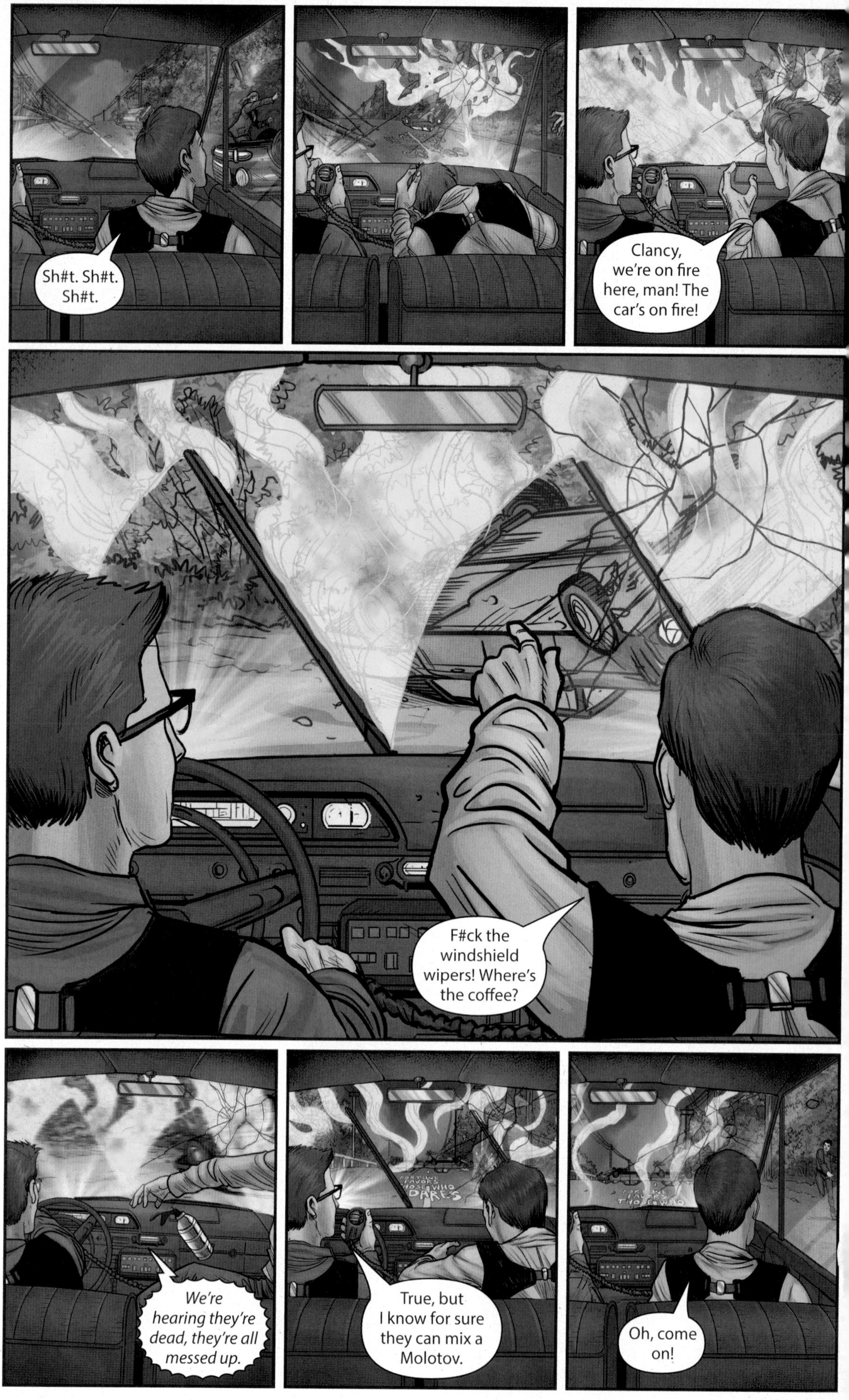
Sh#t. Sh#t. Sh#t.
Clancy, we're on fire here, man! The car's on fire!
F#ck the windshield wipers! Where's the coffee?
We're hearing they're dead, they're all messed up.
True, but I know for sure they can mix a Molotov.
Oh, come on!

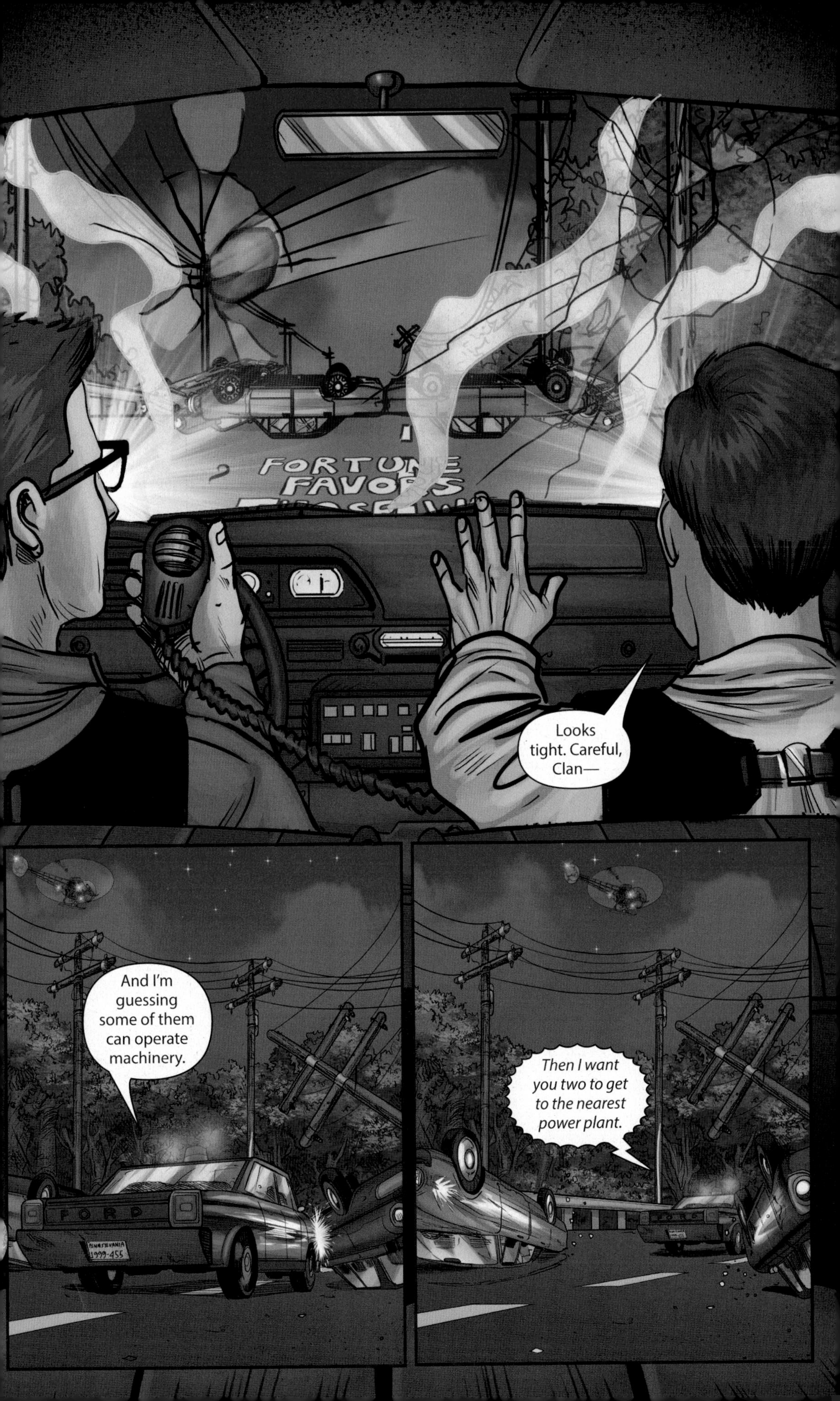
FORTUNE
FAVORS
Looks tight. Careful, Clan—
FORD
PENNSYLVANIA
1999-455
And I'm guessing some of them can operate machinery.
Then I want you two to get to the nearest power plant.

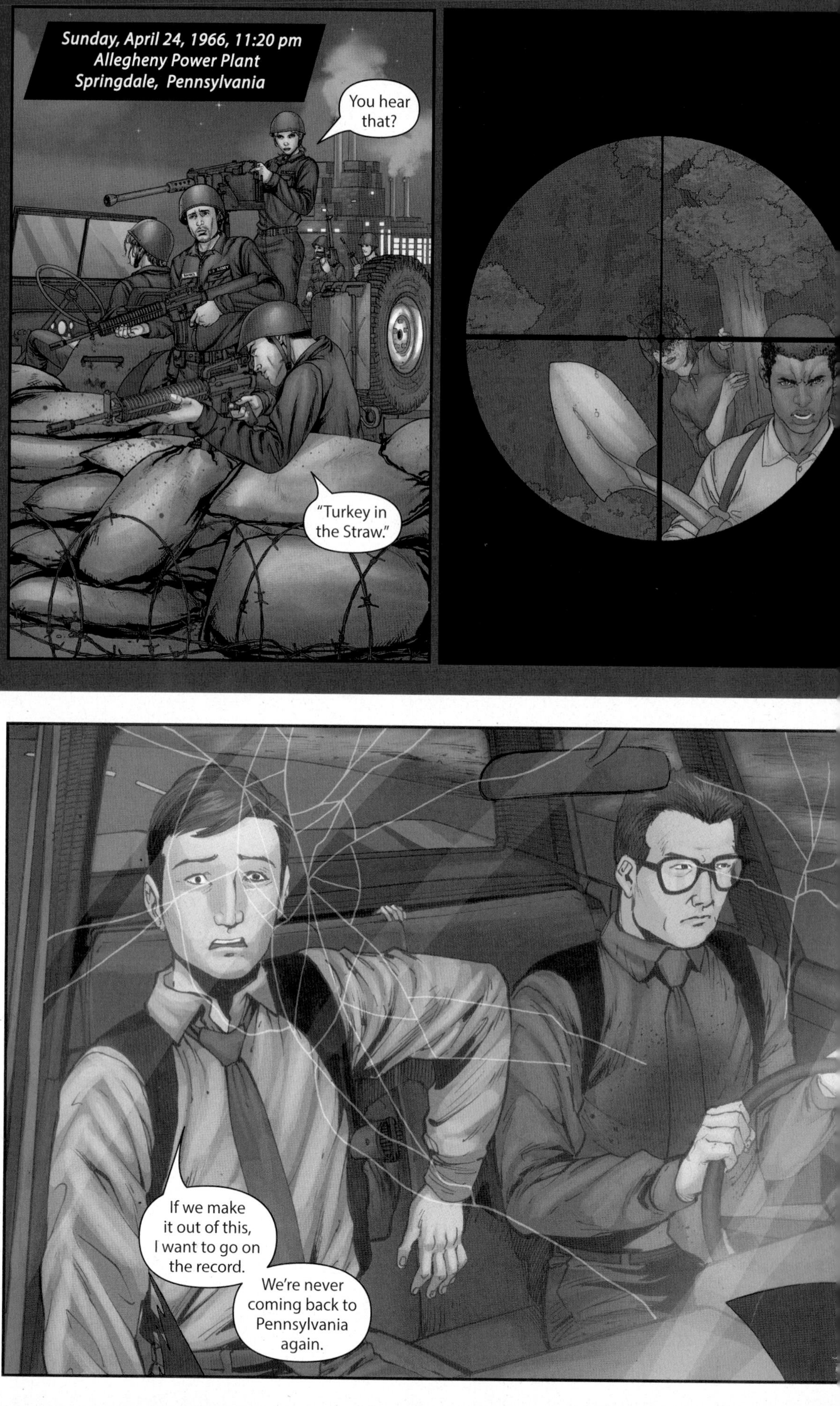
Sunday, April 24, 1966, 11:20 pm
Allegheny Power Plant
Springdale, Pennsylvania
You hear that?
"Turkey in the Straw."
If we make it out of this, I want to go on the record.
We're never coming back to Pennsylvania again.

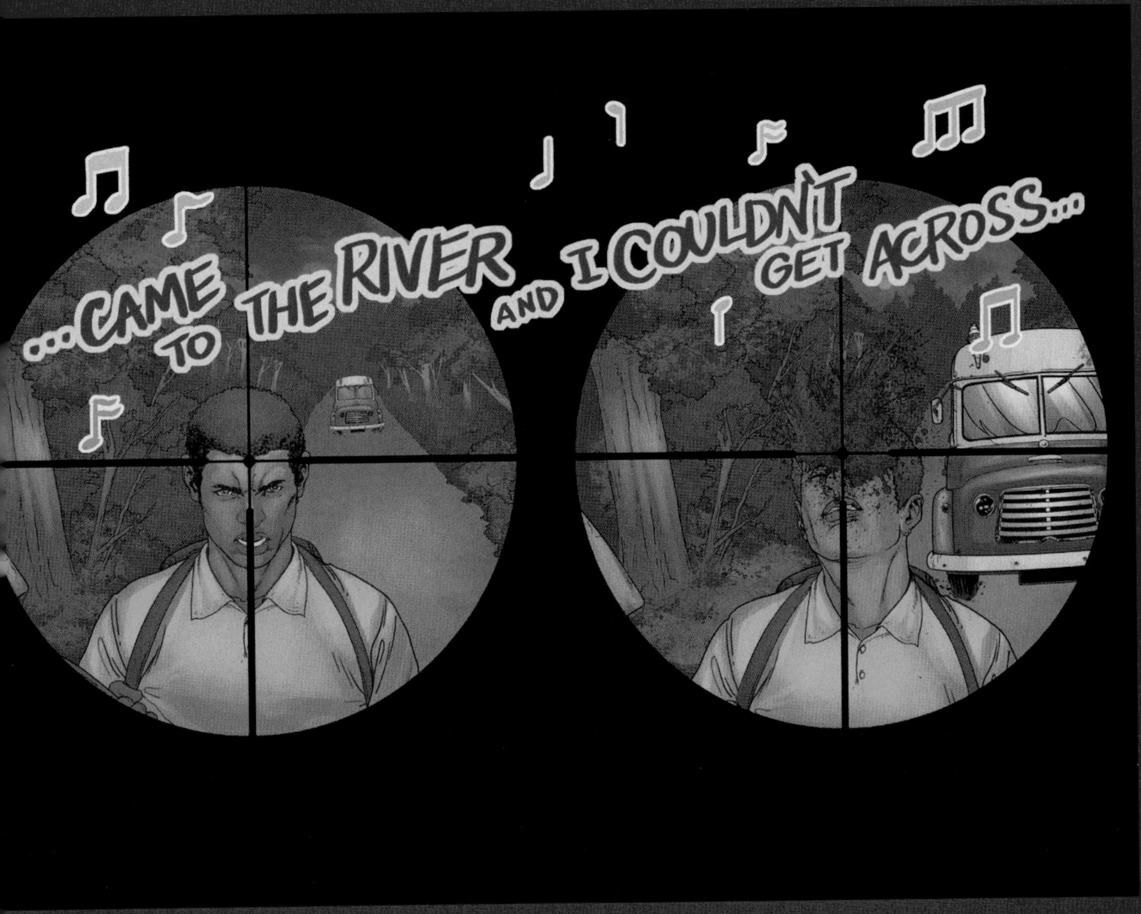
...CAME TO THE RIVER AND I COULDN'T GET ACROSS...

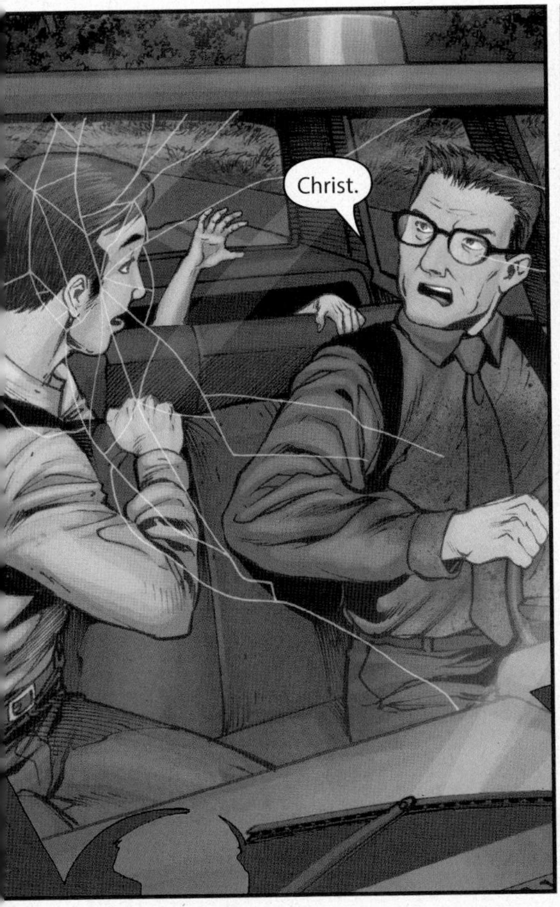
Christ.

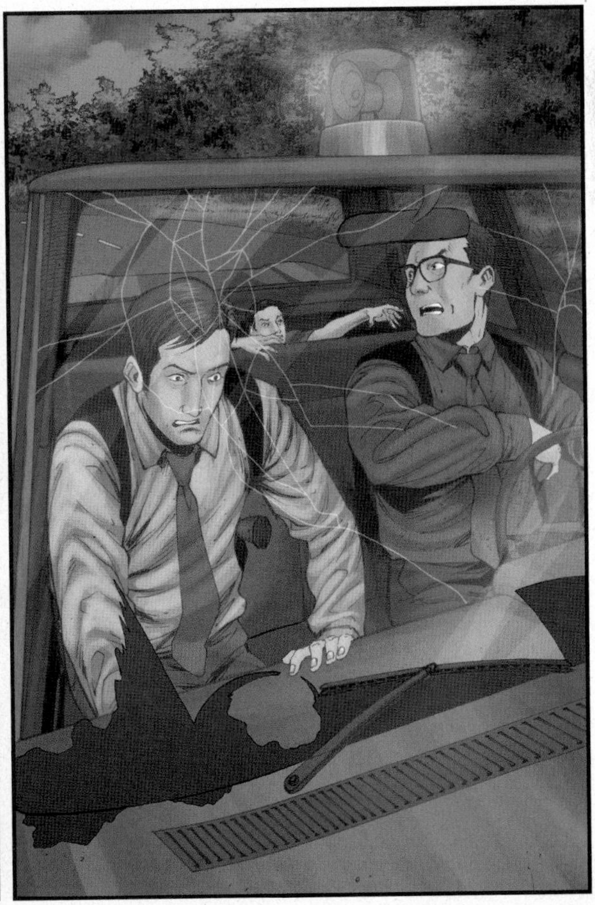

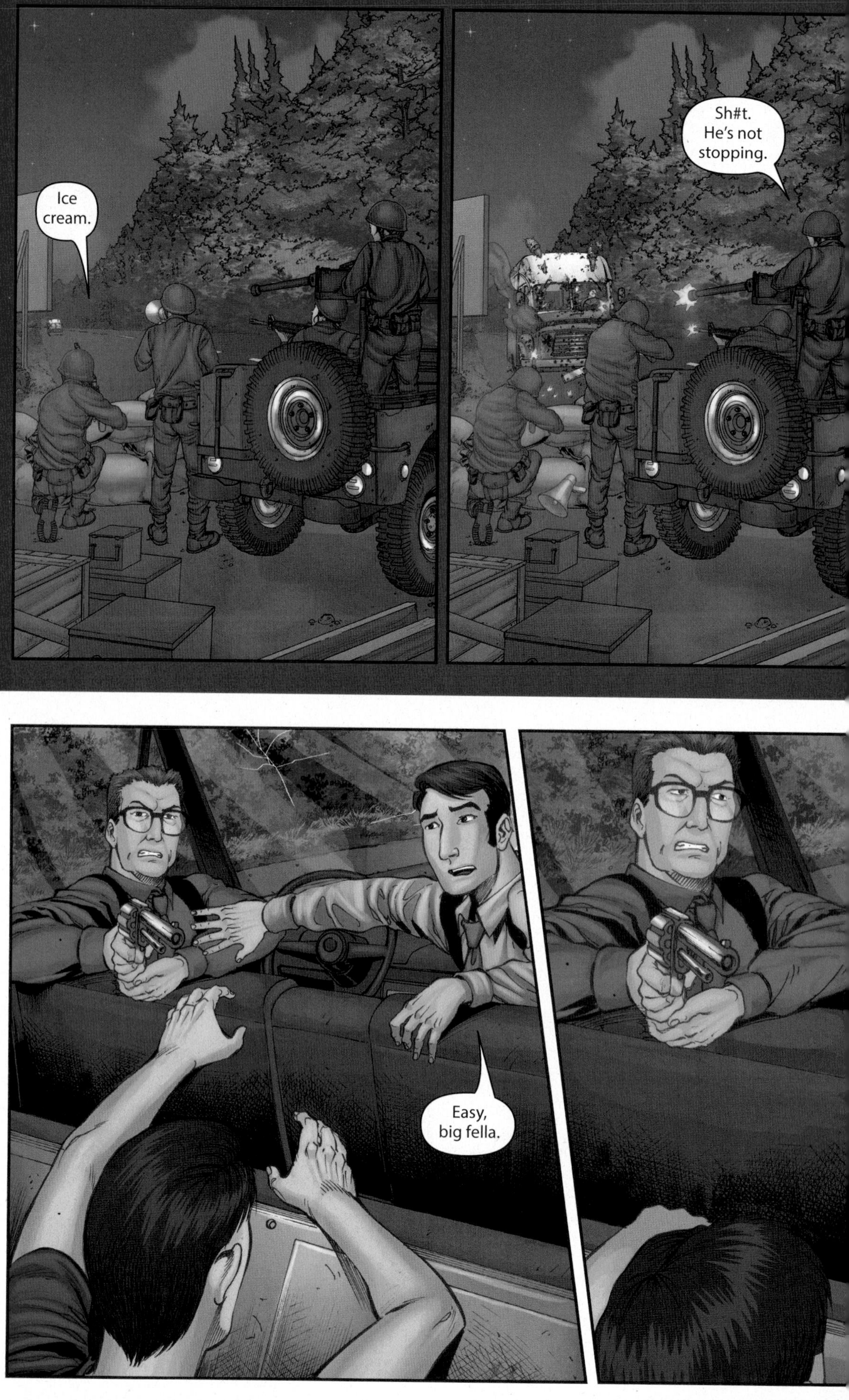
Ice cream.
Sh#t. He's not stopping.
Easy, big fella.

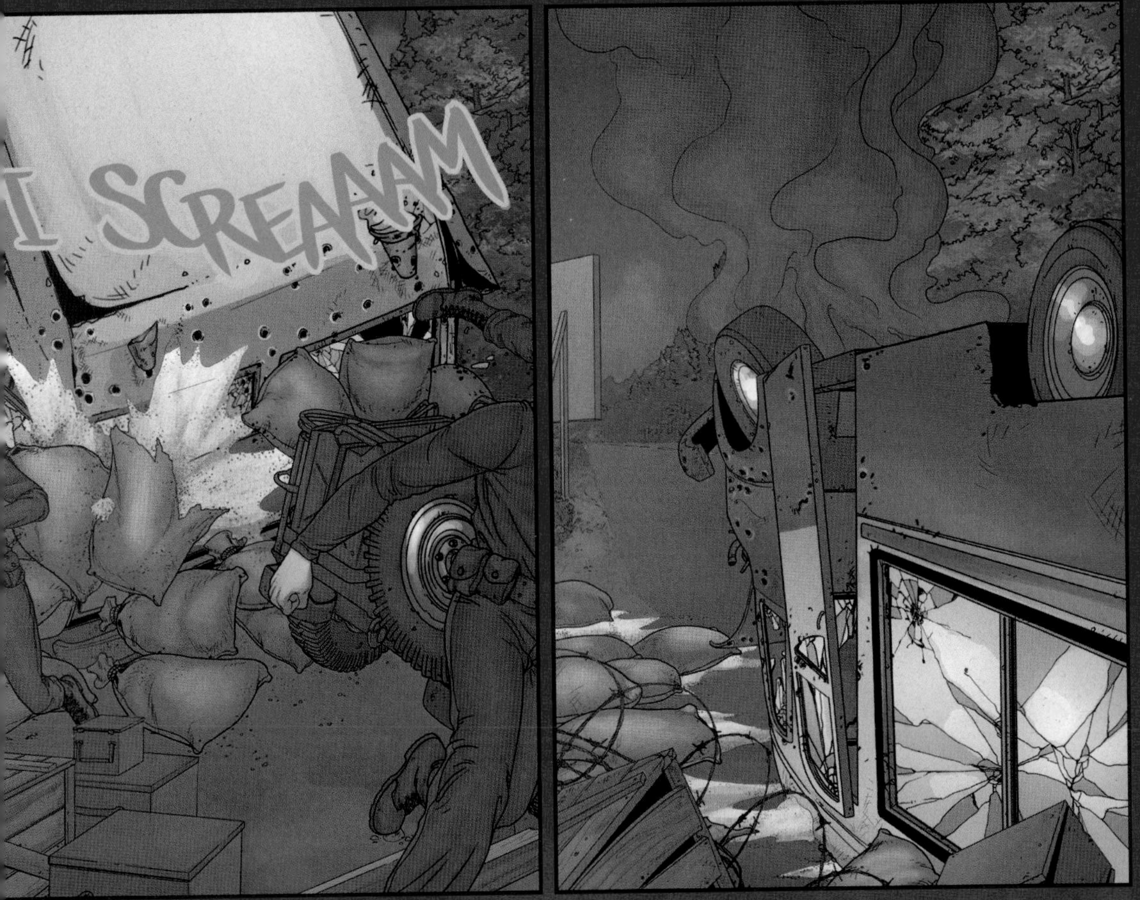
SCREAAAM

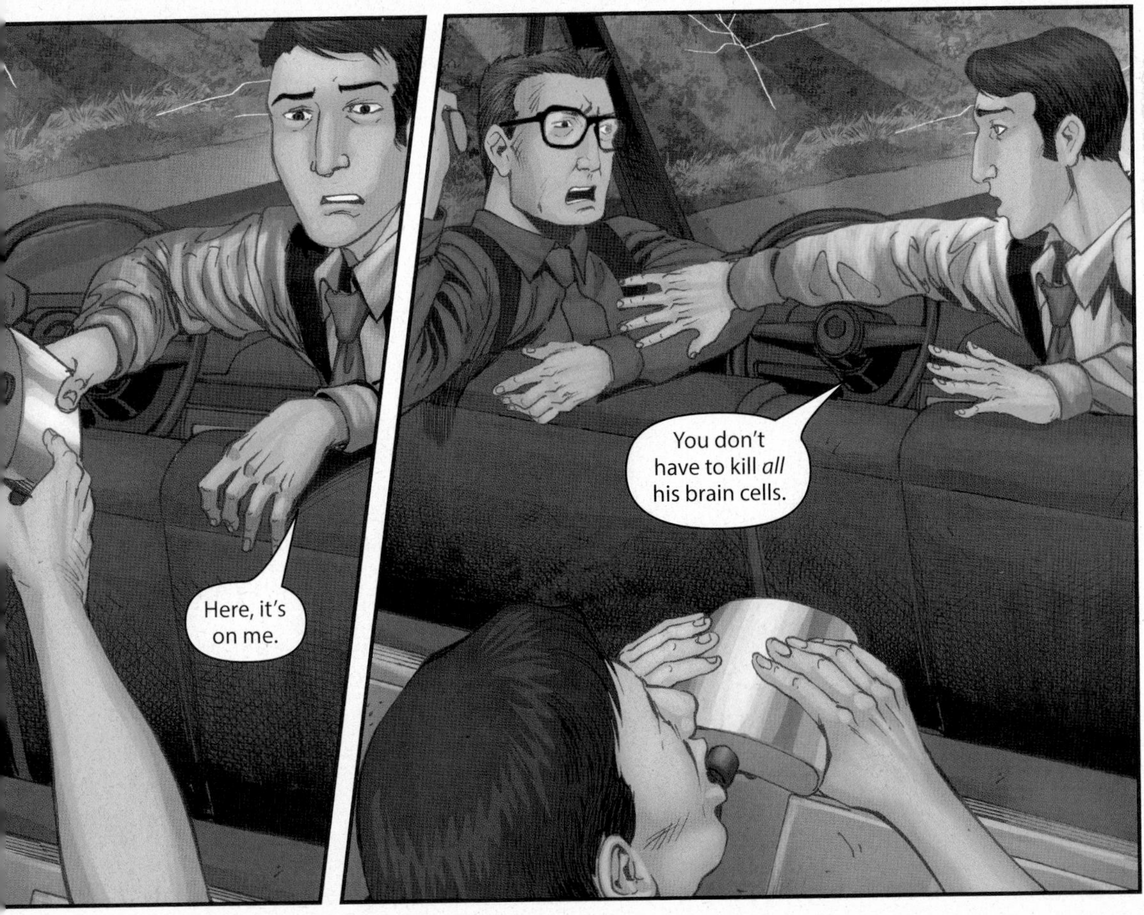
Here, it's on me.
You don't have to kill *all* his brain cells.

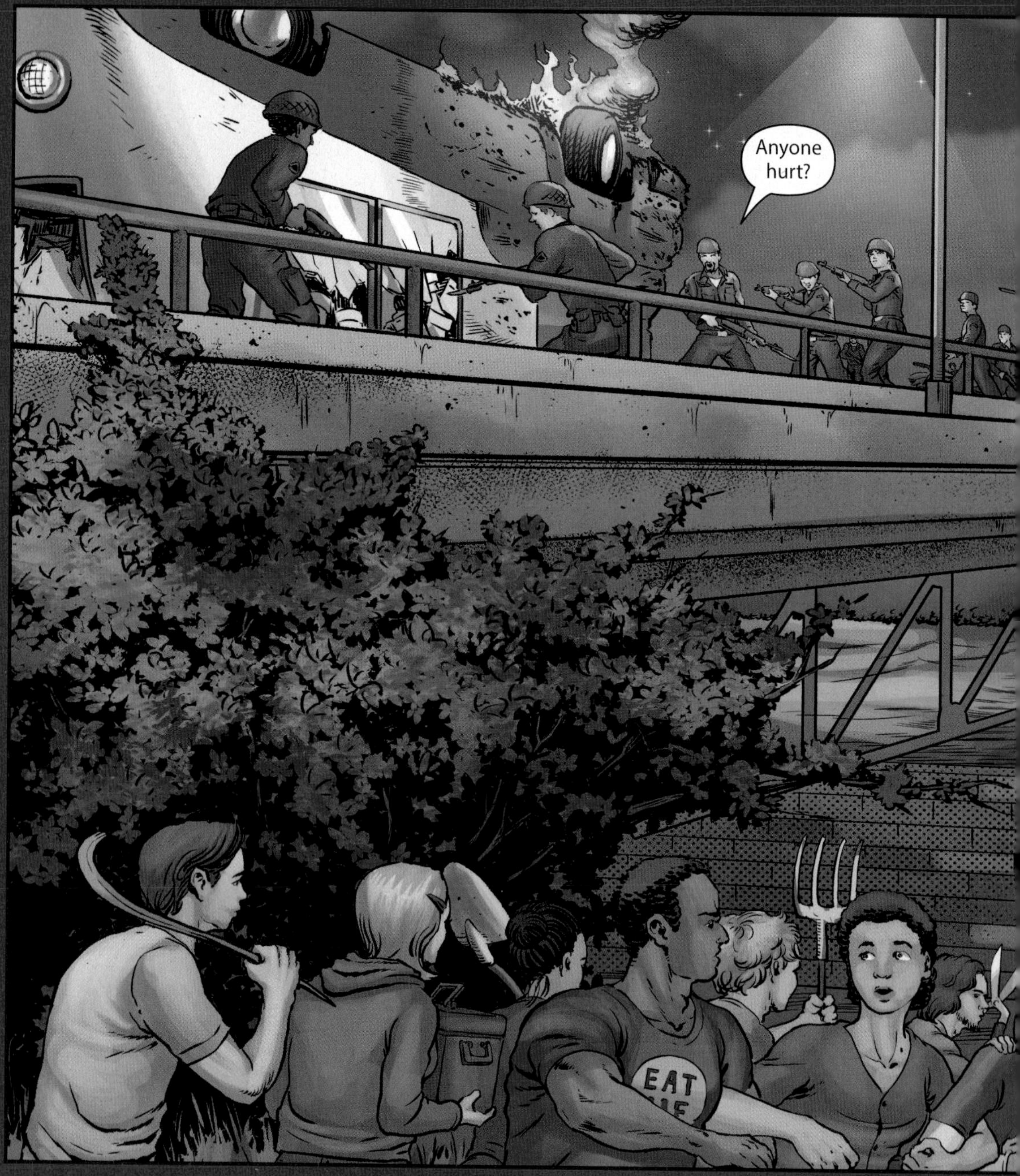
Anyone hurt?
EAT

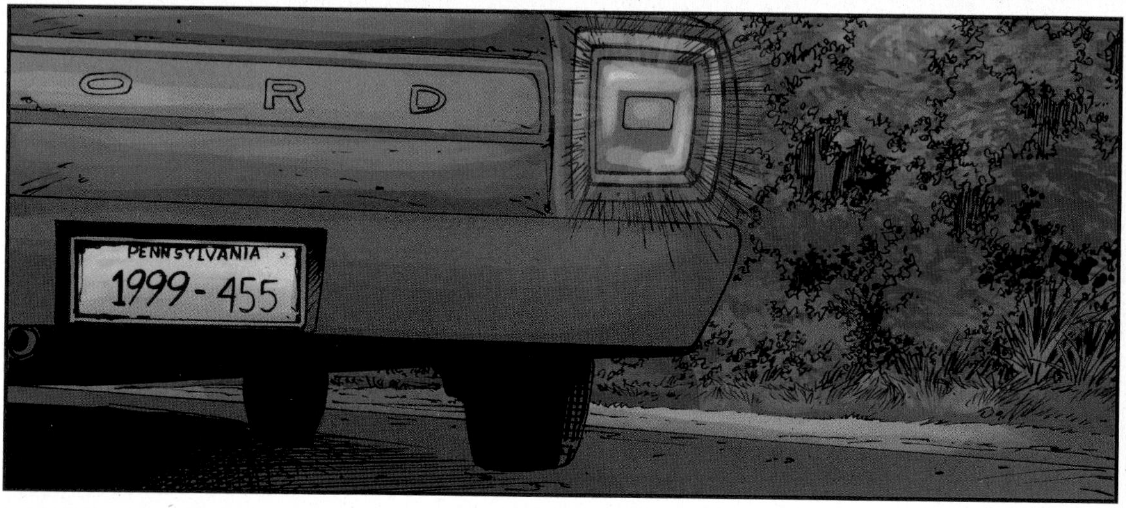
ORD
PENNSYLVANIA
1999-455

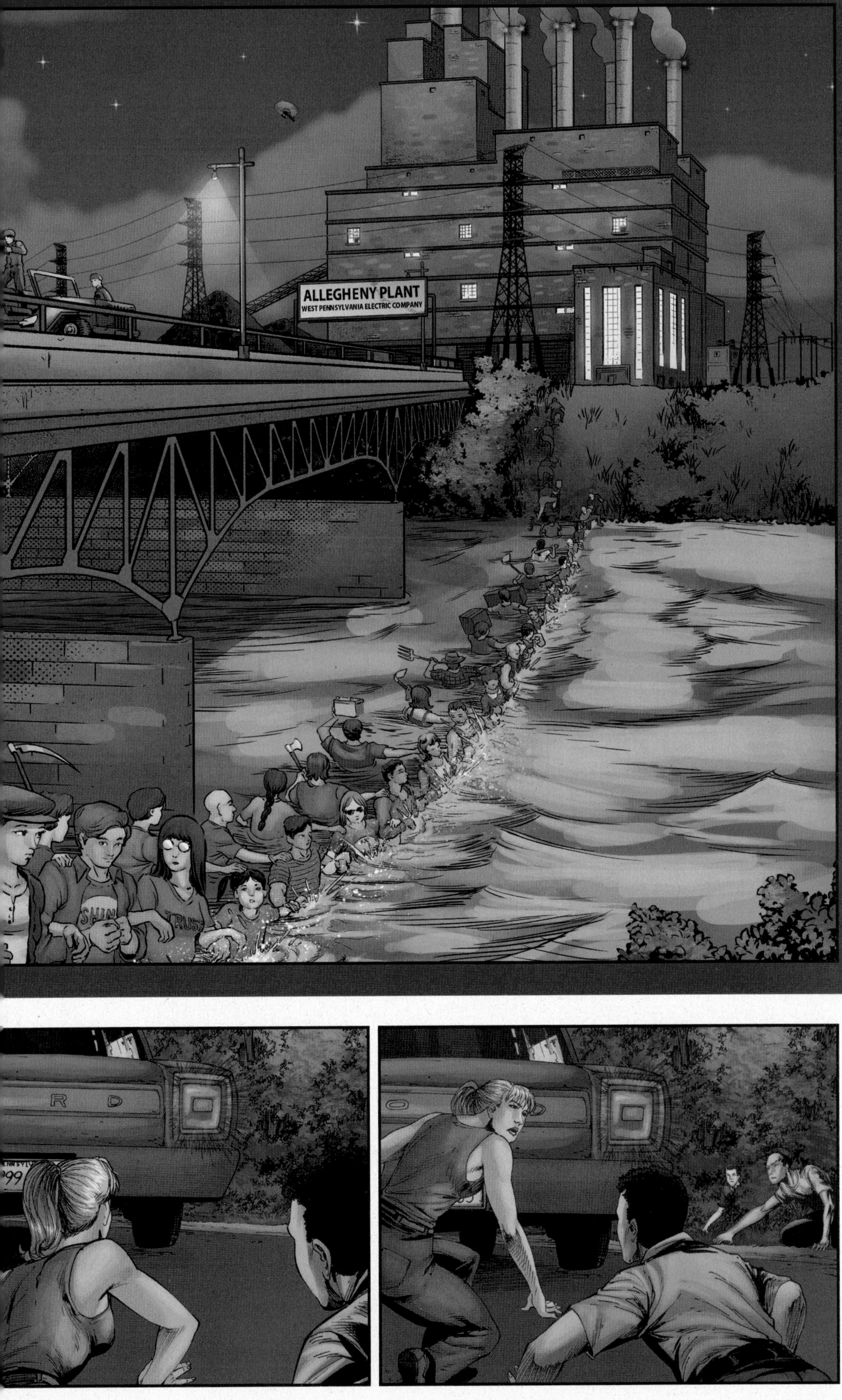
ALLEGHENY PLANT
WEST PENNSYLVANIA ELECTRIC COMPANY

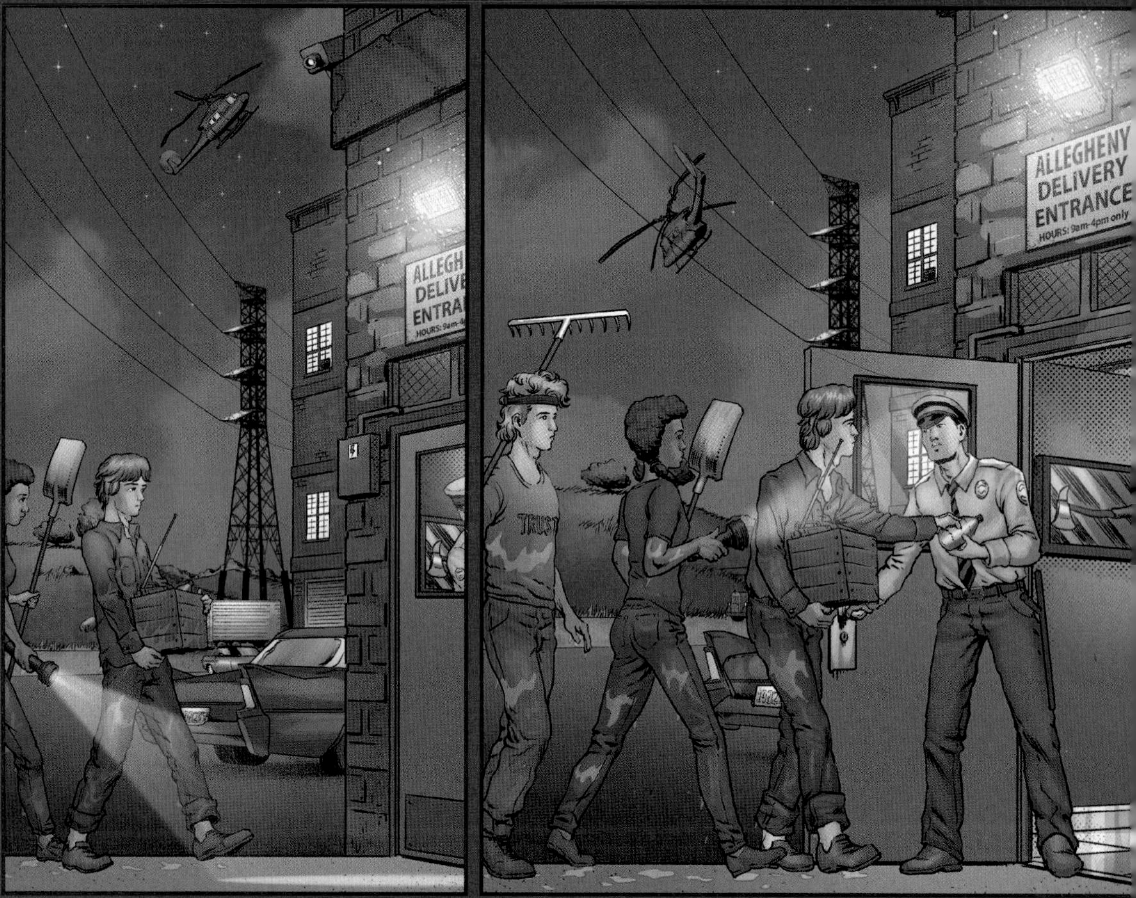
ALLEGHENY
DELIVERY
ENTRANCE
HOURS: 9am-4pm only
TRUST

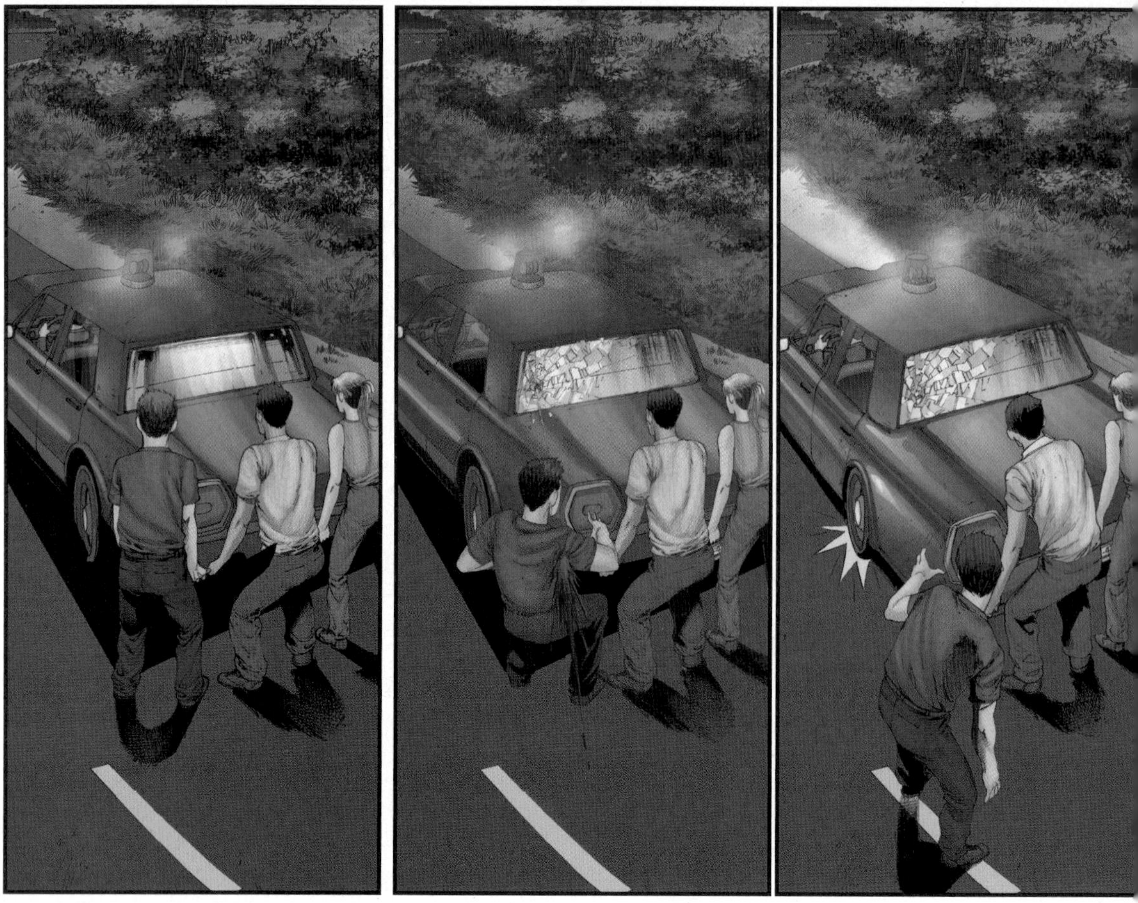

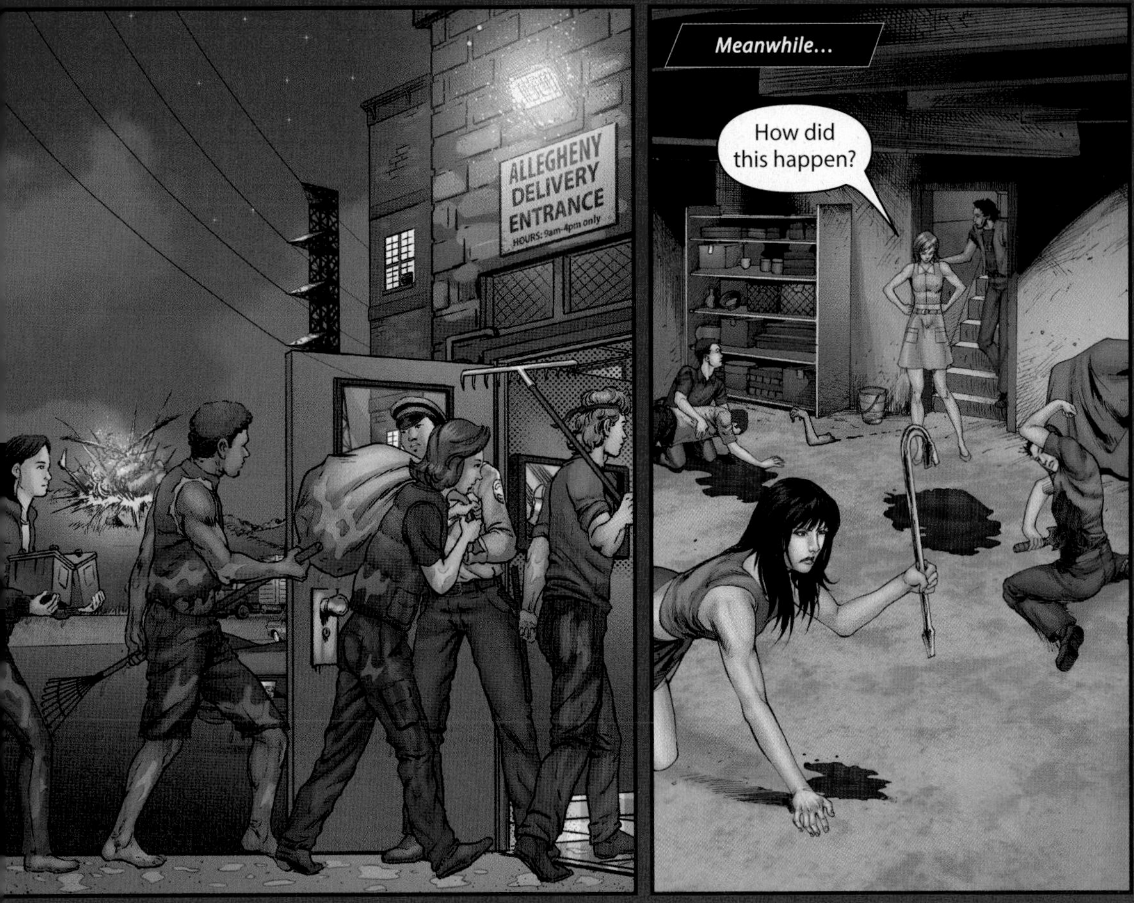
ALLEGHENY
DELIVERY
ENTRANCE
HOURS: 9am-4pm only
Meanwhile...
How did this happen?

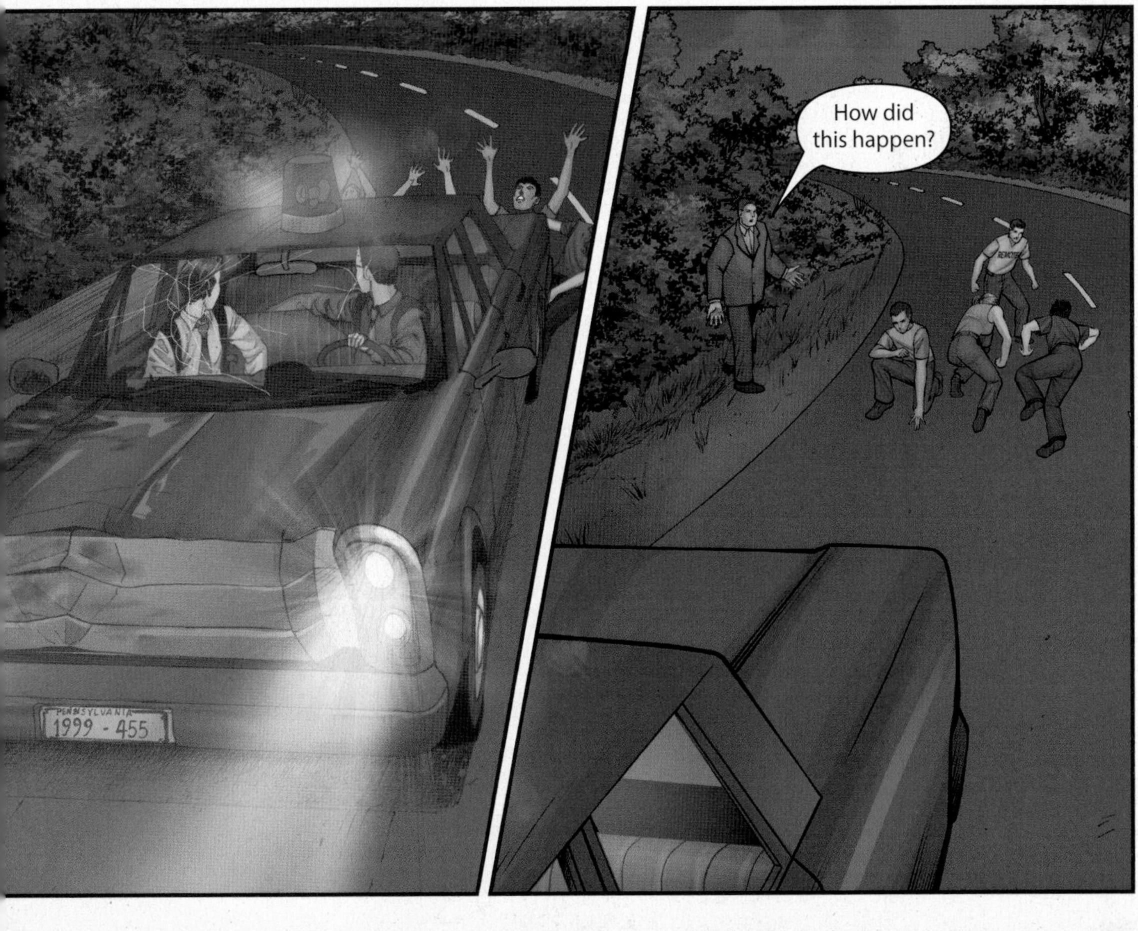
PENNSYLVANIA
1999 - 455
How did this happen?

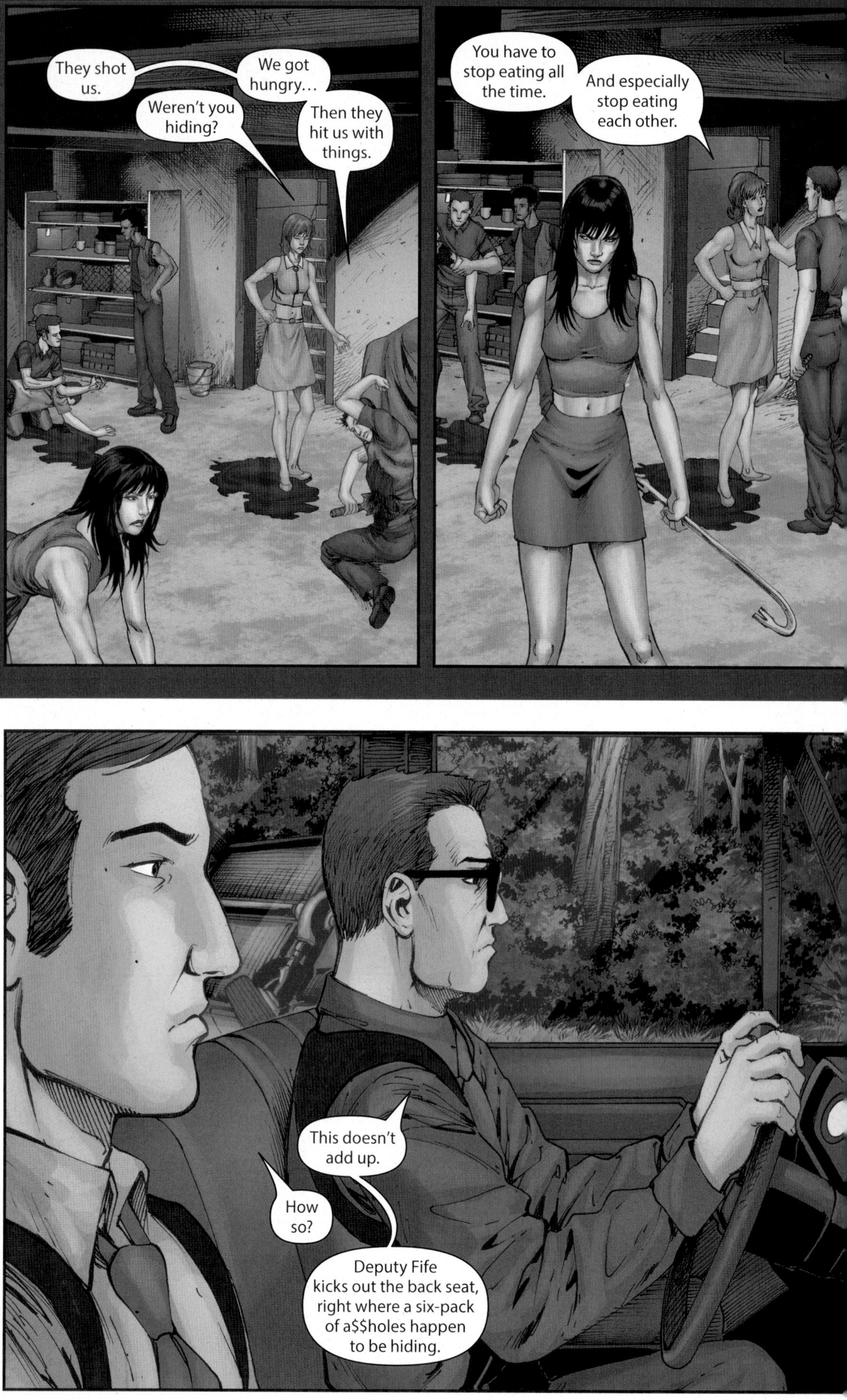
They shot us.
We got hungry…
Weren't you hiding?
Then they hit us with things.
You have to stop eating all the time.
And especially stop eating each other.
This doesn't add up.
How so?
Deputy Fife kicks out the back seat, right where a six-pack of a$$holes happen to be hiding.

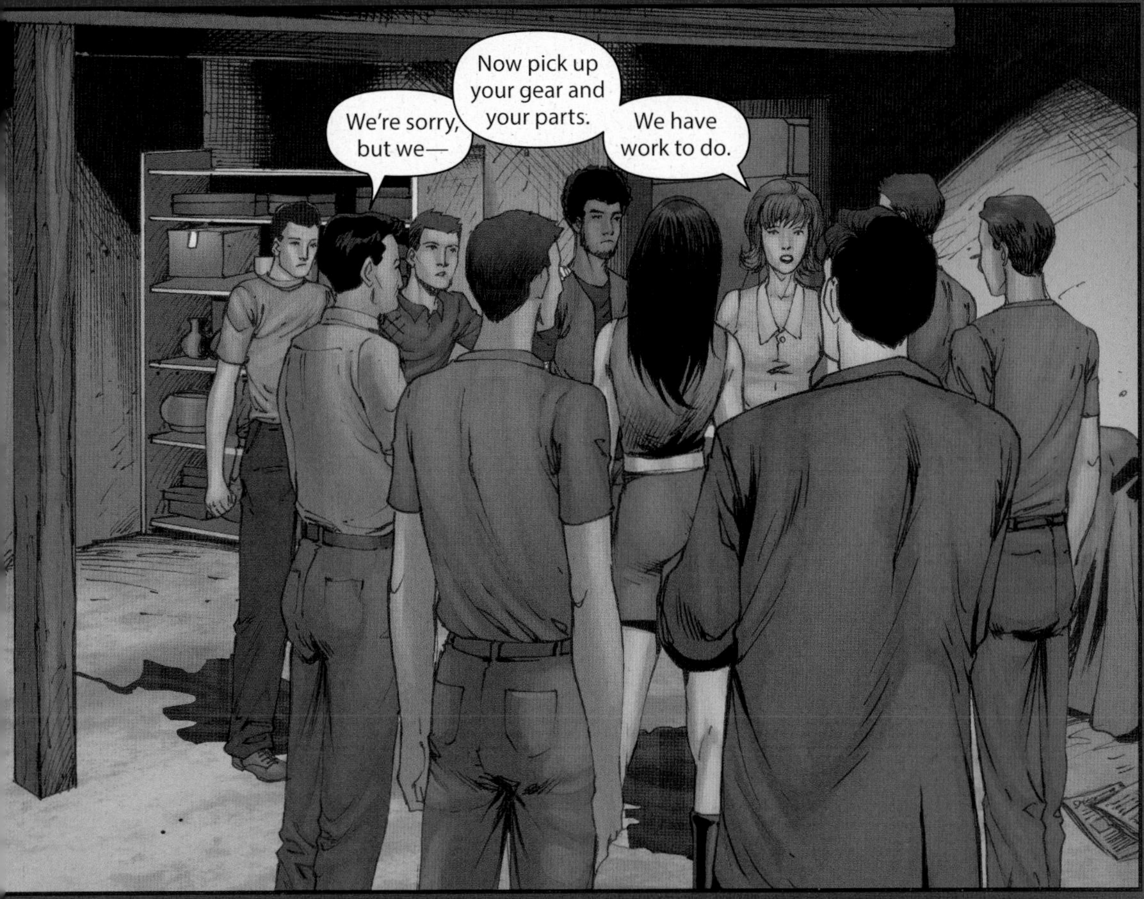
We're sorry, but we—
Now pick up your gear and your parts.
We have work to do.

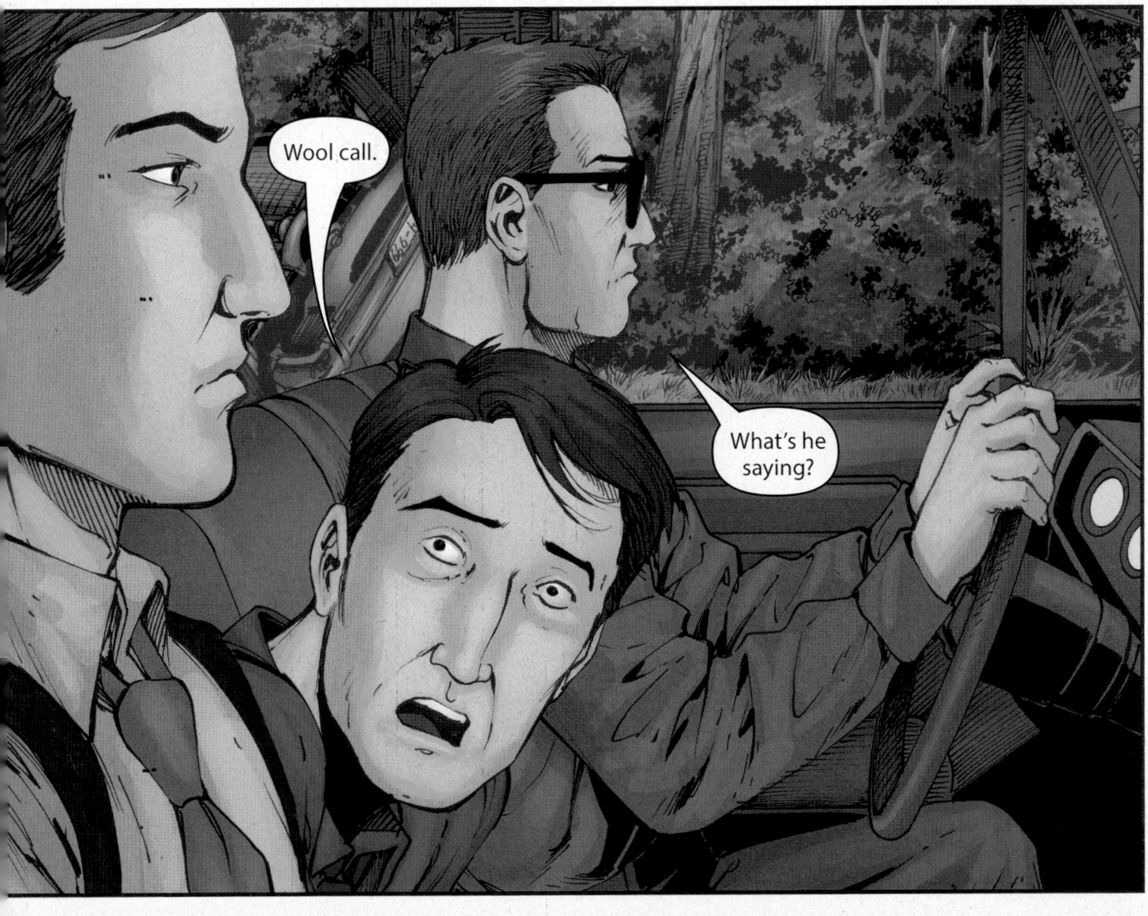
Wool call.
What's he saying?

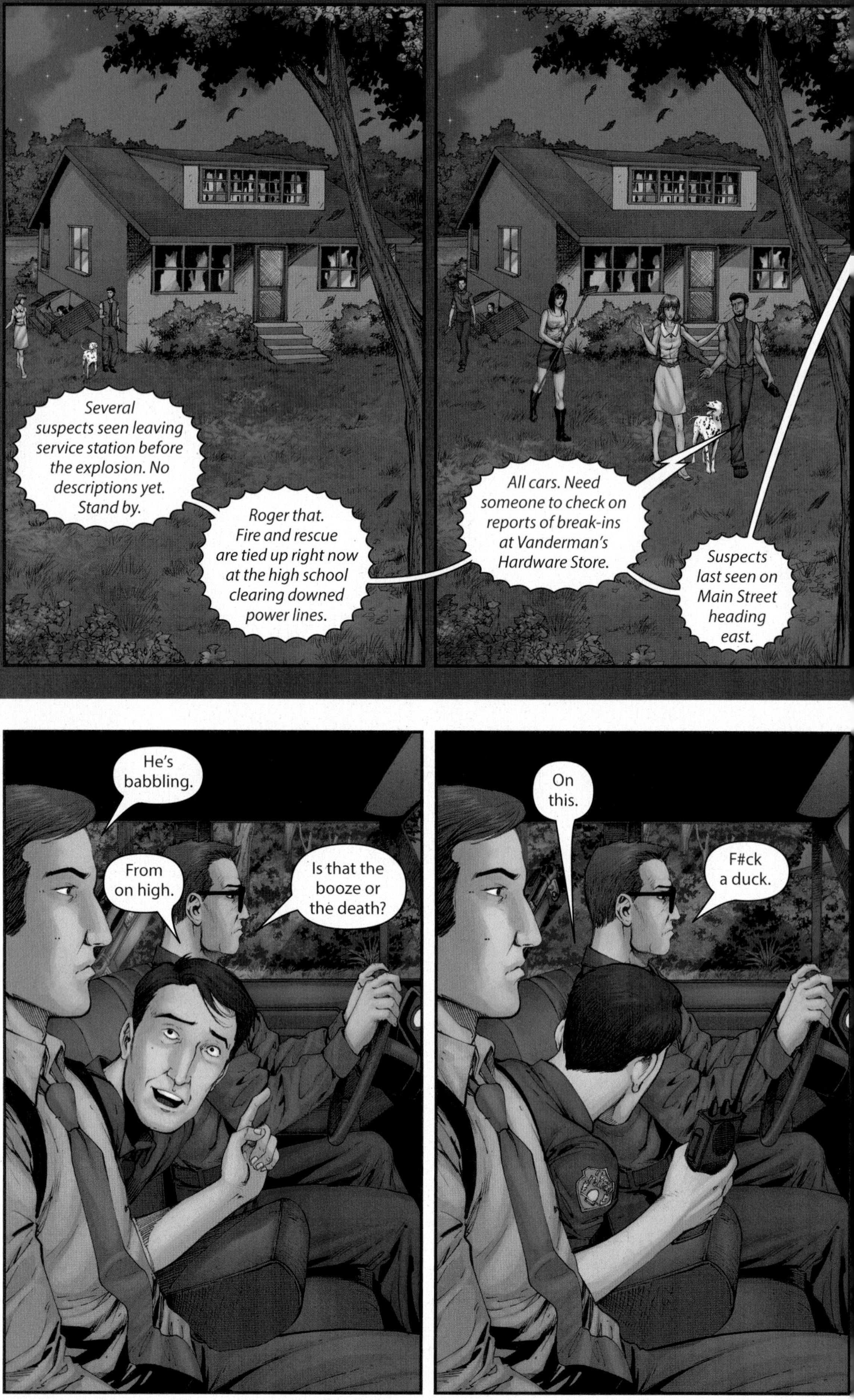
Several suspects seen leaving service station before the explosion. No descriptions yet. Stand by.
Roger that. Fire and rescue are tied up right now at the high school clearing downed power lines.
All cars. Need someone to check on reports of break-ins at Vanderman's Hardware Store.
Suspects last seen on Main Street heading east.
He's babbling.
From on high.
Is that the booze or the death?
On this.
F#ck a duck.

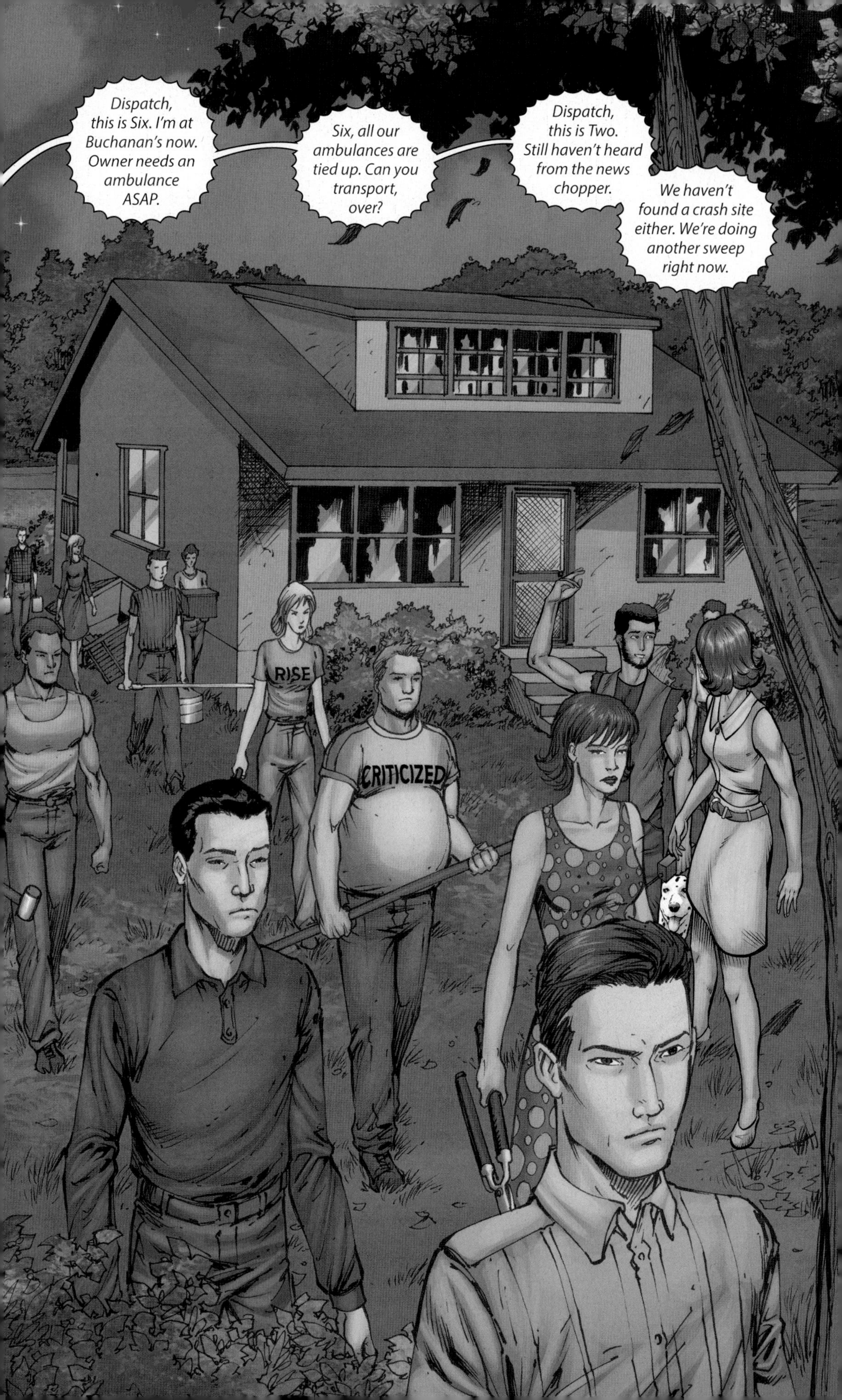

Dispatch, this is Six. I'm at Buchanan's now. Owner needs an ambulance ASAP.
Six, all our ambulances are tied up. Can you transport, over?
Dispatch, this is Two. Still haven't heard from the news chopper.
We haven't found a crash site either. We're doing another sweep right now.
RISE
CRITICIZED

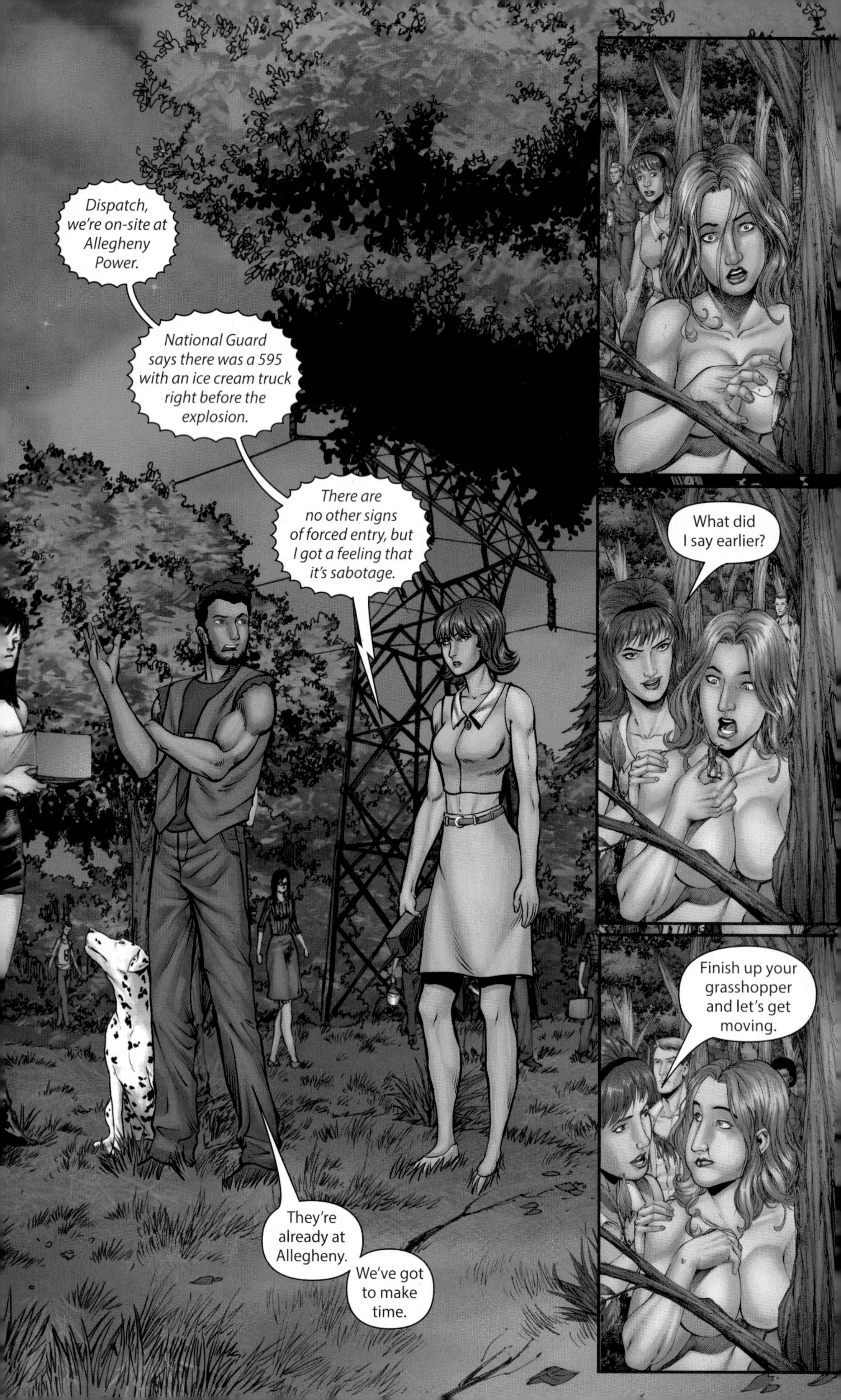
Dispatch, we're on-site at Allegheny Power.
National Guard says there was a 595 with an ice cream truck right before the explosion.
There are no other signs of forced entry, but I got a feeling that it's sabotage.
They're already at Allegheny.
We've got to make time.
What did I say earlier?
Finish up your grasshopper and let's get moving.

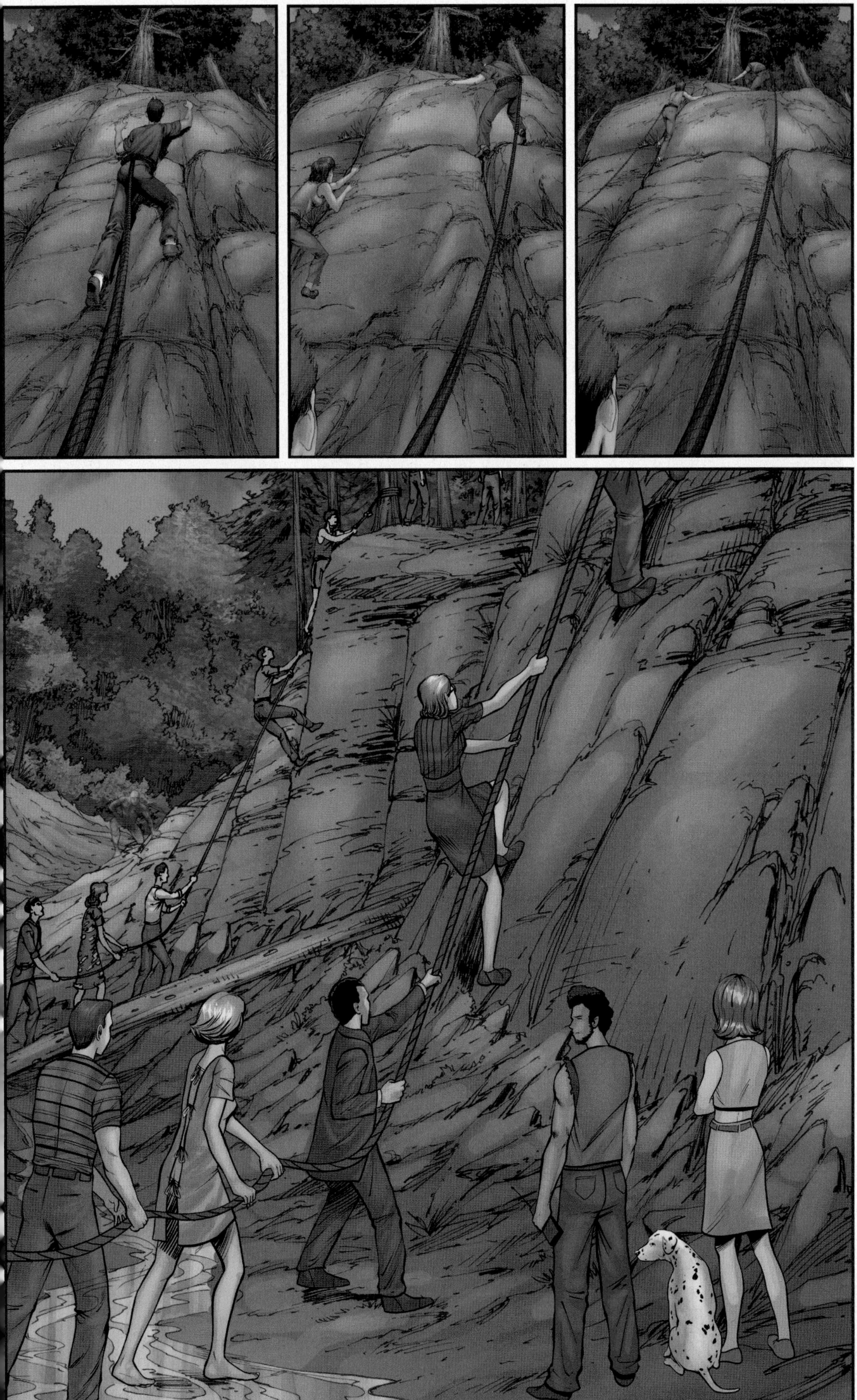

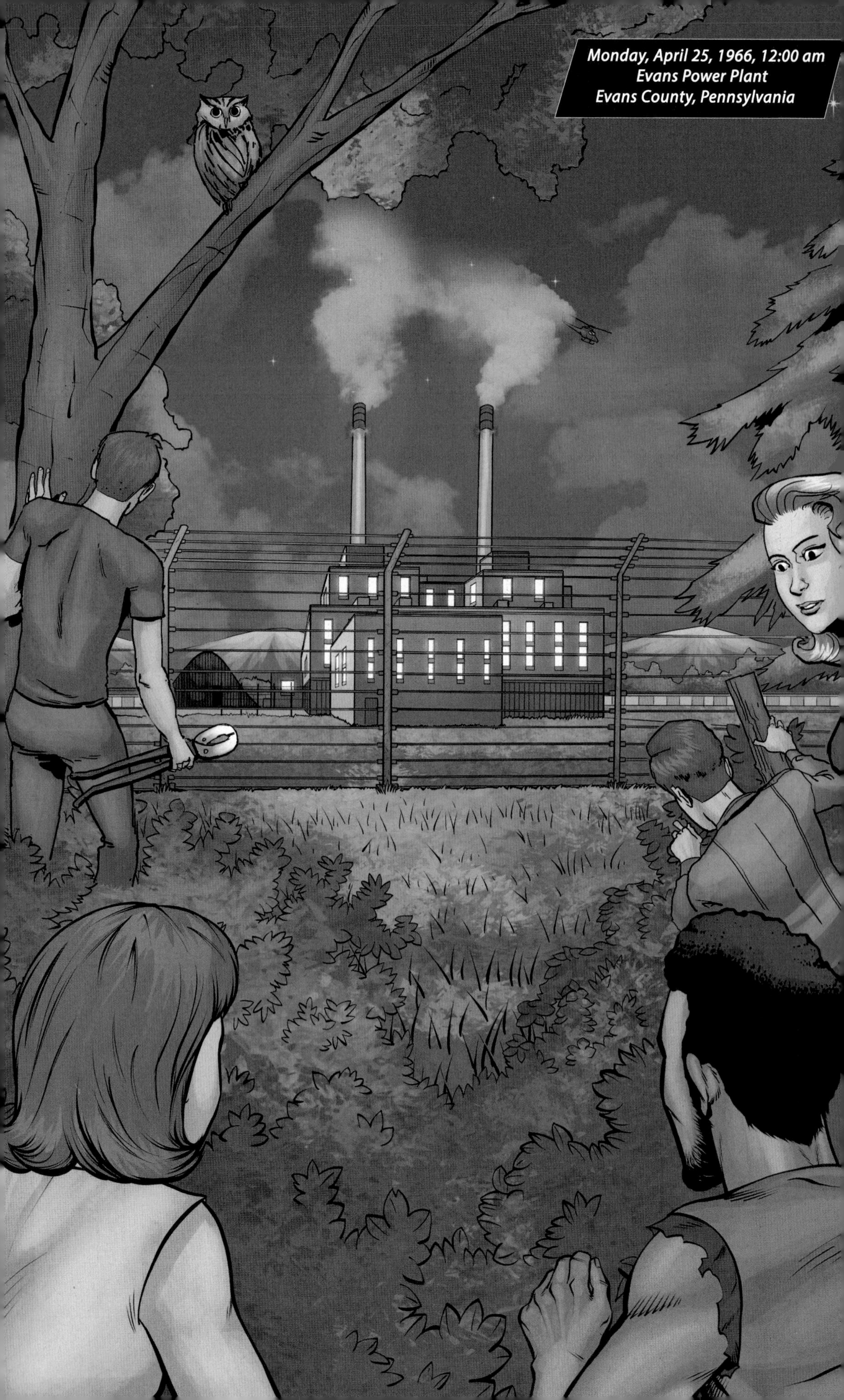
Monday, April 25, 1966, 12:00 am
Evans Power Plant
Evans County, Pennsylvania

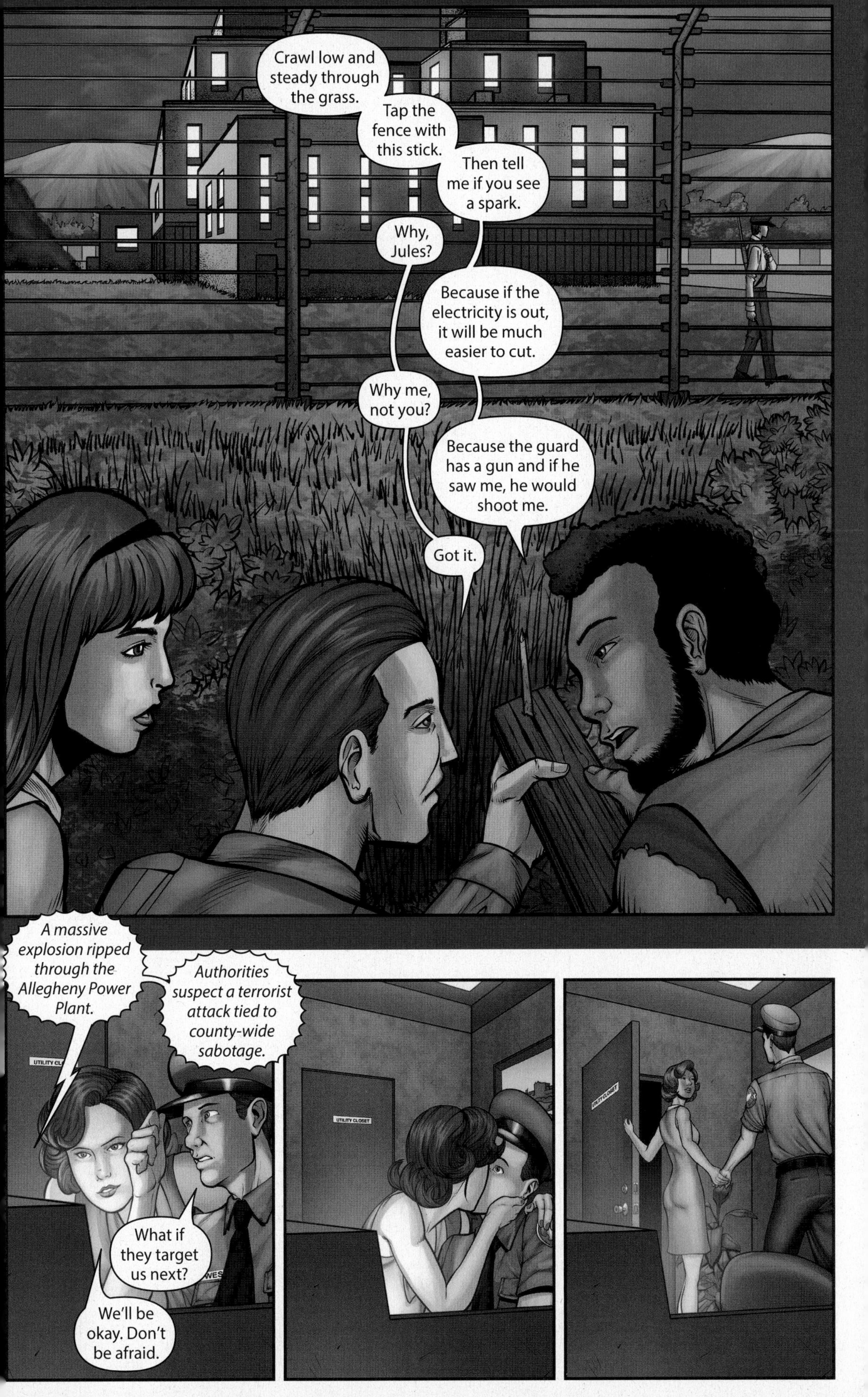
Crawl low and steady through the grass.
Tap the fence with this stick.
Then tell me if you see a spark.
Why, Jules?
Because if the electricity is out, it will be much easier to cut.
Why me, not you?
Because the guard has a gun and if he saw me, he would shoot me.
Got it.
A massive explosion ripped through the Allegheny Power Plant.
Authorities suspect a terrorist attack tied to county-wide sabotage.
What if they target us next?
We'll be okay. Don't be afraid.
UTILITY CLOSET

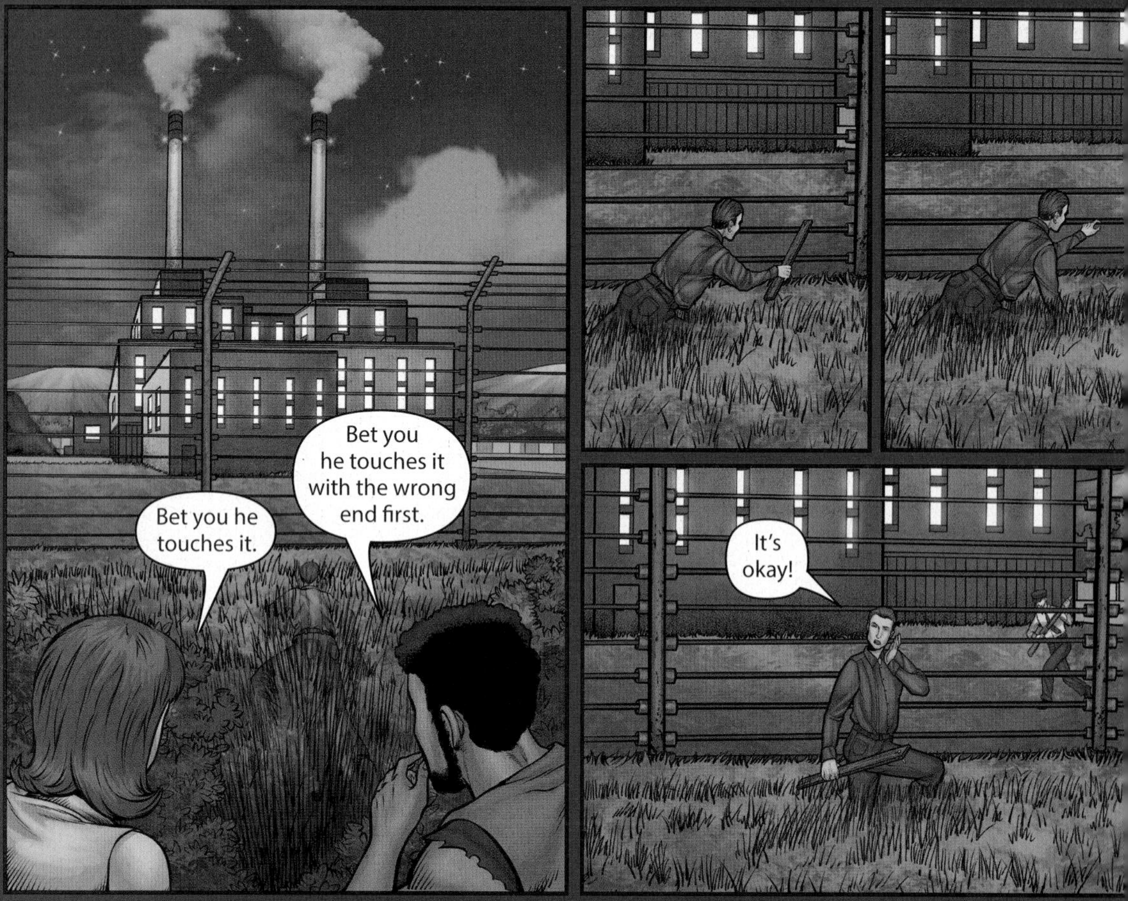
Bet you he touches it.
Bet you he touches it with the wrong end first.
It's okay!

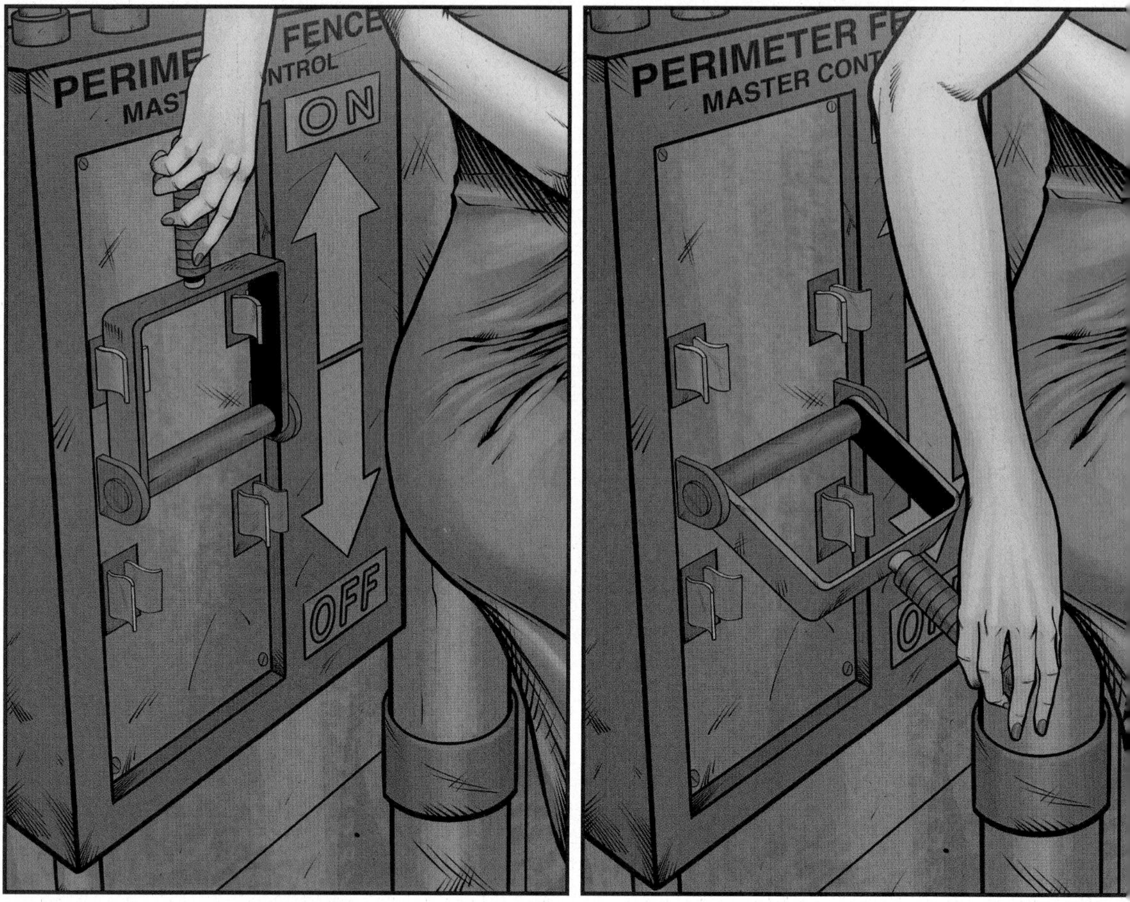
ON
OFF
PERIMETER

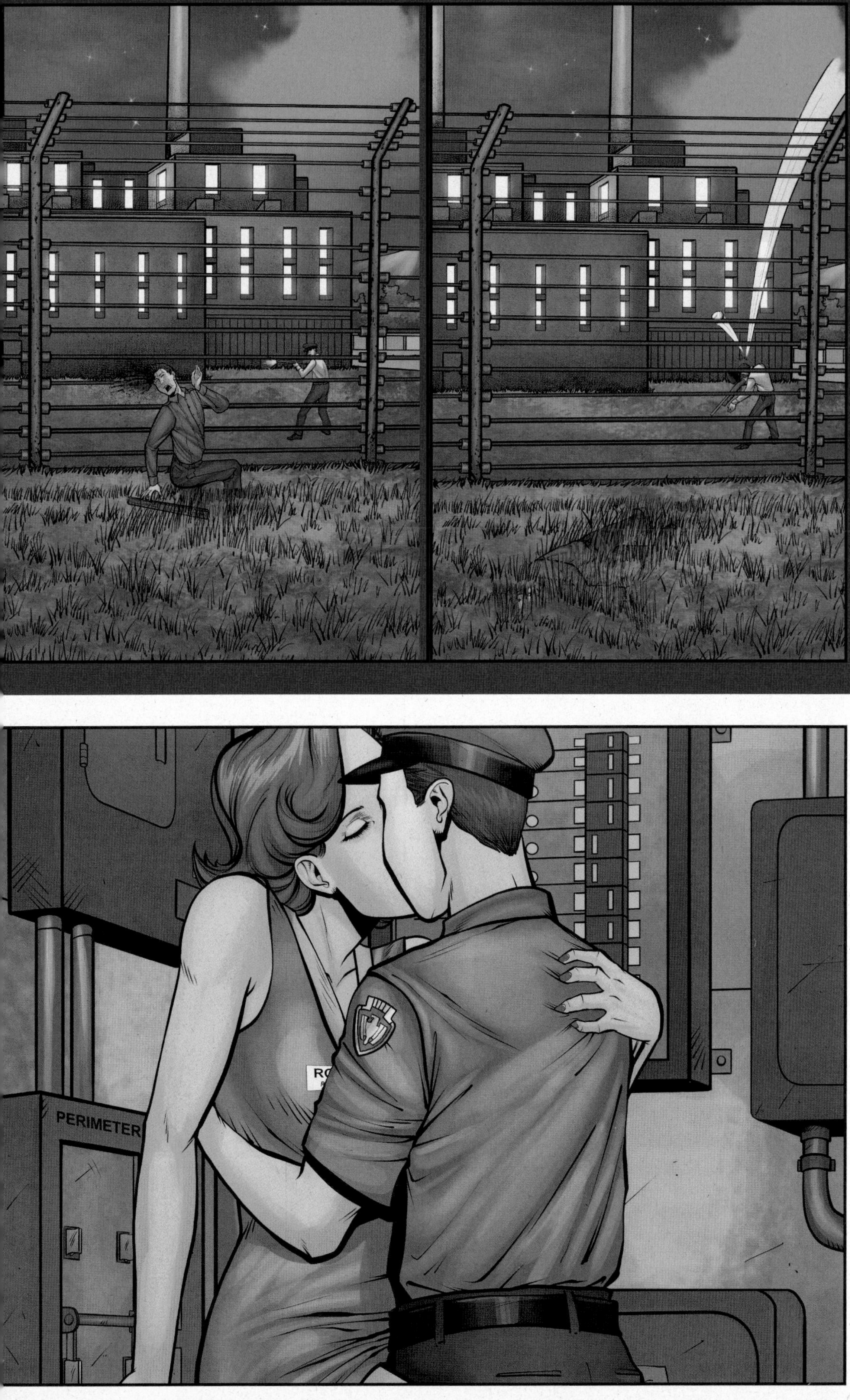
PERIMETER

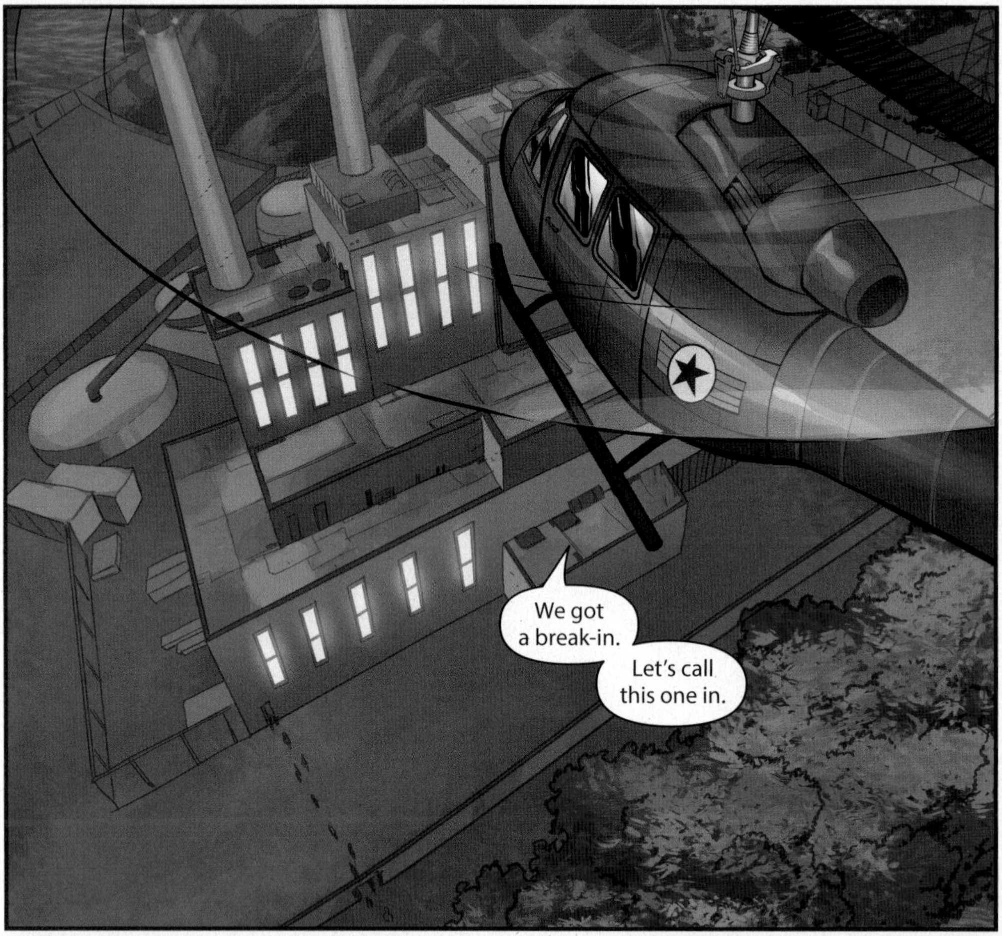
We got a break-in.
Let's call this one in.

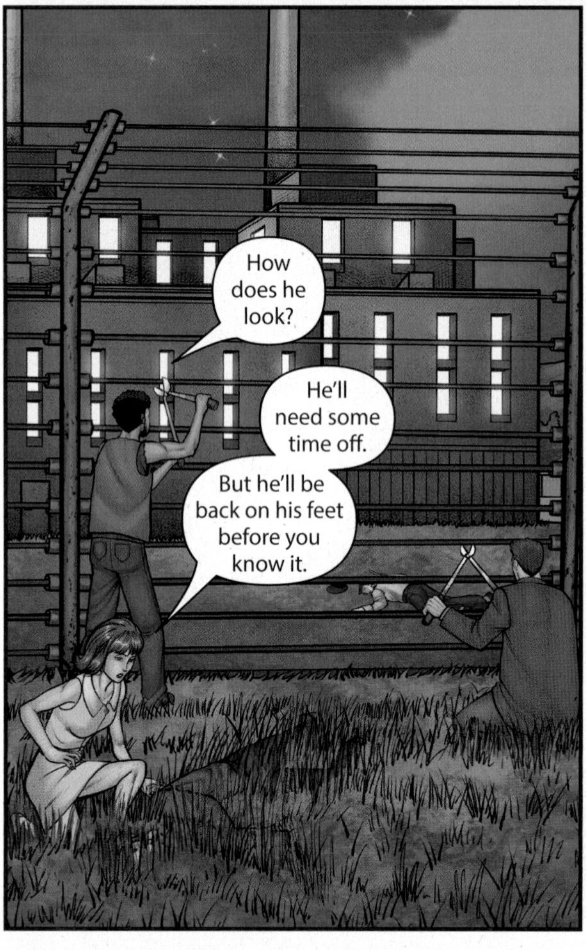
How does he look?
He'll need some time off.
But he'll be back on his feet before you know it.

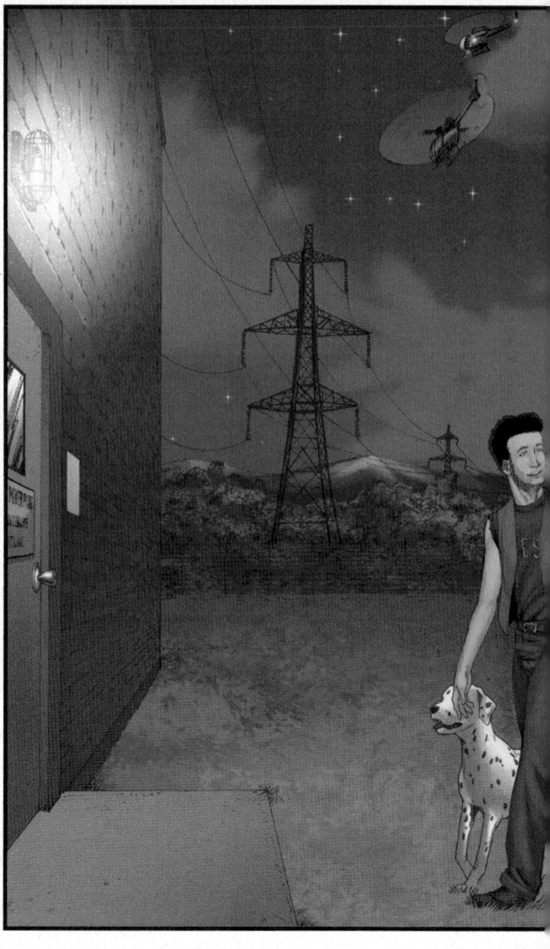

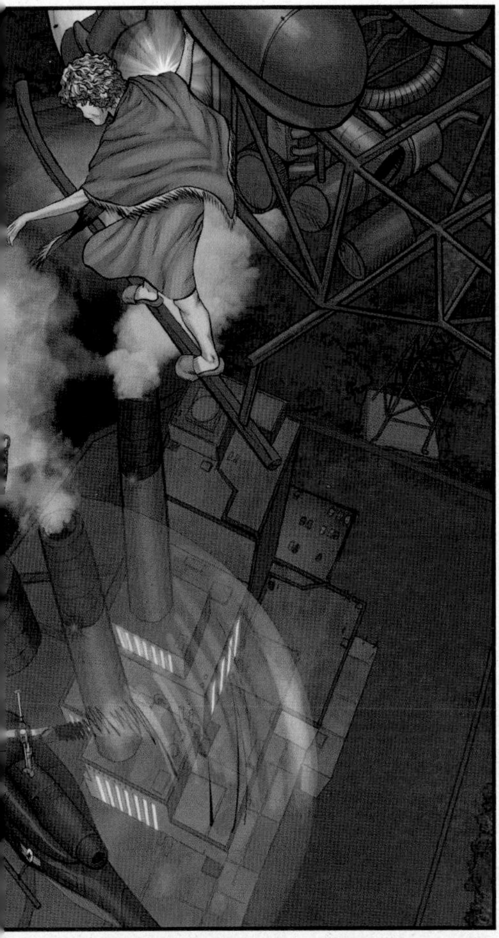

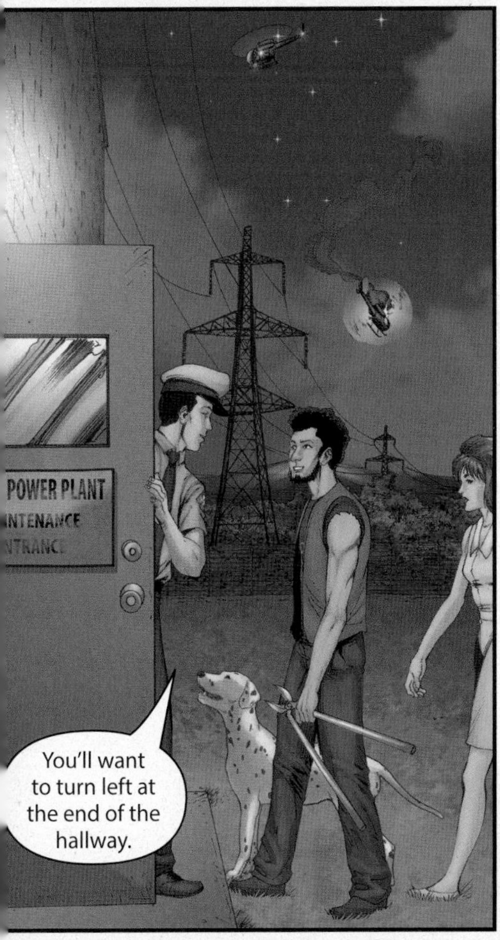
POWER PLANT
You'll want to turn left at the end of the hallway.

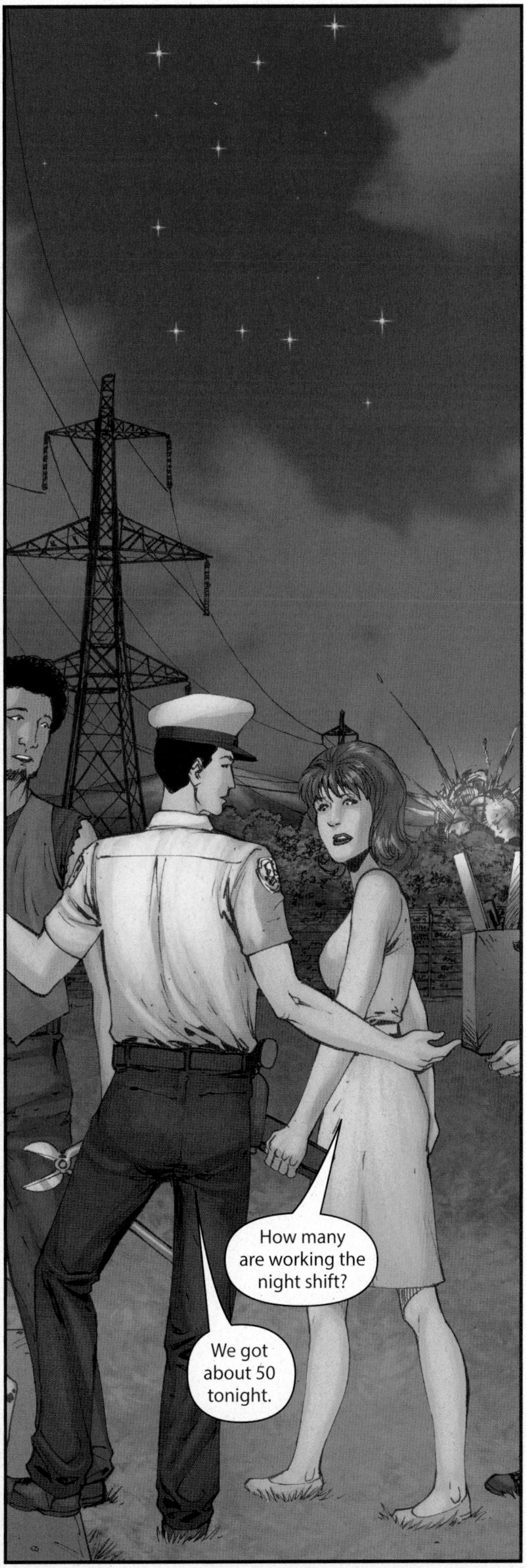
How many are working the night shift?
We got about 50 tonight.

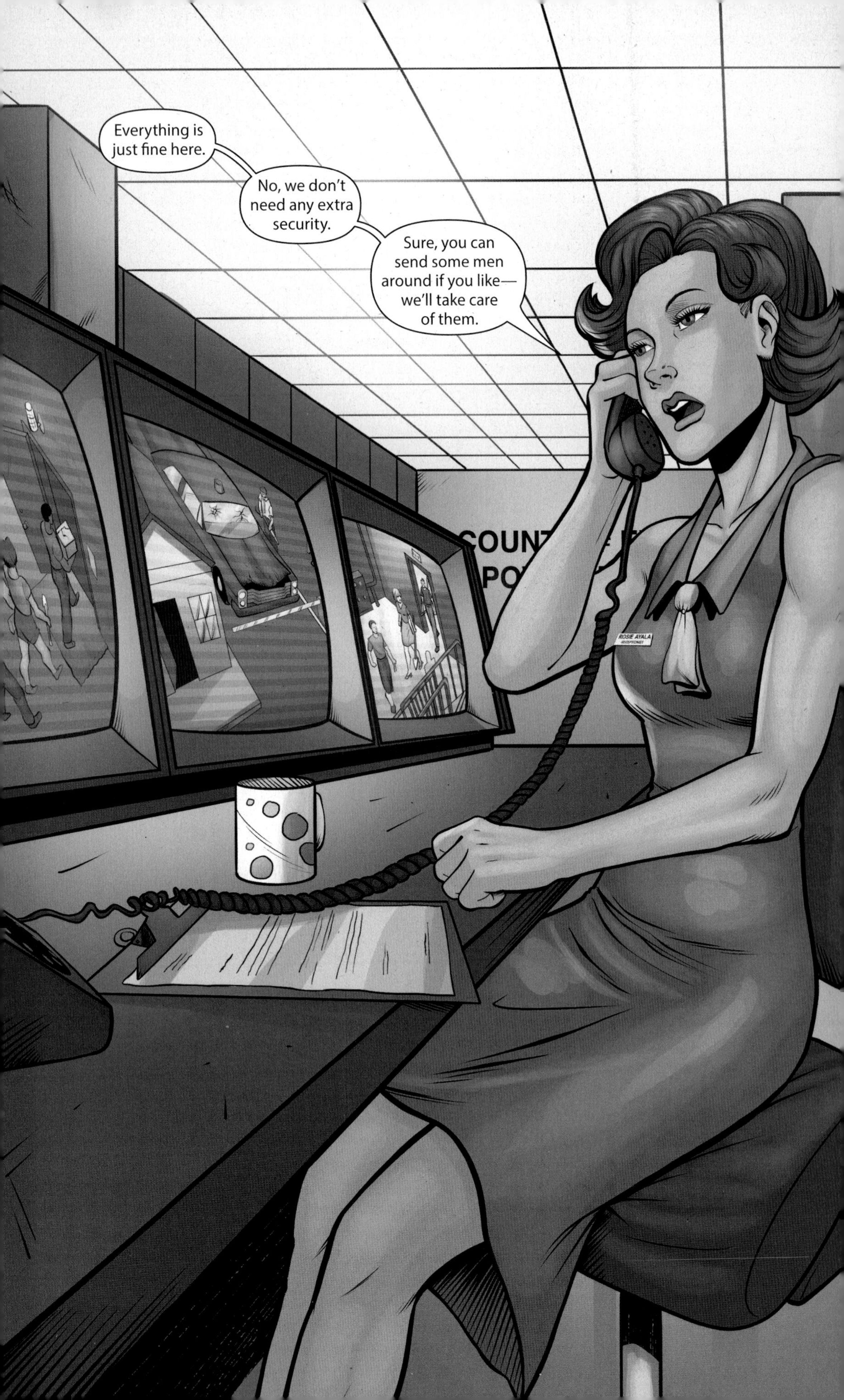
Everything is just fine here.
No, we don't need any extra security.
Sure, you can send some men around if you like—we'll take care of them.
ROSIE AYALA

"Start at the Beginning"

ASSOCIATE EDITOR ELYSIA LIANG

This is one of the cornerstones of Double Take's tradecraft, and as I type this on my phone during my subway ride home, I'm learning that it's also a convenient way to fill a blank page.

Here's my beginning. I interviewed at Double Take on a cold January day filled with sidewalk slush. I remember liking the artwork on the walls and the couches that have since been moved to the front of the office. There are the usual questions about my qualifications, but because I went to school in Chicago, I'm also asked if I'd ever been to Hot Doug's. There's a point where I admit that I'm not a comic book reader, and I quietly hope that this does not count against me. I talk about the storyboard for *Soul* because I liked how one of the scenes used a first-person point of view. I'm glad that I brought copies of my resume.

Beginnings were everywhere when I arrived at Double Take for my first day of work. The office was preparing to put together their first books for publication. Some series had entire scenes penciled. Other books only had a few scattered ideas or perhaps a handful of frames for an opening scene. We had four illustrations in our cover bank instead of 50. Email inboxes were full of test panels, and binders of portfolios showed up on our desks. There was plenty of trial and error. I had to watch *Night of the Living Dead* twice before I remembered the names of all the characters. My first draft of our universe's timeline took 14 pages to print and had font too small to be readable from our bulletin board.

Eventually, our fledging books looked more like things that could be displayed on a comic bookstore shelf. The pockets of our brand new universe began to take shape. We now have emails from artists who have worked on multiple books and new binders with our favorite print layouts. Our universe timeline now lives on a giant whiteboard, readable and color-coded thanks to our story editor. These pictures give you a glimpse of how far we've come. They're a throwback to a time when Double Take's first 50 issues were still in the distant future.

Luckily, I still get to witness a lot of beginnings. With the release of our graphic novels, we can start working on new story arcs and even a new series or two. Publishing books "every month" is a lot of work, but there's always the excitement of starting with a new book. It feels like standing on the edge of another frontier.

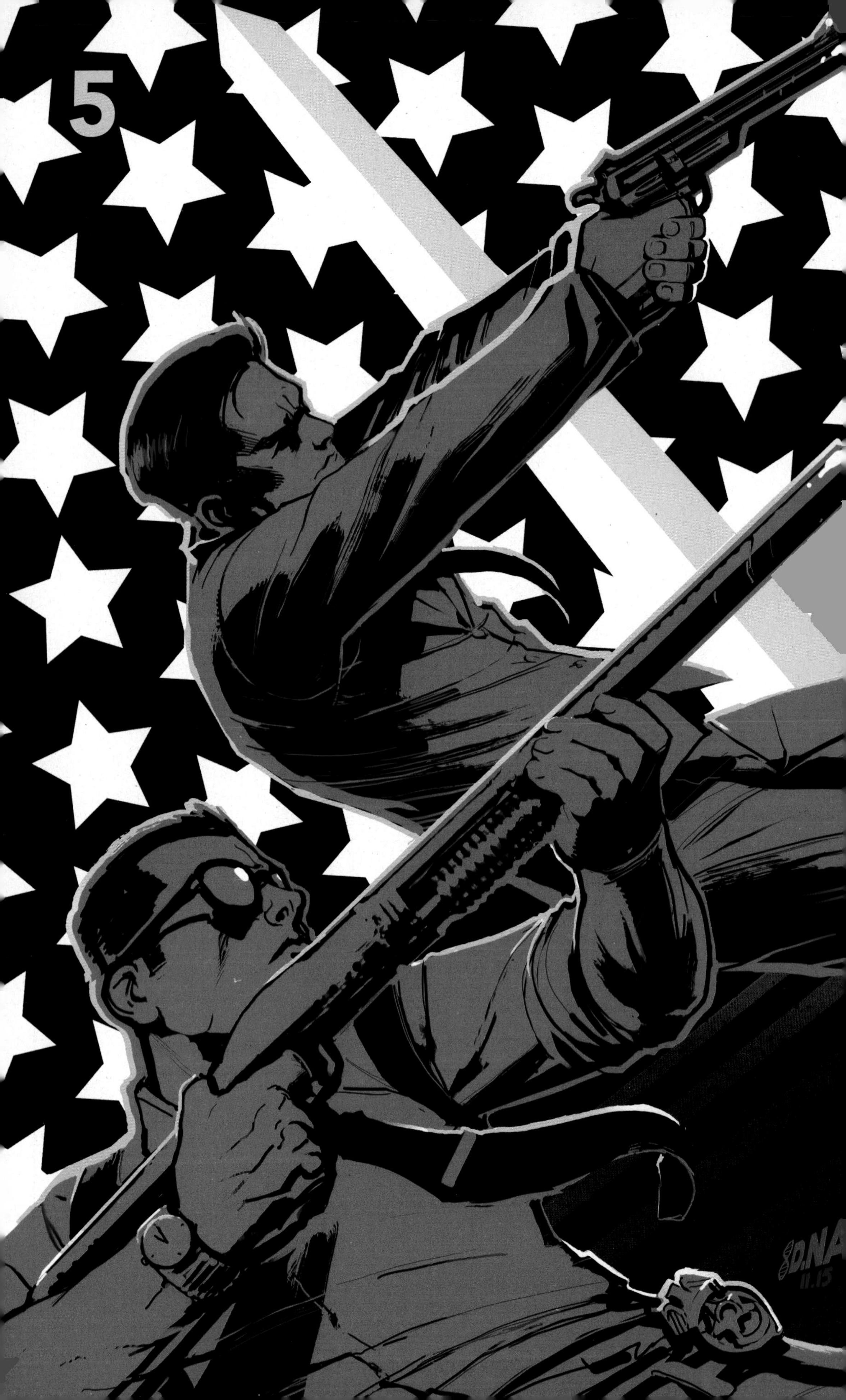
5
D.NA
11.15

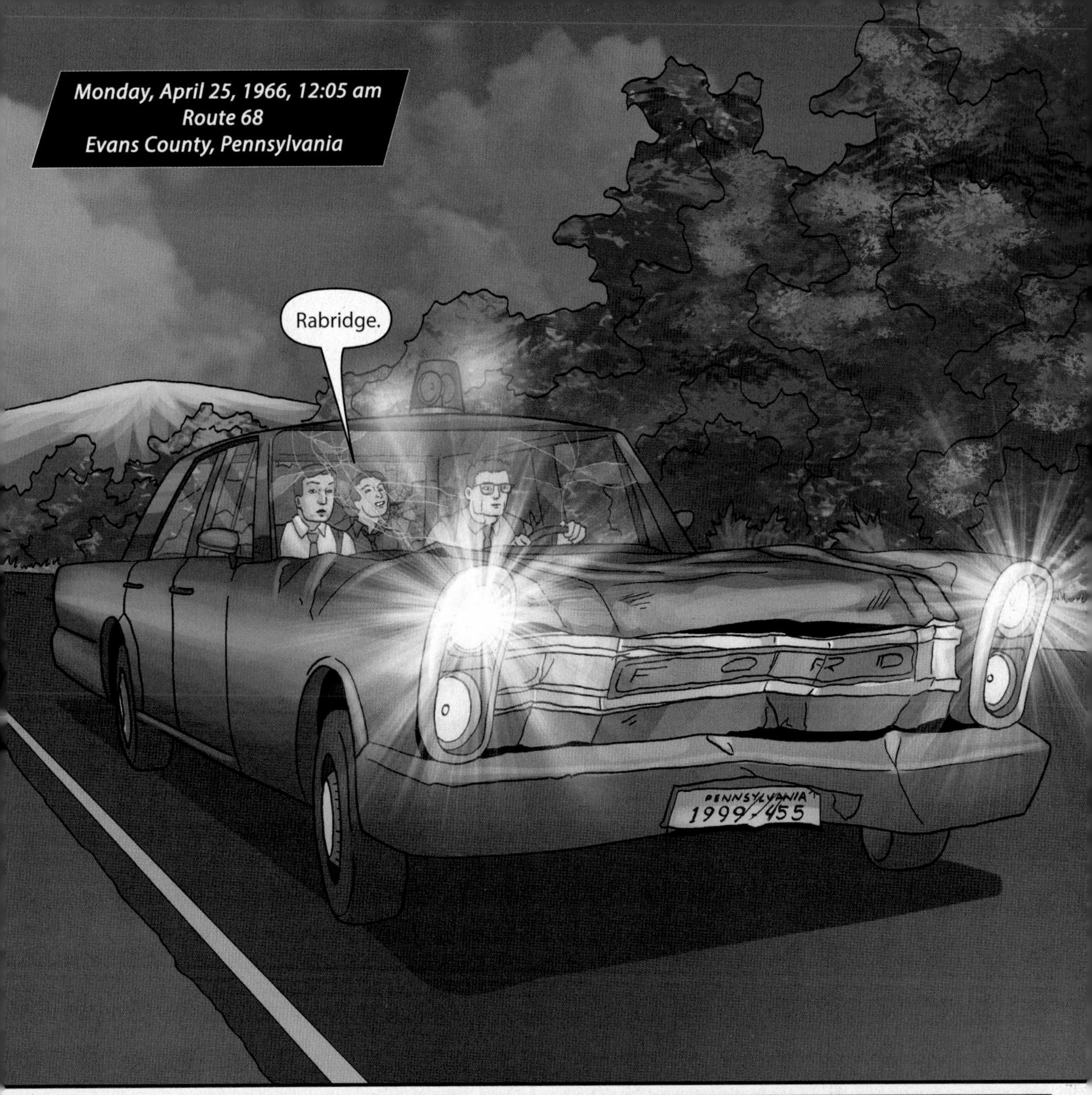
Monday, April 25, 1966, 12:05 am
Route 68
Evans County, Pennsylvania
Rabridge.
FORD
PENNSYLVANIA
1999-455

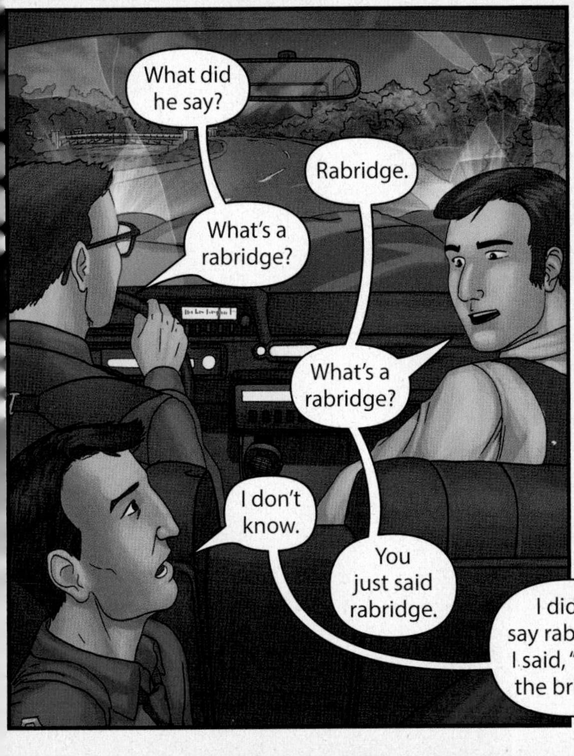
What did he say?
Rabridge.
What's a rabridge?
What's a rabridge?
I don't know.
You just said rabridge.
I didn't say rabridge. I said, "Raise the bridge."

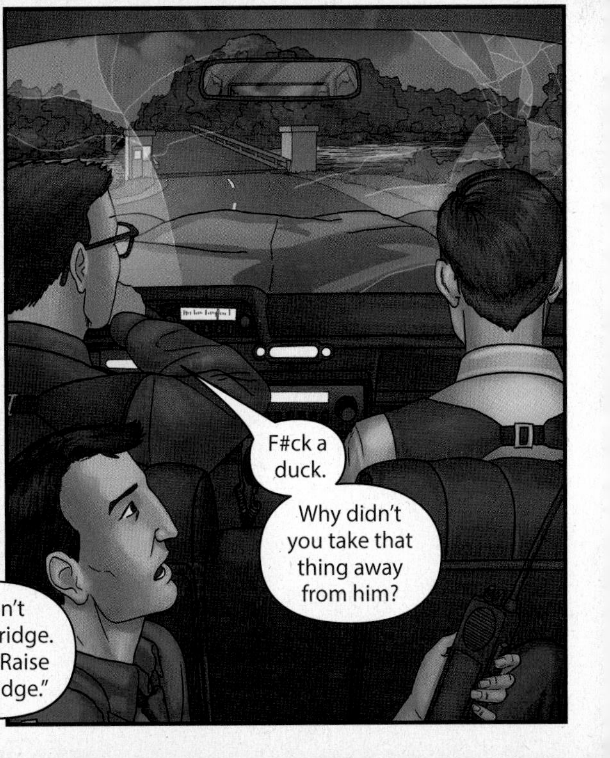
F#ck a duck.
Why didn't you take that thing away from him?

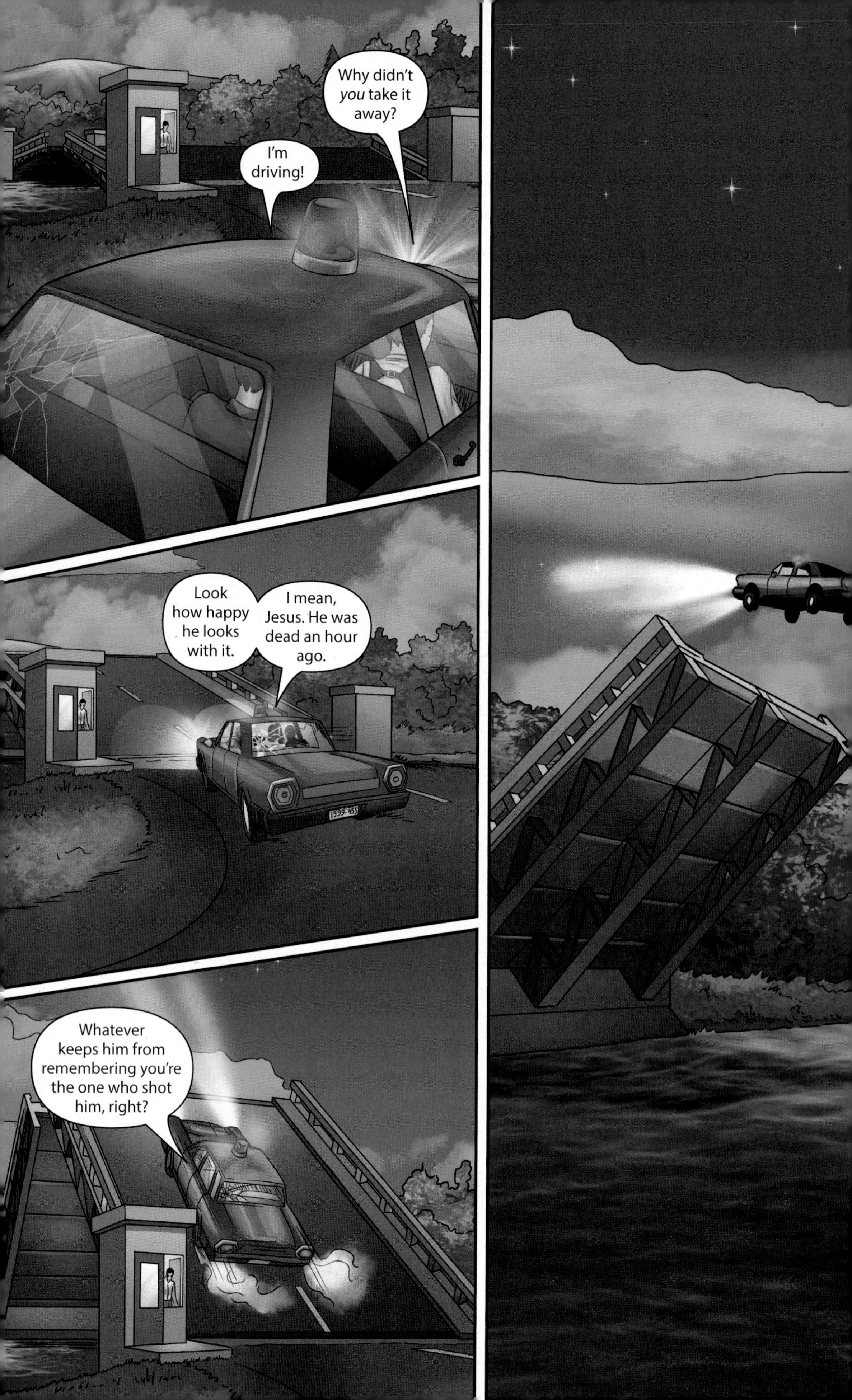
Why didn't *you* take it away?
I'm driving!
Look how happy he looks with it.
I mean, Jesus. He was dead an hour ago.
1999-455
Whatever keeps him from remembering you're the one who shot him, right?

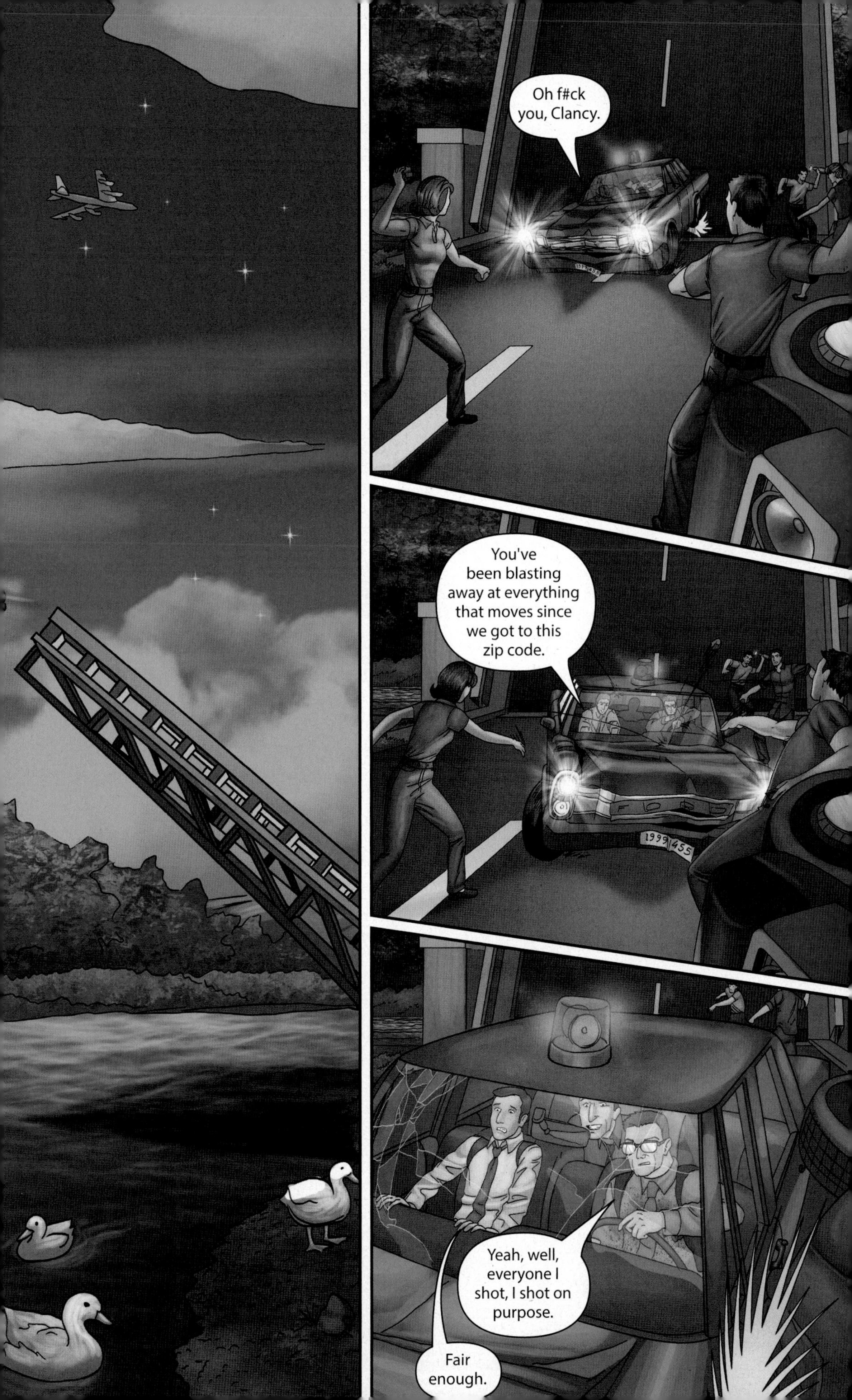

Oh f#ck you, Clancy.
You've been blasting away at everything that moves since we got to this zip code.
FORD
Yeah, well, everyone I shot, I shot on purpose.
Fair enough.

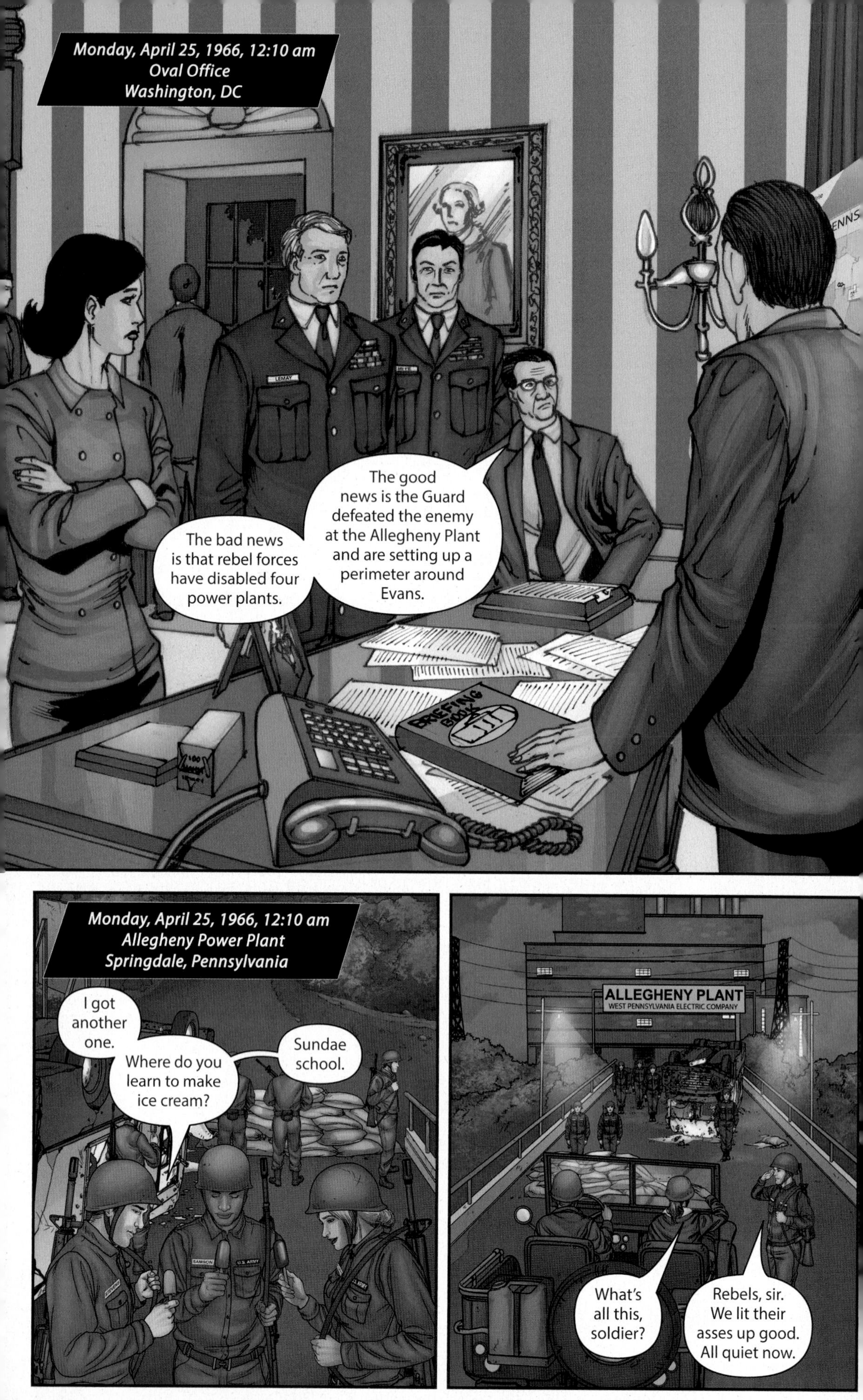
Monday, April 25, 1966, 12:10 am
Oval Office
Washington, DC
LEMAY
The bad news is that rebel forces have disabled four power plants.
The good news is the Guard defeated the enemy at the Allegheny Plant and are setting up a perimeter around Evans.
BRIEFING BOOK
Monday, April 25, 1966, 12:10 am
Allegheny Power Plant
Springdale, Pennsylvania
I got another one.
Where do you learn to make ice cream?
Sundae school.
SAMSON
U.S. ARMY
ALLEGHENY PLANT
WEST PENNSYLVANIA ELECTRIC COMPANY
What's all this, soldier?
Rebels, sir. We lit their asses up good. All quiet now.

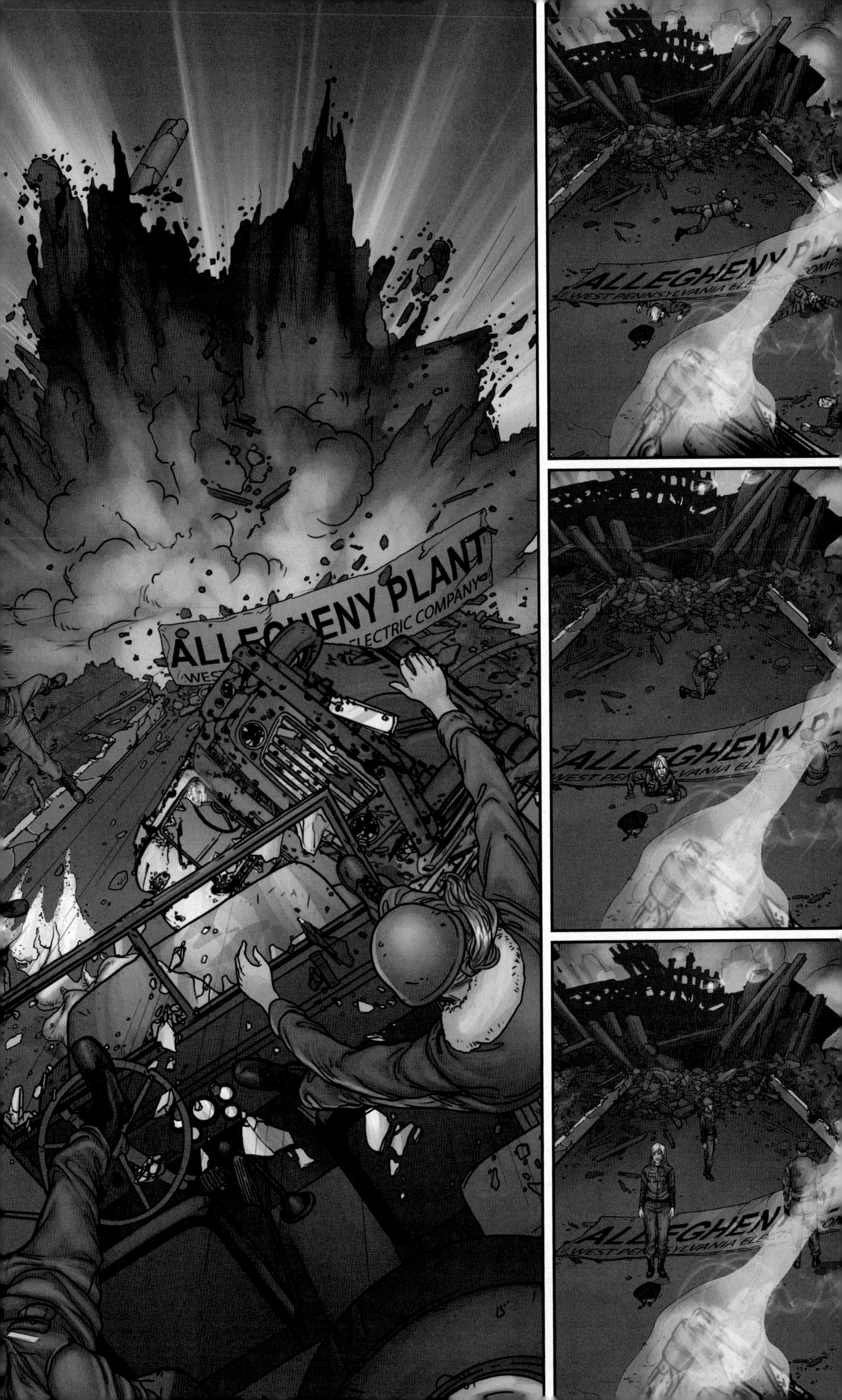
ALLEGHENY PLANT
ELECTRIC COMPANY
ALLEGHENY PLA
WEST PENNSYLVANIA ELECT
ALLEGHENY PL
WEST PENNSYLVANIA ELECTR
ALLEGHENY
WEST PENNSYLVANIA ELECTR

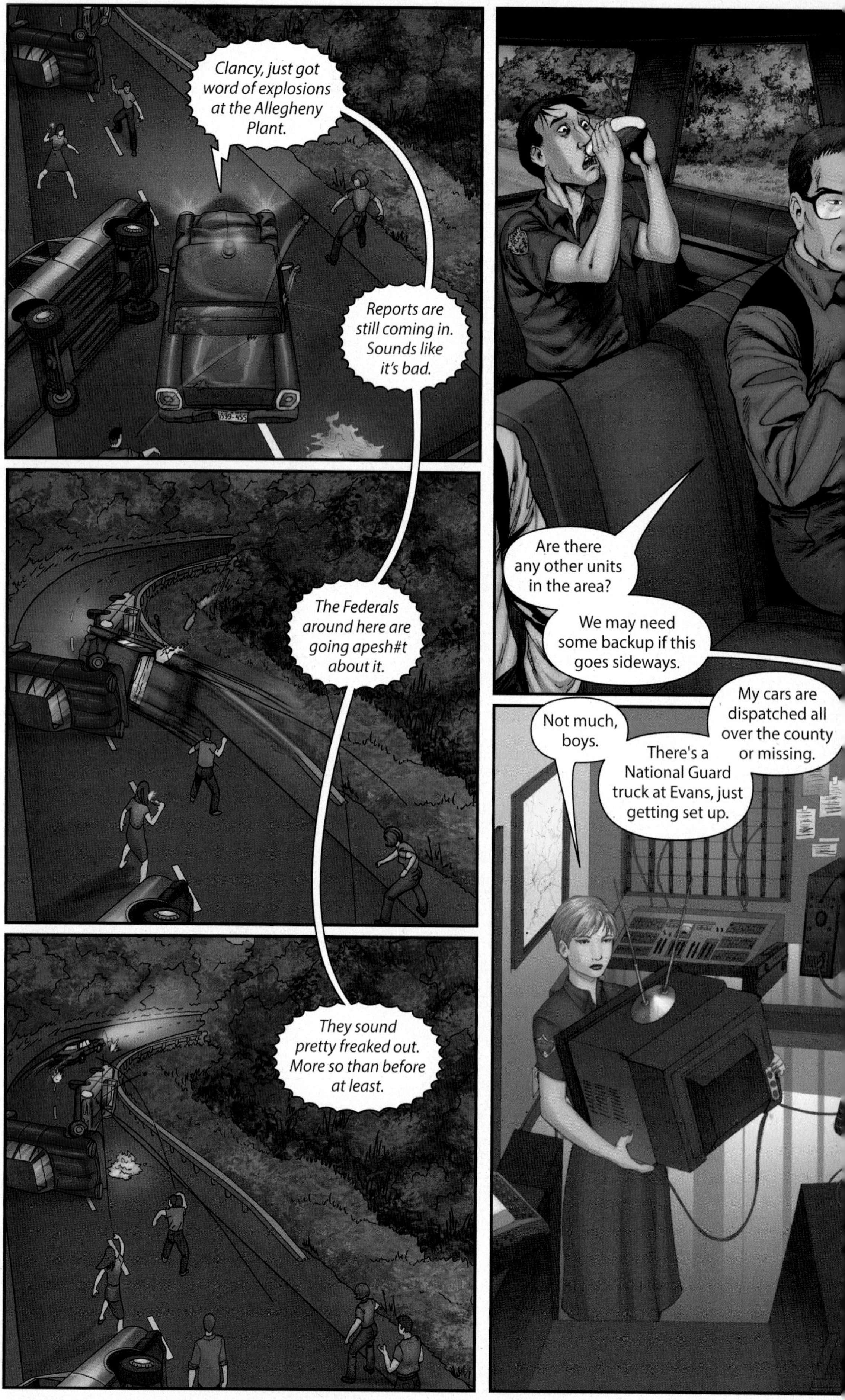
Clancy, just got word of explosions at the Allegheny Plant.
Reports are still coming in. Sounds like it's bad.
The Federals around here are going apesh#t about it.
They sound pretty freaked out. More so than before at least.
Are there any other units in the area?
We may need some backup if this goes sideways.
Not much, boys.
My cars are dispatched all over the county or missing.
There's a National Guard truck at Evans, just getting set up.

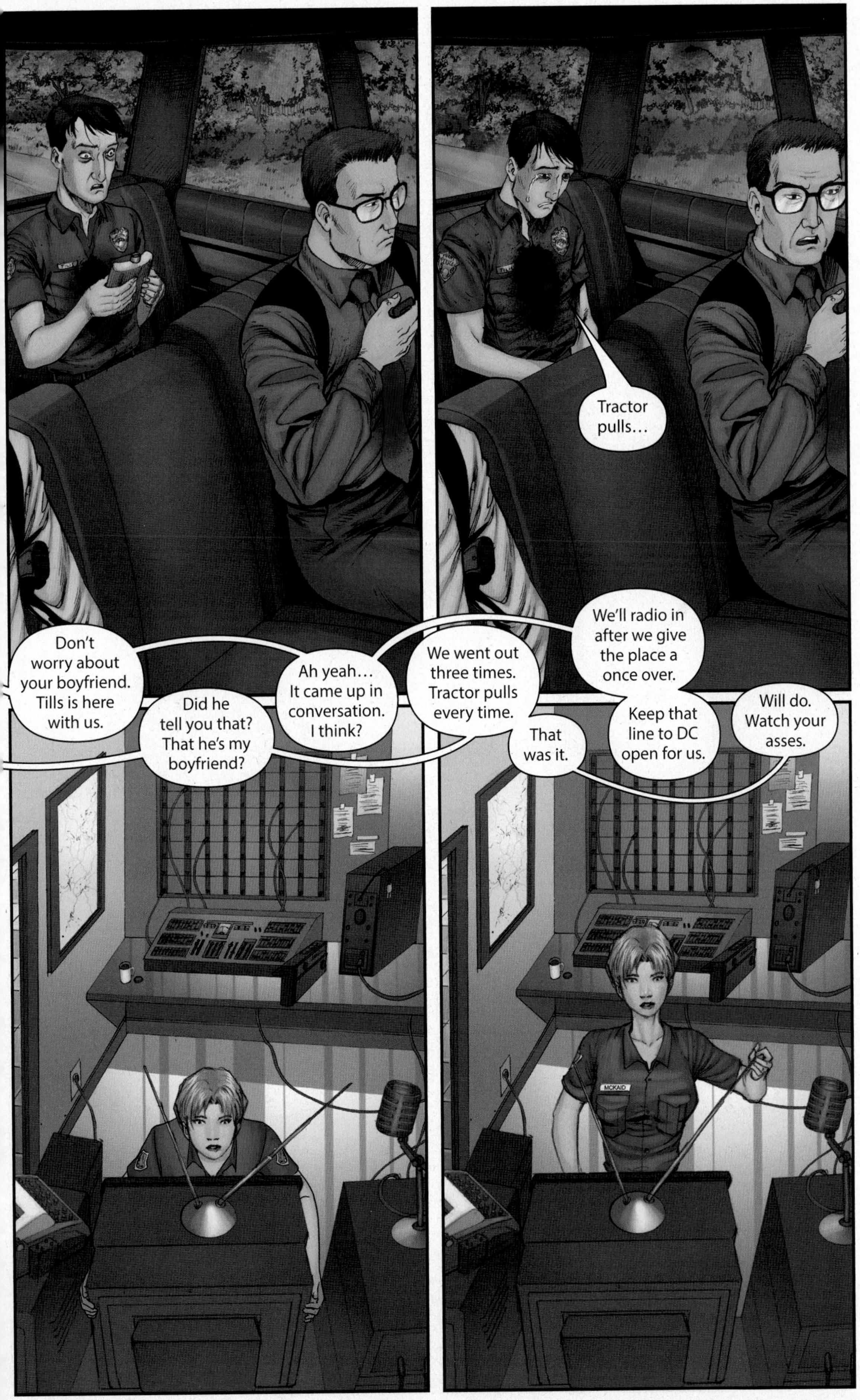
Tractor pulls…
Don't worry about your boyfriend. Tills is here with us.
Did he tell you that? That he's my boyfriend?
Ah yeah… It came up in conversation. I think?
We went out three times. Tractor pulls every time.
That was it.
We'll radio in after we give the place a once over.
Keep that line to DC open for us.
Will do. Watch your asses.
MCKAID

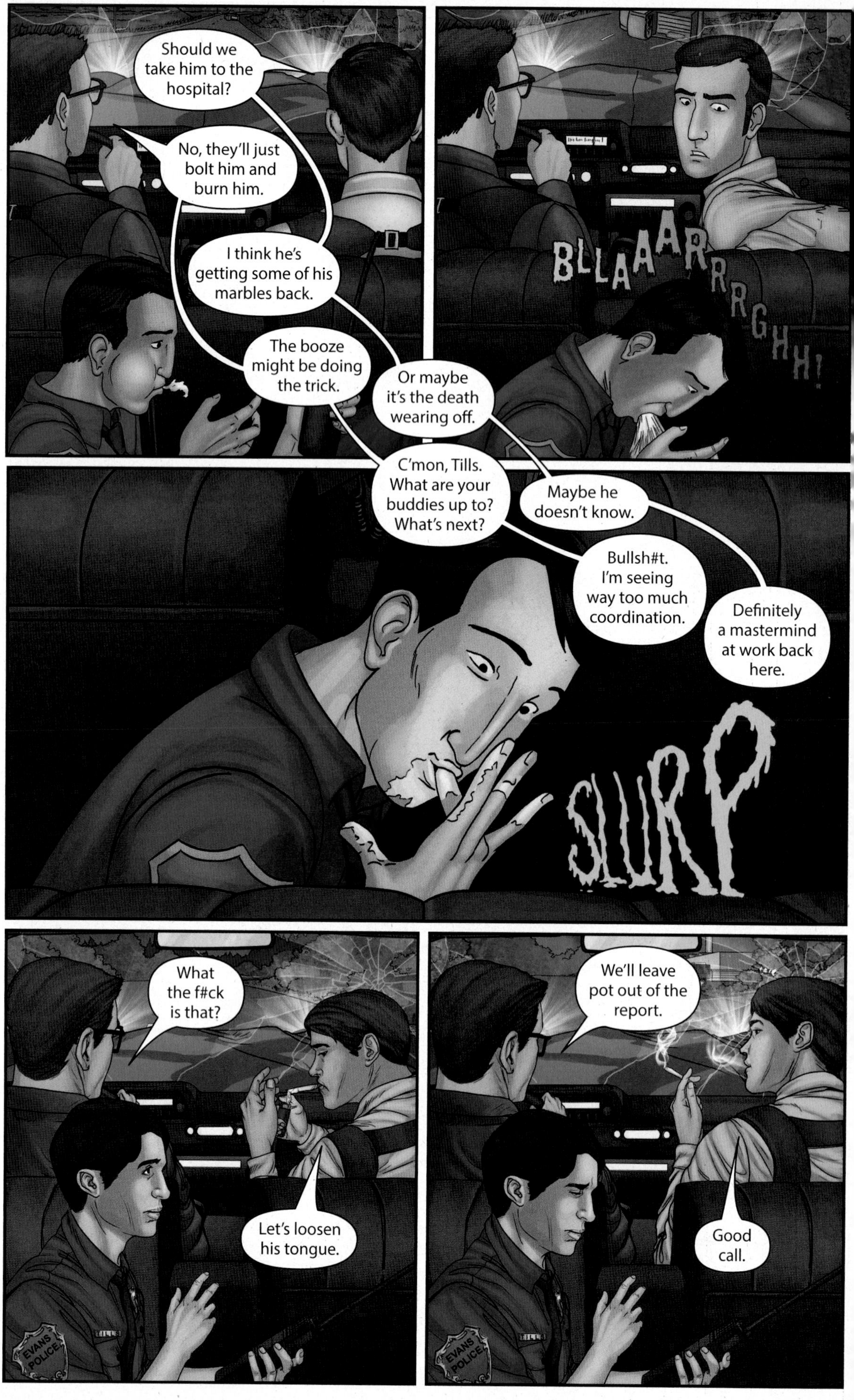
Should we take him to the hospital?
No, they'll just bolt him and burn him.
I think he's getting some of his marbles back.
The booze might be doing the trick.
Or maybe it's the death wearing off.
BLLAAARRRGHH!
C'mon, Tills. What are your buddies up to? What's next?
Maybe he doesn't know.
Bullsh#t. I'm seeing way too much coordination.
Definitely a mastermind at work back here.
SLURP
What the f#ck is that?
Let's loosen his tongue.
EVANS POLICE
TILLS
We'll leave pot out of the report.
Good call.
EVANS POLICE
TILLS

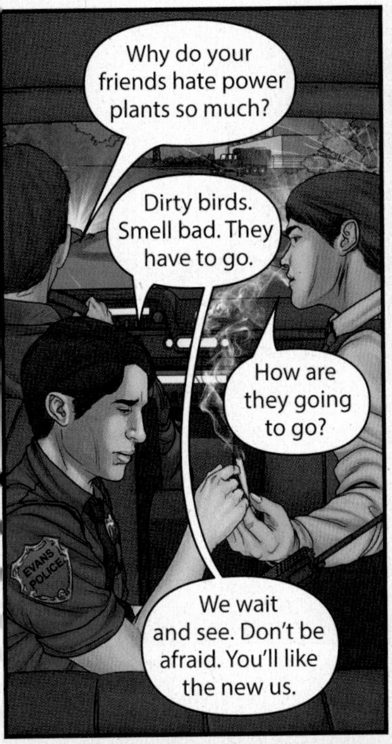
Why do your friends hate power plants so much?
Dirty birds. Smell bad. They have to go.
How are they going to go?
We wait and see. Don't be afraid. You'll like the new us.
EVANS POLICE

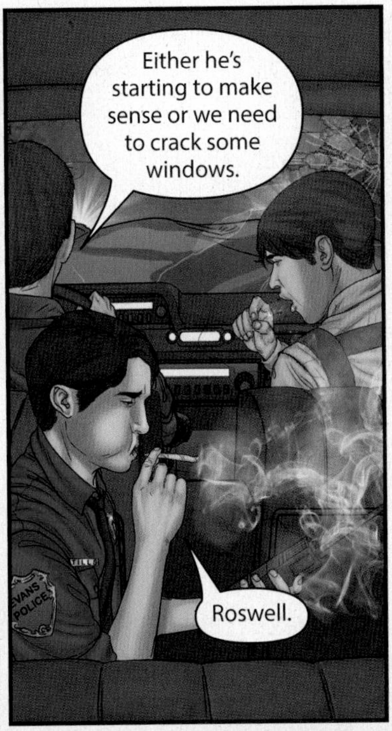
Either he's starting to make sense or we need to crack some windows.
Roswell.
EVANS POLICE

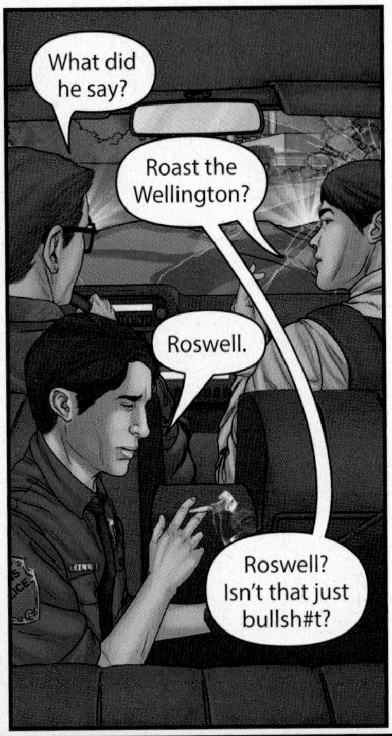
What did he say?
Roast the Wellington?
Roswell.
Roswell? Isn't that just bullsh#t?

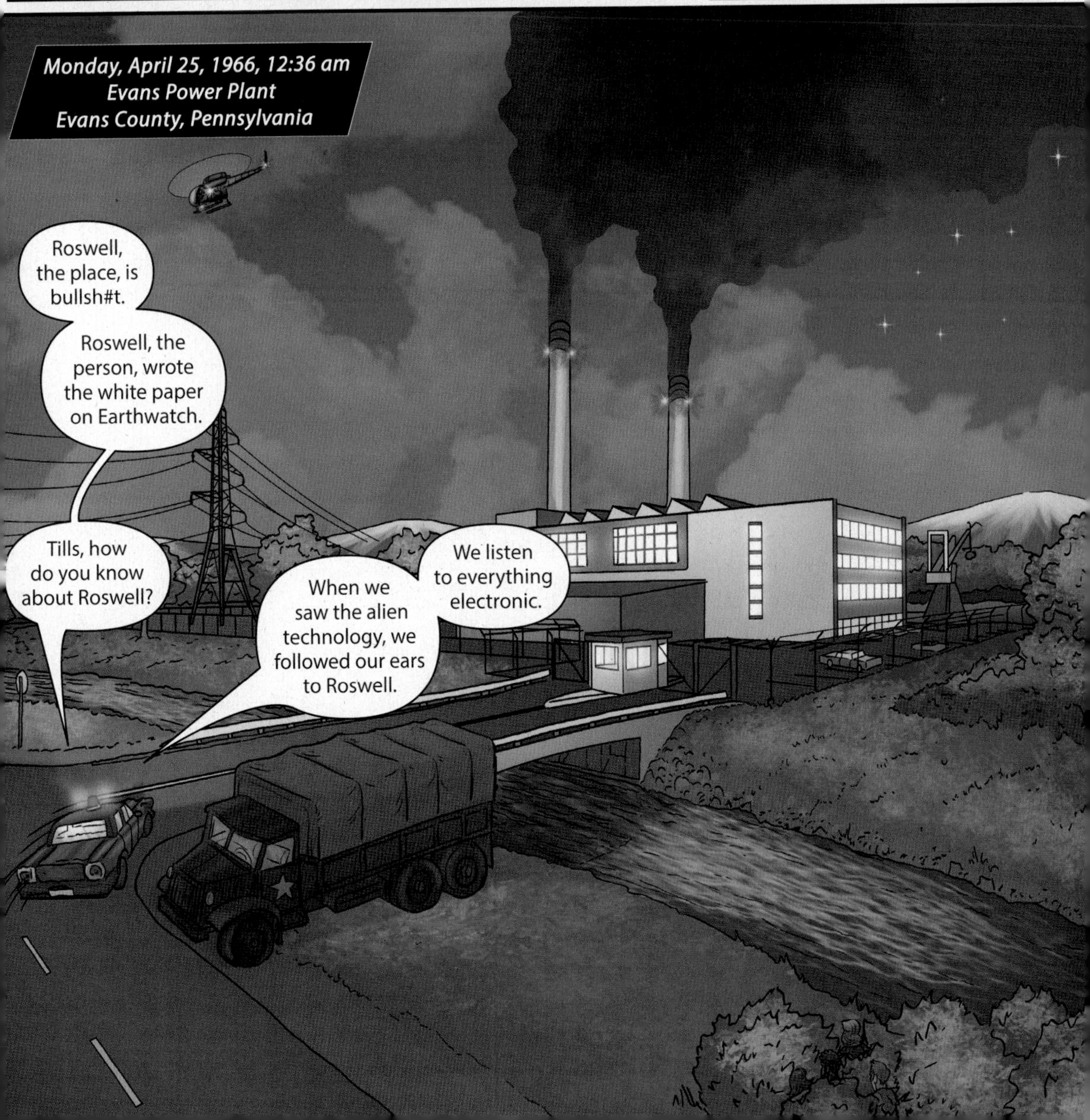
Monday, April 25, 1966, 12:36 am
Evans Power Plant
Evans County, Pennsylvania
Roswell, the place, is bullsh#t.
Roswell, the person, wrote the white paper on Earthwatch.
Tills, how do you know about Roswell?
When we saw the alien technology, we followed our ears to Roswell.
We listen to everything electronic.

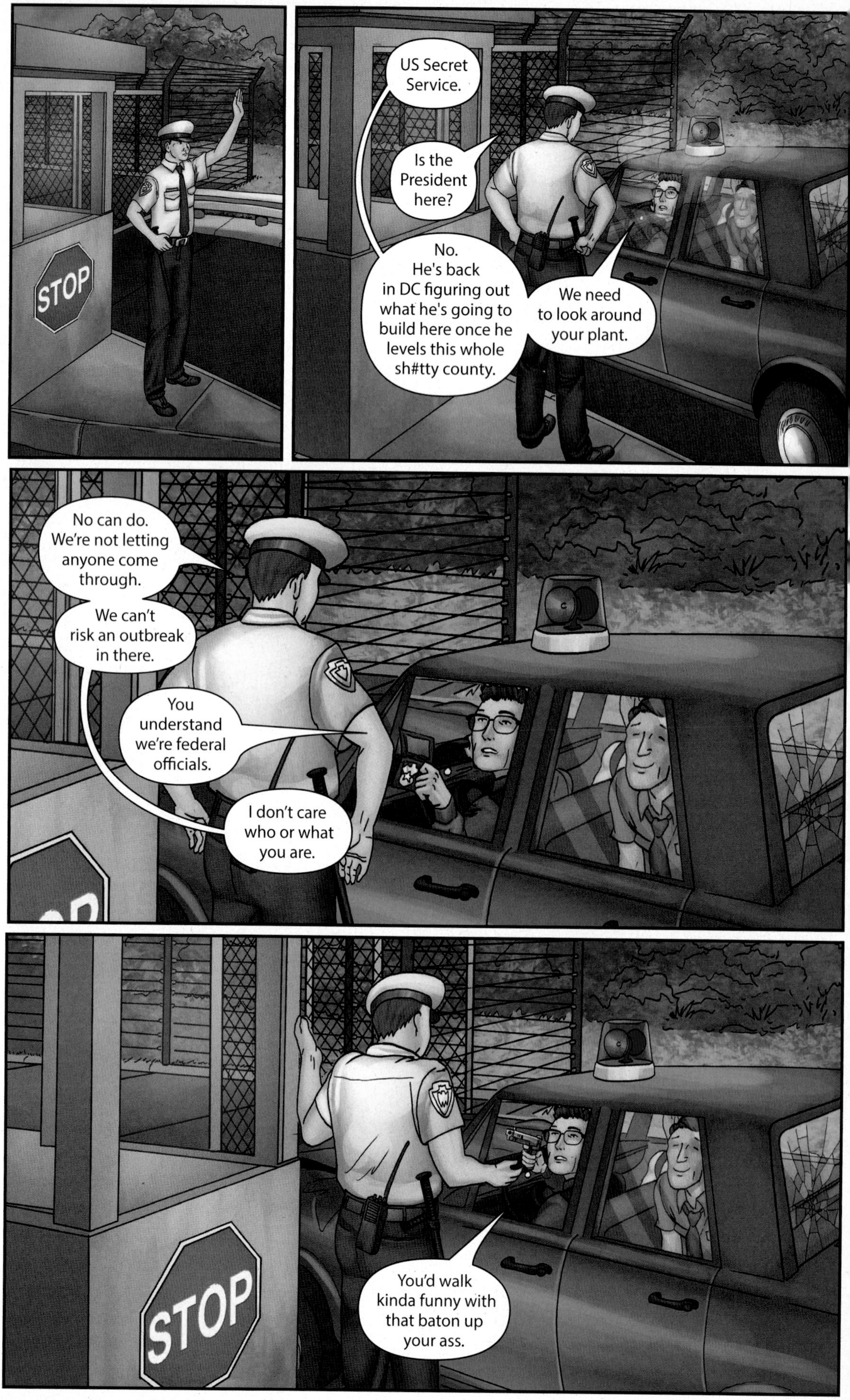
STOP
US Secret Service.
Is the President here?
No. He's back in DC figuring out what he's going to build here once he levels this whole sh#tty county.
We need to look around your plant.
No can do. We're not letting anyone come through.
We can't risk an outbreak in there.
You understand we're federal officials.
I don't care who or what you are.
STOP
You'd walk kinda funny with that baton up your ass.

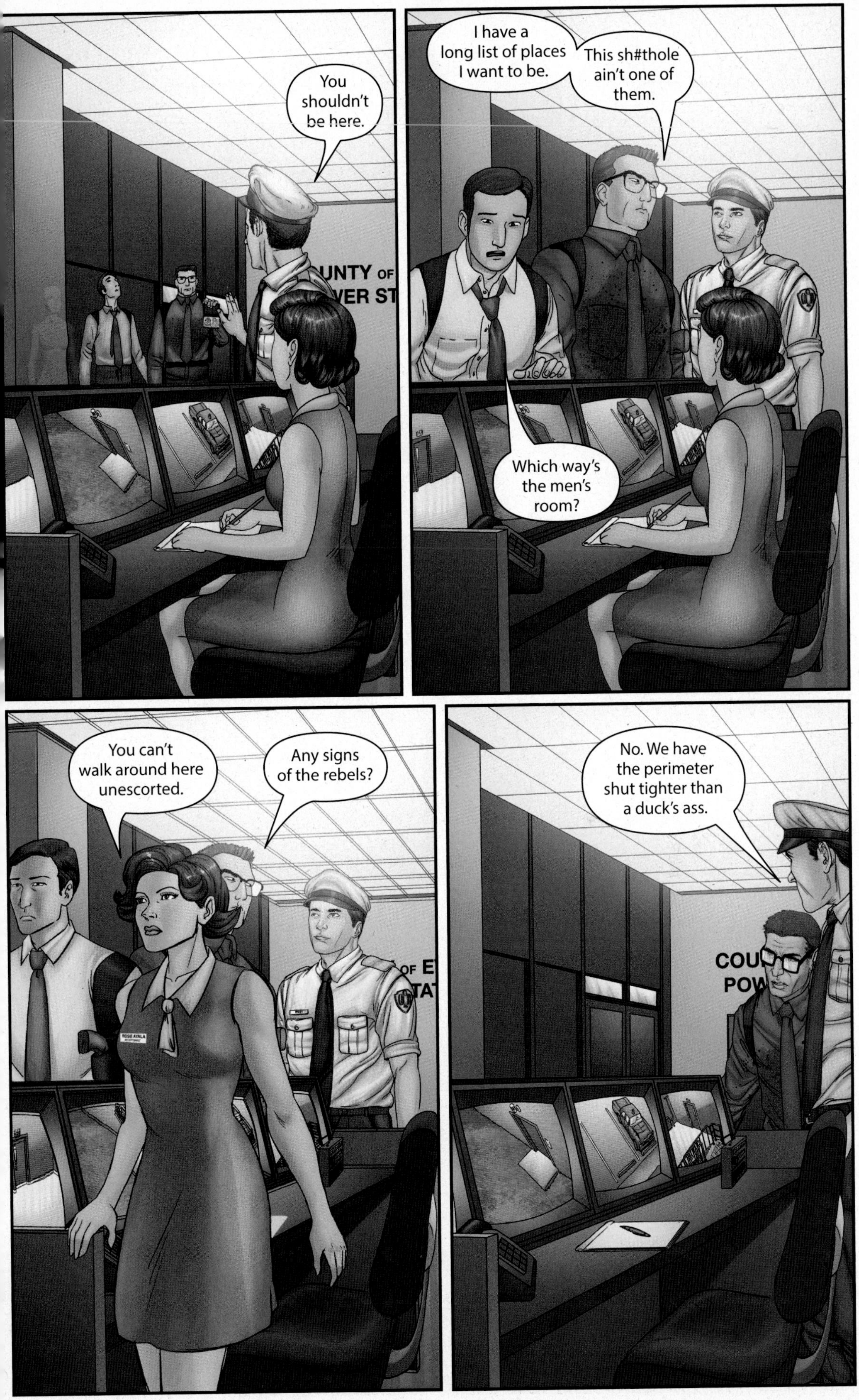
You shouldn't be here.
I have a long list of places I want to be.
This sh#thole ain't one of them.
Which way's the men's room?
You can't walk around here unescorted.
ROSIE AYALA
Any signs of the rebels?
No. We have the perimeter shut tighter than a duck's ass.

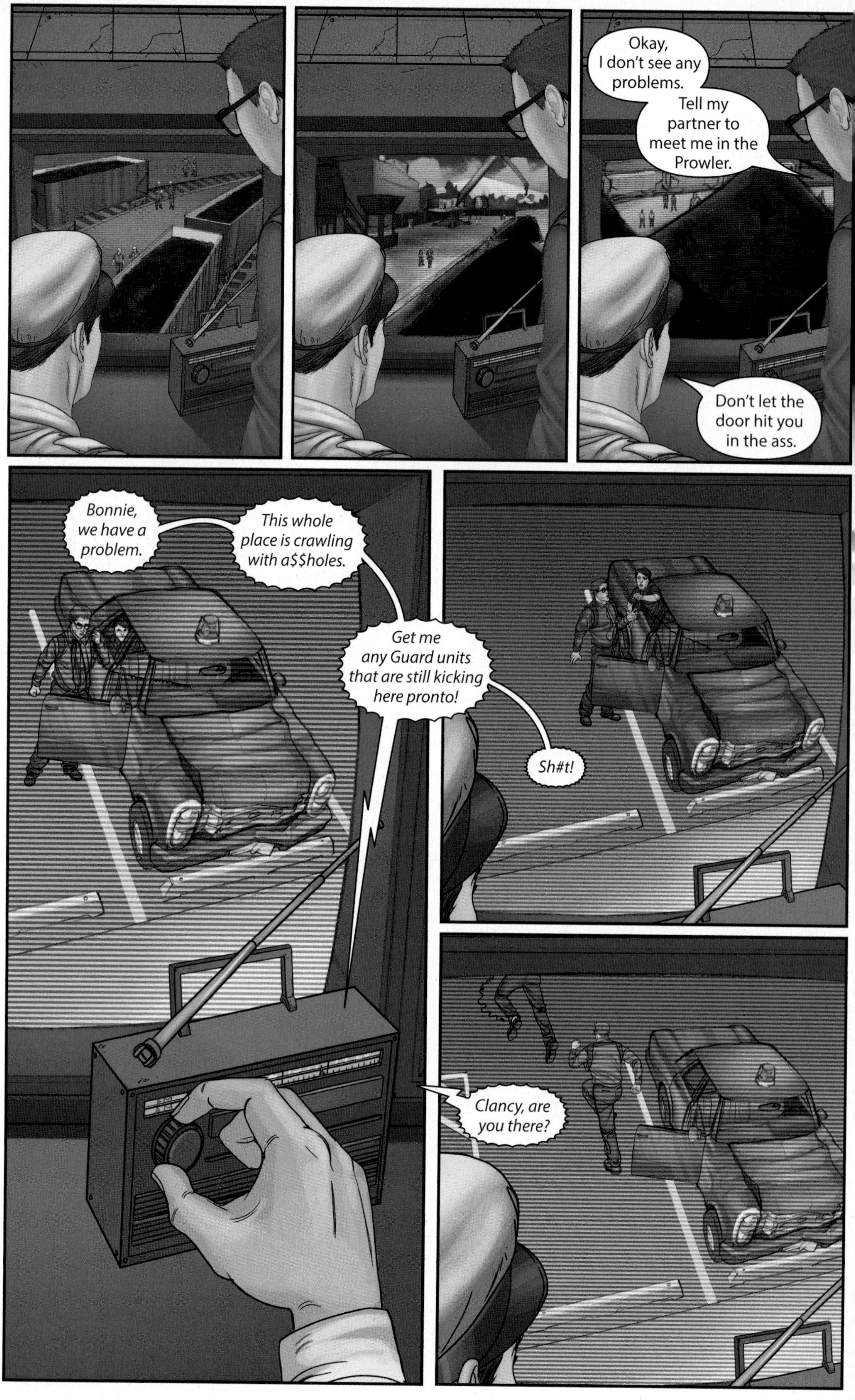
Okay, I don't see any problems.
Tell my partner to meet me in the Prowler.
Don't let the door hit you in the ass.
Bonnie, we have a problem.
This whole place is crawling with a$$holes.
Get me any Guard units that are still kicking here pronto!
Sh#t!
Clancy, are you there?

NATURAL RESOURCES

CUMULATIVE DEFORESTATION

WORLD FOREST COVER (in billion hectares)			
Pre-Industrial	**1966**	**2016**	**2066***
5.9	4.3	4.0	3.7

Between the 1960s and today, humans have destroyed over 300 million hectares of forest. This is roughly the size of the contiguous western United States.

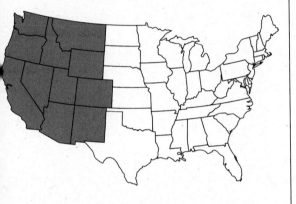

SOIL DEGRADATION

WORLD POPULATION		
1966	**2016**	**2060***
3.1 billion	6.3 billion	9.6 billion
HECTARES OF ARABLE LAND PER CAPITA		
0.42	0.23	0.18

Forty percent of the soil used for agricuture around the world is degraded or seriously degraded from our modern farming practices. Soil is now being lost at between 10 and 40 times the rate at which it can be naturally replenished. Today, the world has a rough estimate of 60 years of topsoil left.

FRESH WATER DEPLETION

Aquifers around the world cannot keep up with our consumption either. Today, 21 out of the 37 largest aquifers in the world are being tapped at unsustainable rates. In the US, the High Plains (HP) Aquifer system is one of the world's largest, spanning portions of 8 states (approximately 174,000 square miles).

DEPLETION OF SUPPLY IN THE HP AQUIFER		
1966	**2016**	**2066***
3%	30%	69%

Once depleted, the HP Aquifer will take 500 to 1,300 years to completely refill.

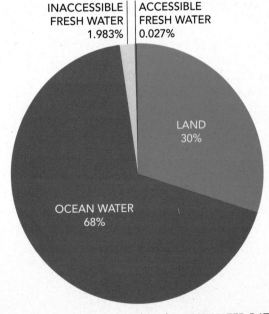

INACCESSIBLE FRESH WATER 1.983% ACCESSIBLE FRESH WATER 0.027%

LAND 30%

OCEAN WATER 68%

*ESTIMATED DATA

THE NATIONAL AIR AND SPACE ADMINISTRATION

October 4, 1957 – The Soviet Union launched *Sputnik*, the world's first man-made satellite, into space.

November 3, 1957 – The Soviet Union followed with *Sputnik 2*, which carried Laika, a canine. Laika survived the trip into space but died when the oxygen supply ran out.

January 31, 1958 – The United States launched its first satellite, *Explorer 1*.

August 19, 1960 – The Soviet Union launched *Sputnik 5* with a grey rabbit, 42 mice, two rats, flies, several plants, fungi, and two canines, Belka and Strelka; all passengers survived the trip to and from space.

April 12, 1961 – Soviet cosmonaut Yuri Gagarin became the first human in space.

May 5, 1961 – Alan Shepard became the first American in space.

May 25, 1961 – President John F. Kennedy rallied Congress and the nation to support the first manned mission to the moon, which became the Apollo program.

February 3, 1966 – The Soviet Union landed the first spacecraft on the moon; the United States followed with *Surveyor I* on June 2.

July 2, 1969 – American astronauts Neil Armstrong and "Buzz" Aldrin became the first men on the moon.

September 1976 – American probe *Viking 2* discovered water frost on Mars.

August and September 1977 – *Voyagers 1* and *2* were launched; each would transmit images of the outer planets over the decades while on their (still ongoing) journeys.

April 12, 1981 – The United States launched the first space shuttle *Columbia*.

August 6, 2012 – NASA's *Curiosity* rover landed on Mars.

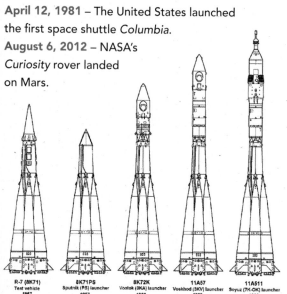

R-7 (8K71)
Test vehicle
1957

8K71PS
Sputnik (PS) launcher
1957

8K72K
Vostok (3KA) launcher
1960

11A57
Voskhod (3KV) launcher
1963

11A511
Soyuz (7K-OK) launcher
1966

SINCE *SPUTNIK'S* LAUNCH IN 1957

SATELLITES SENT INTO ORBIT	2,271
ACTIVE SATELLITES	1,381
UNITED STATES	568
RUSSIA	133
CHINA	177
ALL OTHER COUNTRIES	503
ACTIVE MILITARY SATELLITES	295
UNITED STATES	129
RUSSIA	75
CHINA	35
ALL OTHER COUNTRIES	56

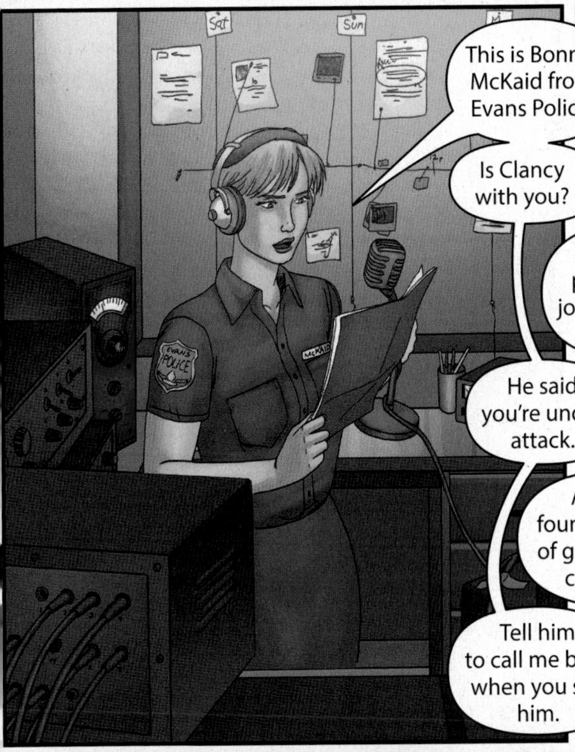
This is Bonnie McKaid from Evans Police.
Is Clancy with you?
He said you're under attack.
Tell him to call me back when you see him.

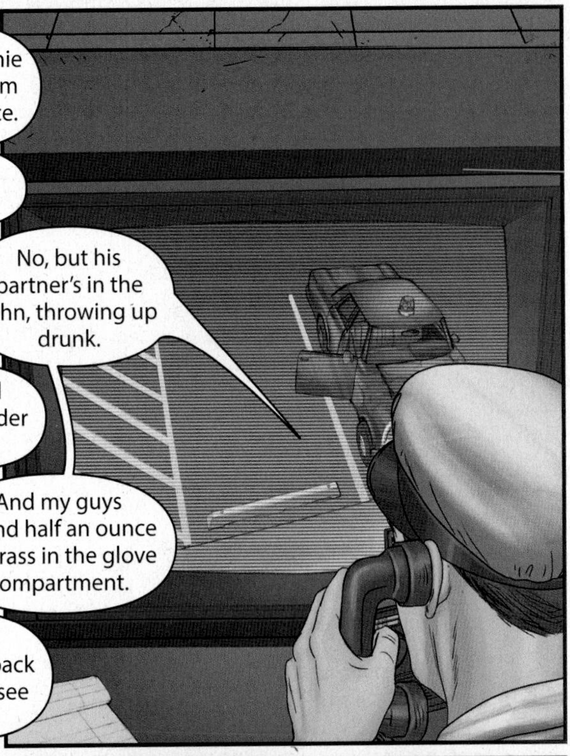
No, but his partner's in the john, throwing up drunk.
And my guys found half an ounce of grass in the glove compartment.

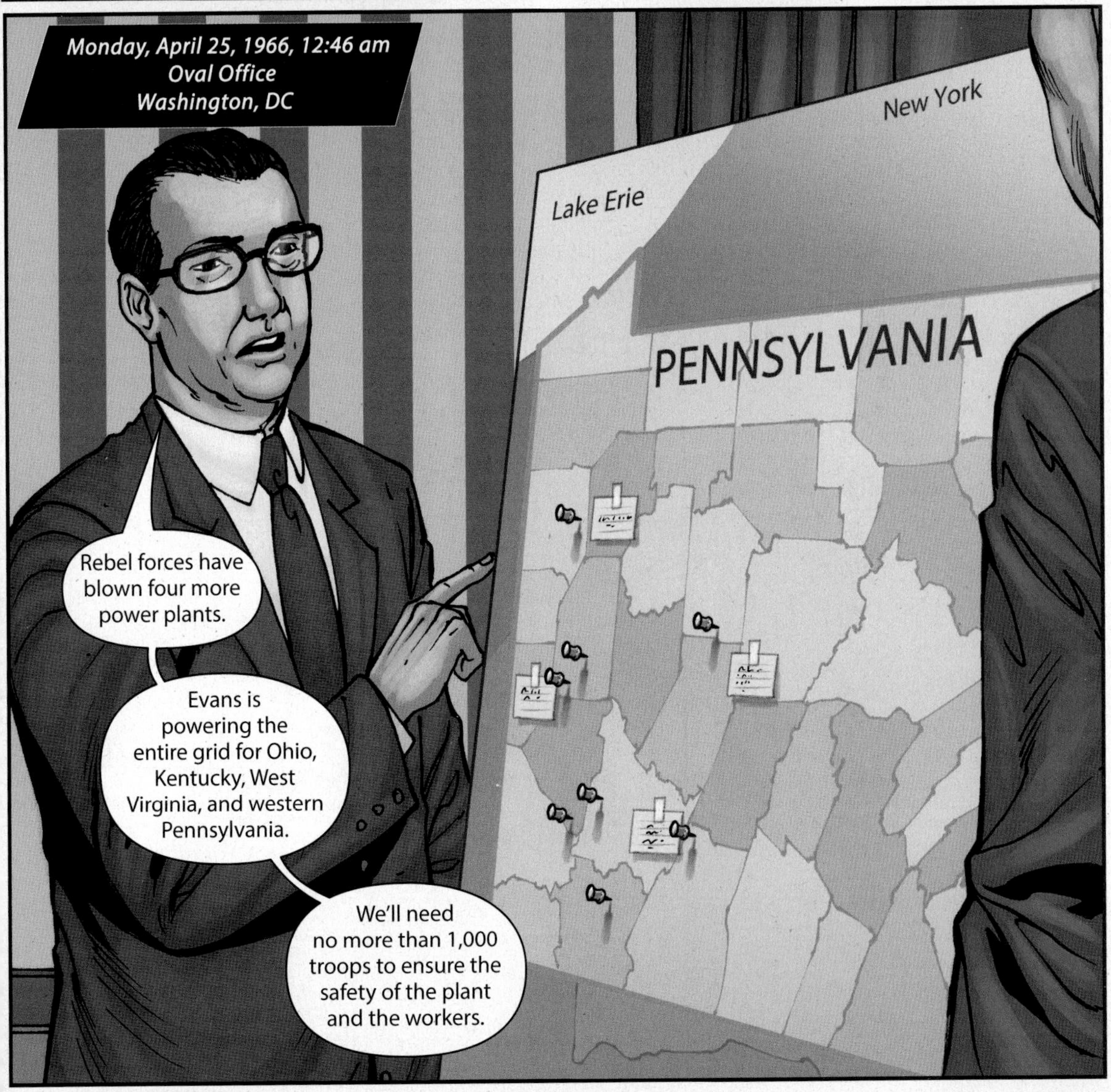
Monday, April 25, 1966, 12:46 am
Oval Office
Washington, DC
New York
Lake Erie
PENNSYLVANIA
Rebel forces have blown four more power plants.
Evans is powering the entire grid for Ohio, Kentucky, West Virginia, and western Pennsylvania.
We'll need no more than 1,000 troops to ensure the safety of the plant and the workers.

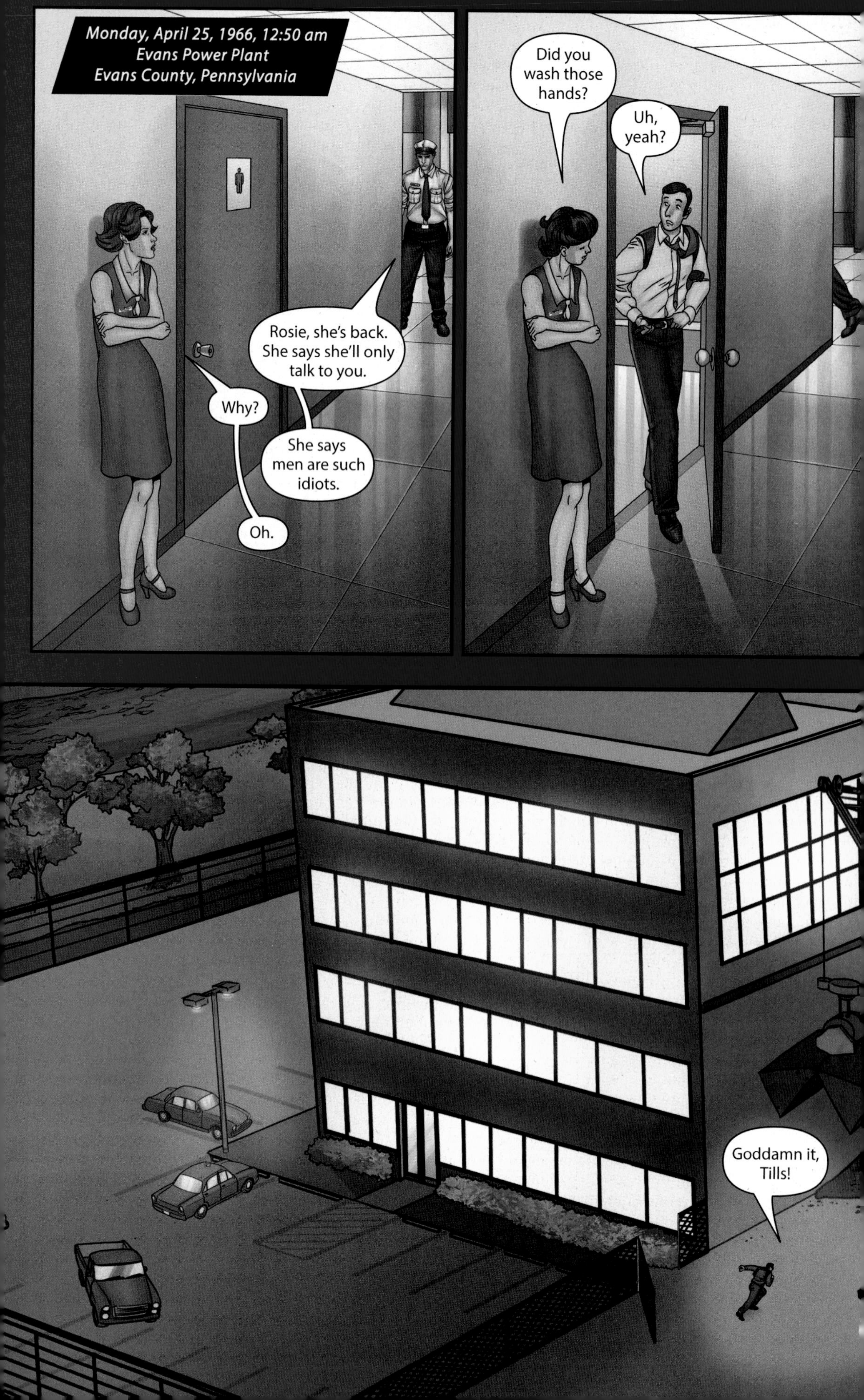
Monday, April 25, 1966, 12:50 am
Evans Power Plant
Evans County, Pennsylvania
Rosie, she's back. She says she'll only talk to you.
Why?
She says men are such idiots.
Oh.
Did you wash those hands?
Uh, yeah?
Goddamn it, Tills!

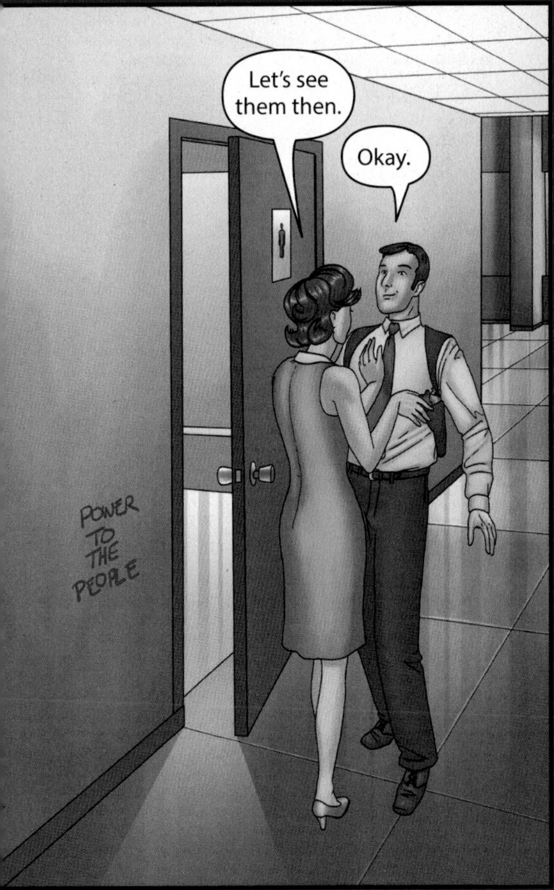
Let's see them then.
Okay.
POWER TO THE PEOPLE

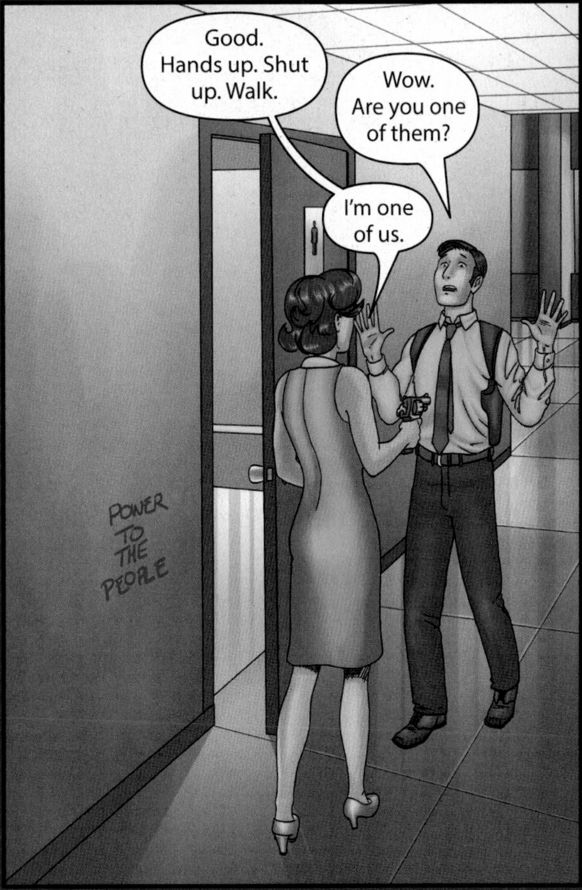
Good. Hands up. Shut up. Walk.
Wow. Are you one of them?
I'm one of us.
POWER TO THE PEOPLE

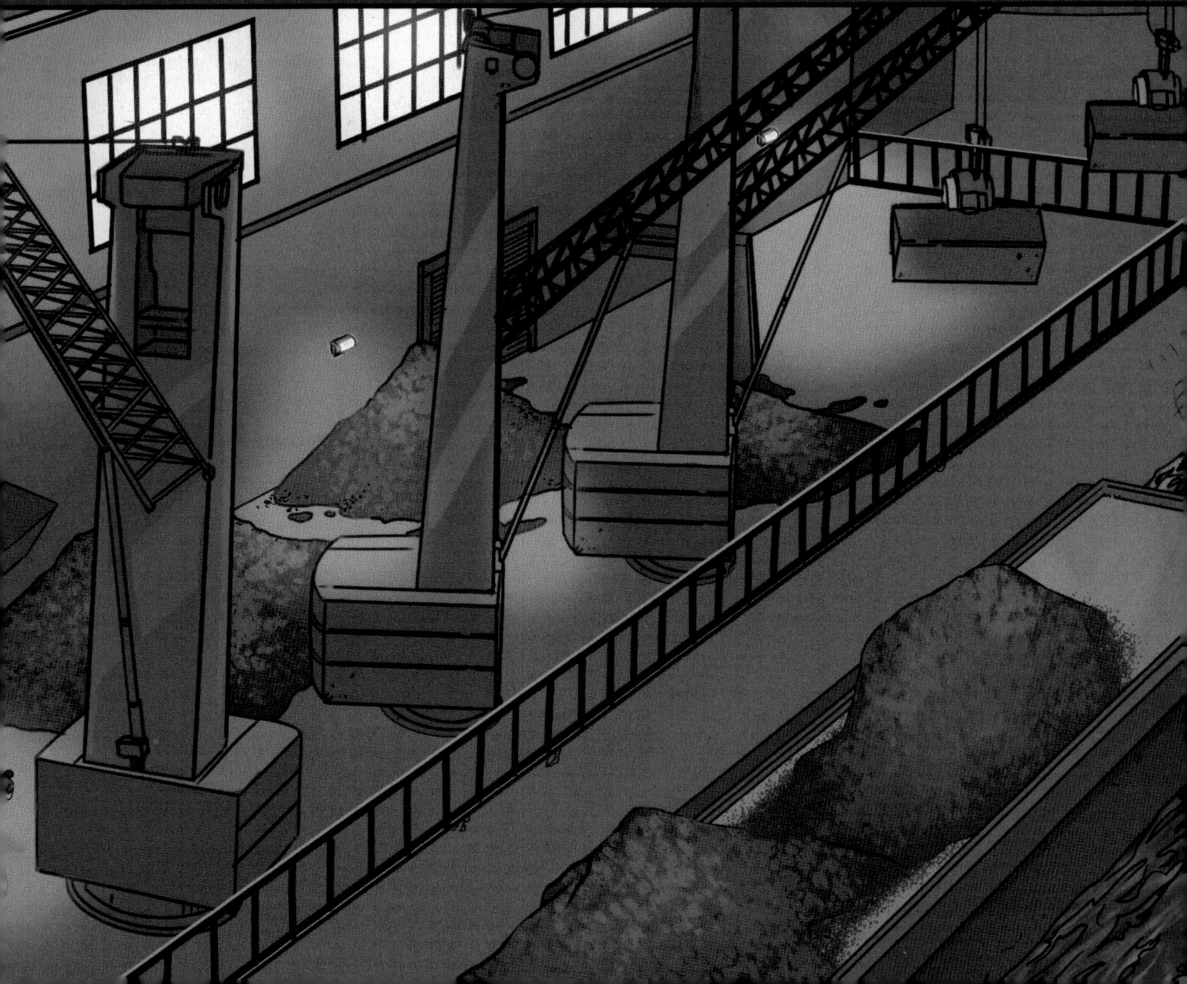

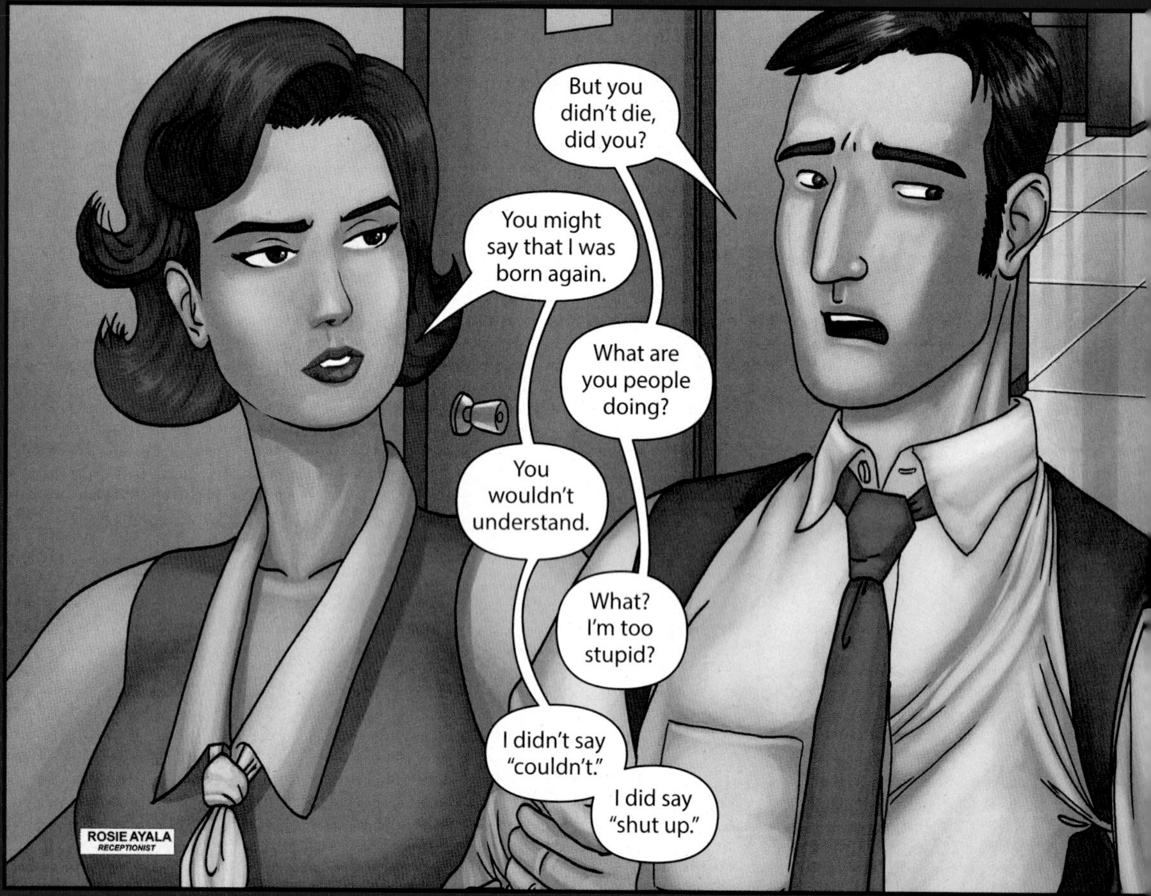
But you didn't die, did you?
You might say that I was born again.
What are you people doing?
You wouldn't understand.
What? I'm too stupid?
I didn't say "couldn't."
I did say "shut up."
ROSIE AYALA
RECEPTIONIST

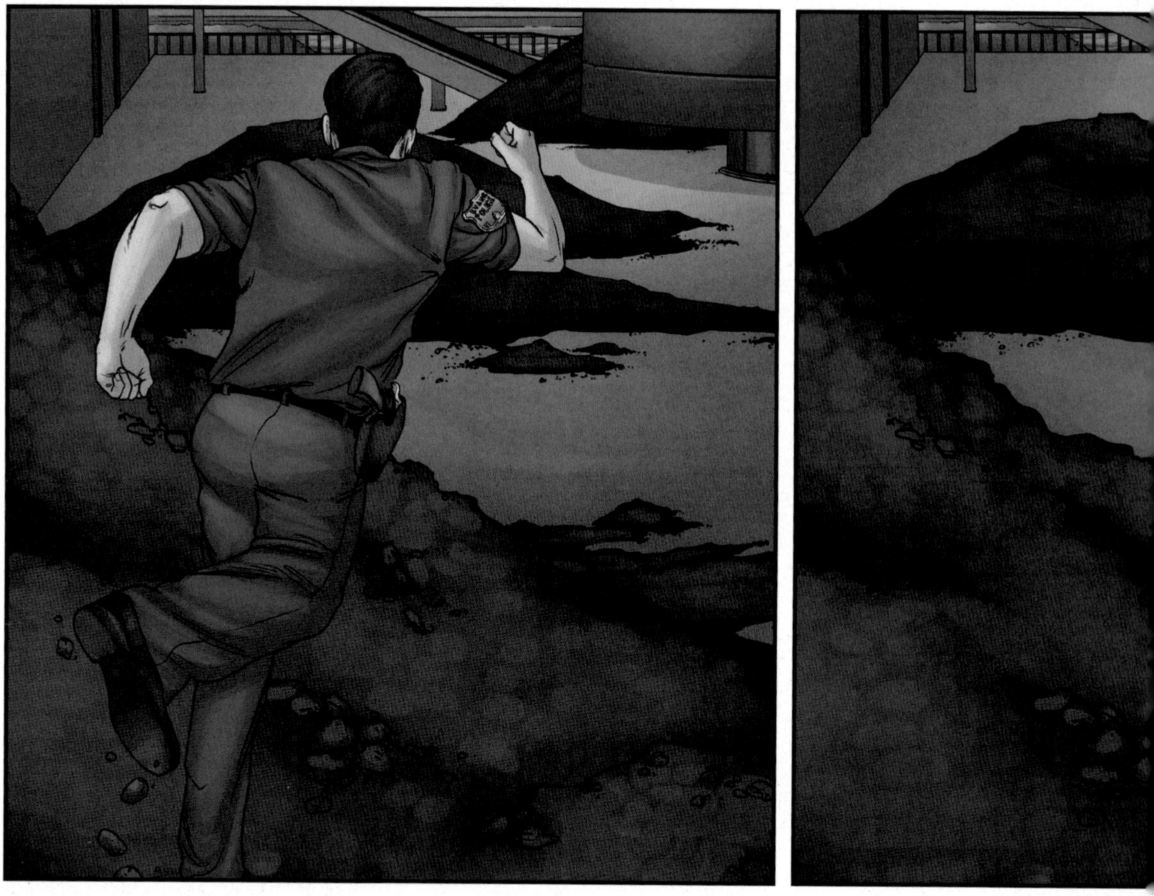

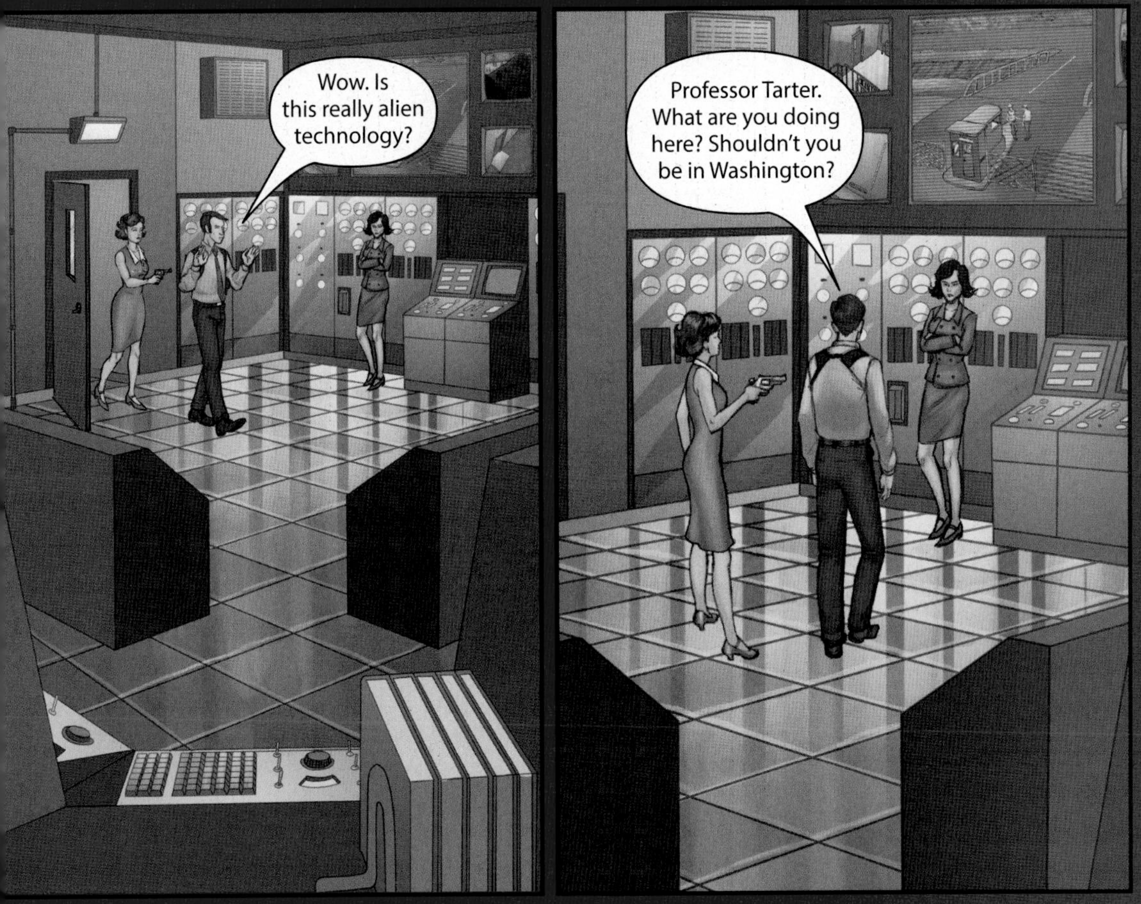
Wow. Is this really alien technology?
Professor Tarter. What are you doing here? Shouldn't you be in Washington?

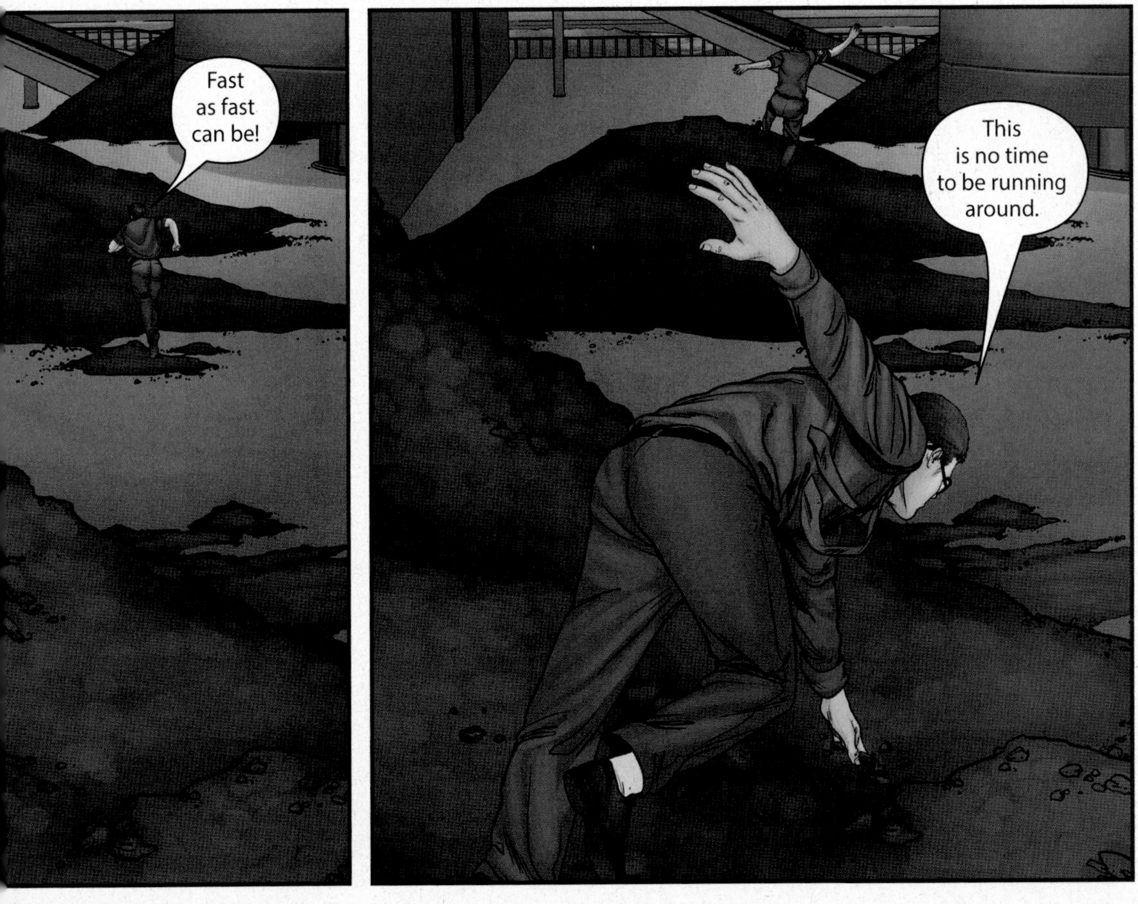
Fast as fast can be!
This is no time to be running around.

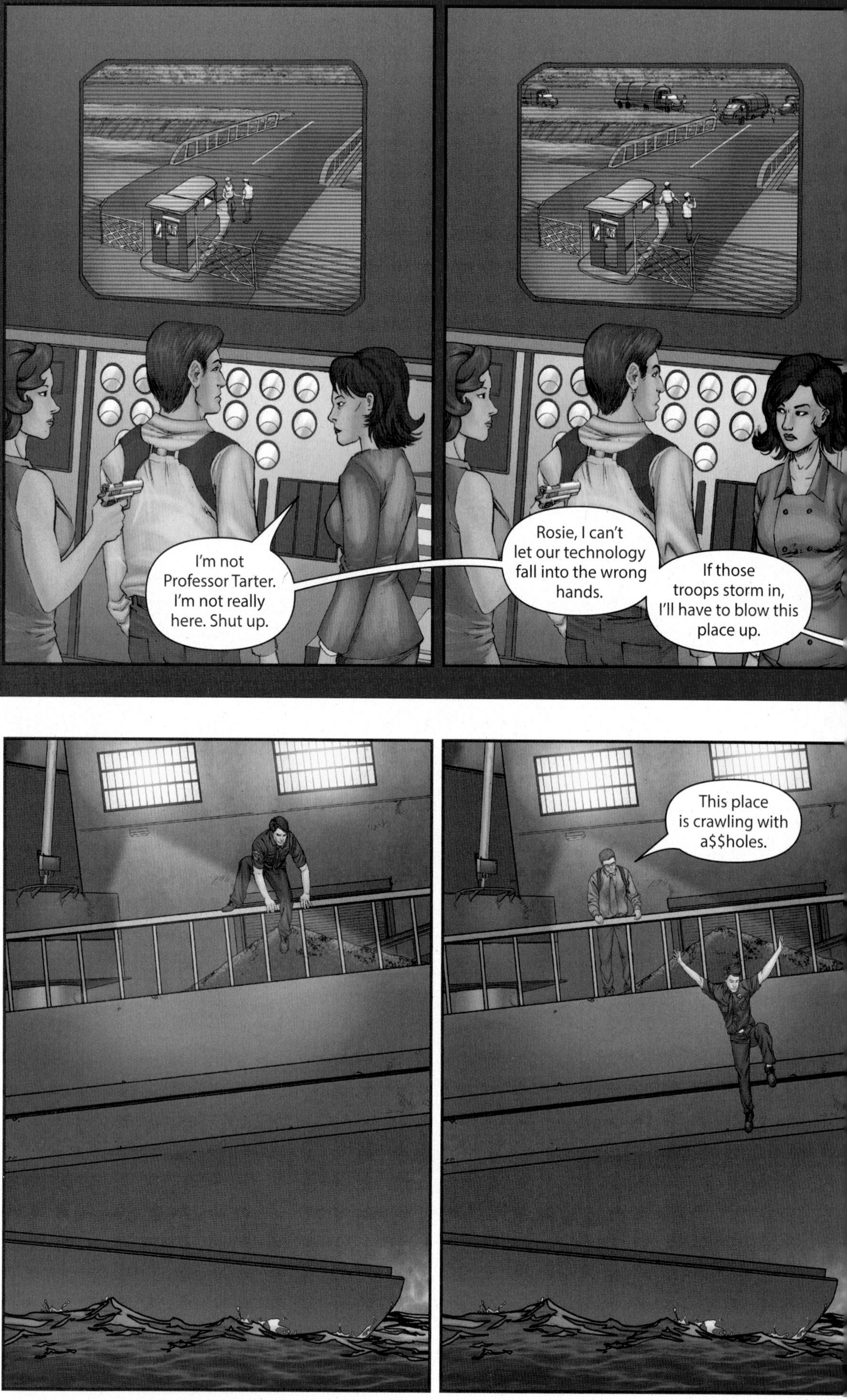
I'm not Professor Tarter. I'm not really here. Shut up.
Rosie, I can't let our technology fall into the wrong hands.
If those troops storm in, I'll have to blow this place up.
This place is crawling with a$$holes.

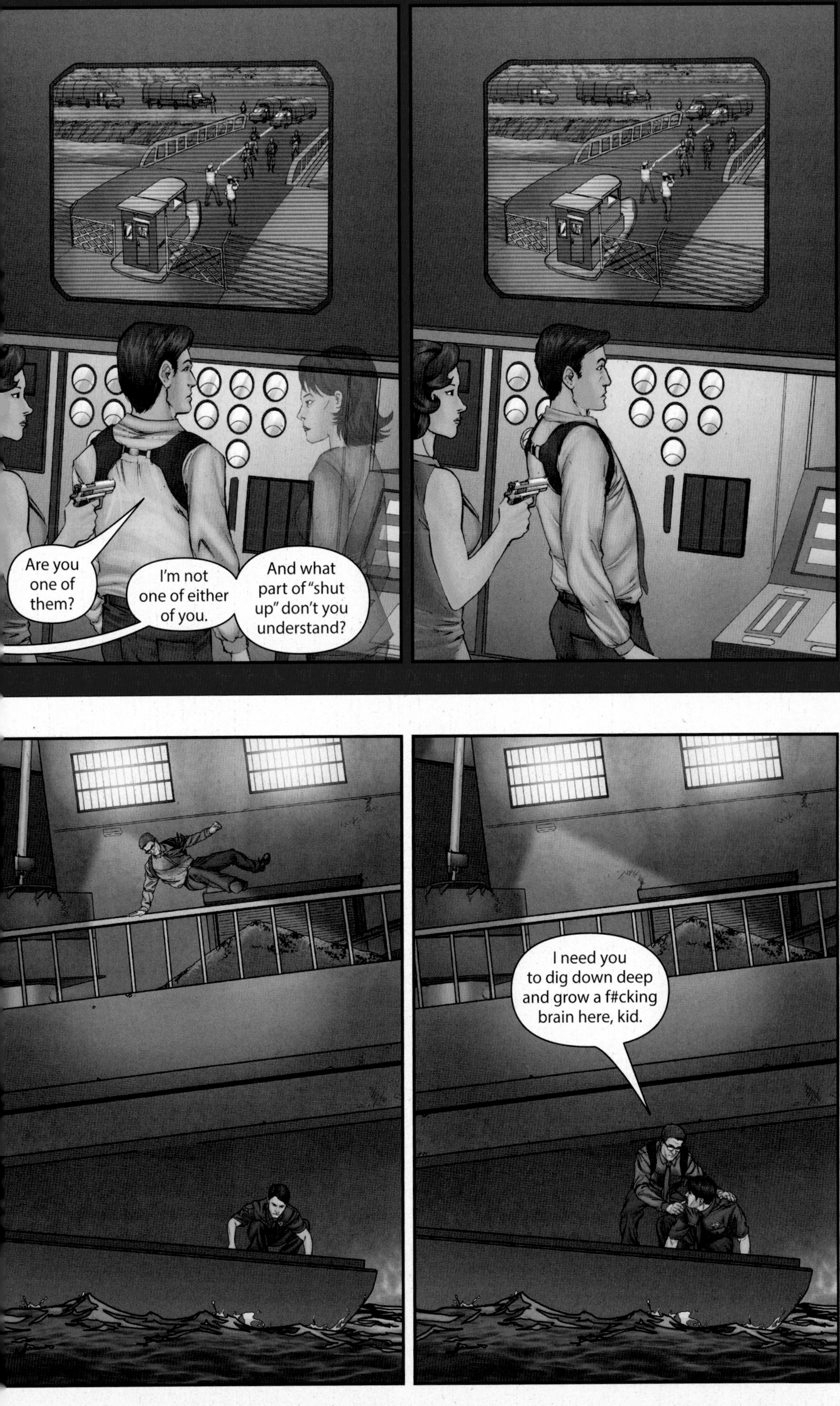
Are you one of them?
I'm not one of either of you.
And what part of "shut up" don't you understand?
I need you to dig down deep and grow a f#cking brain here, kid.

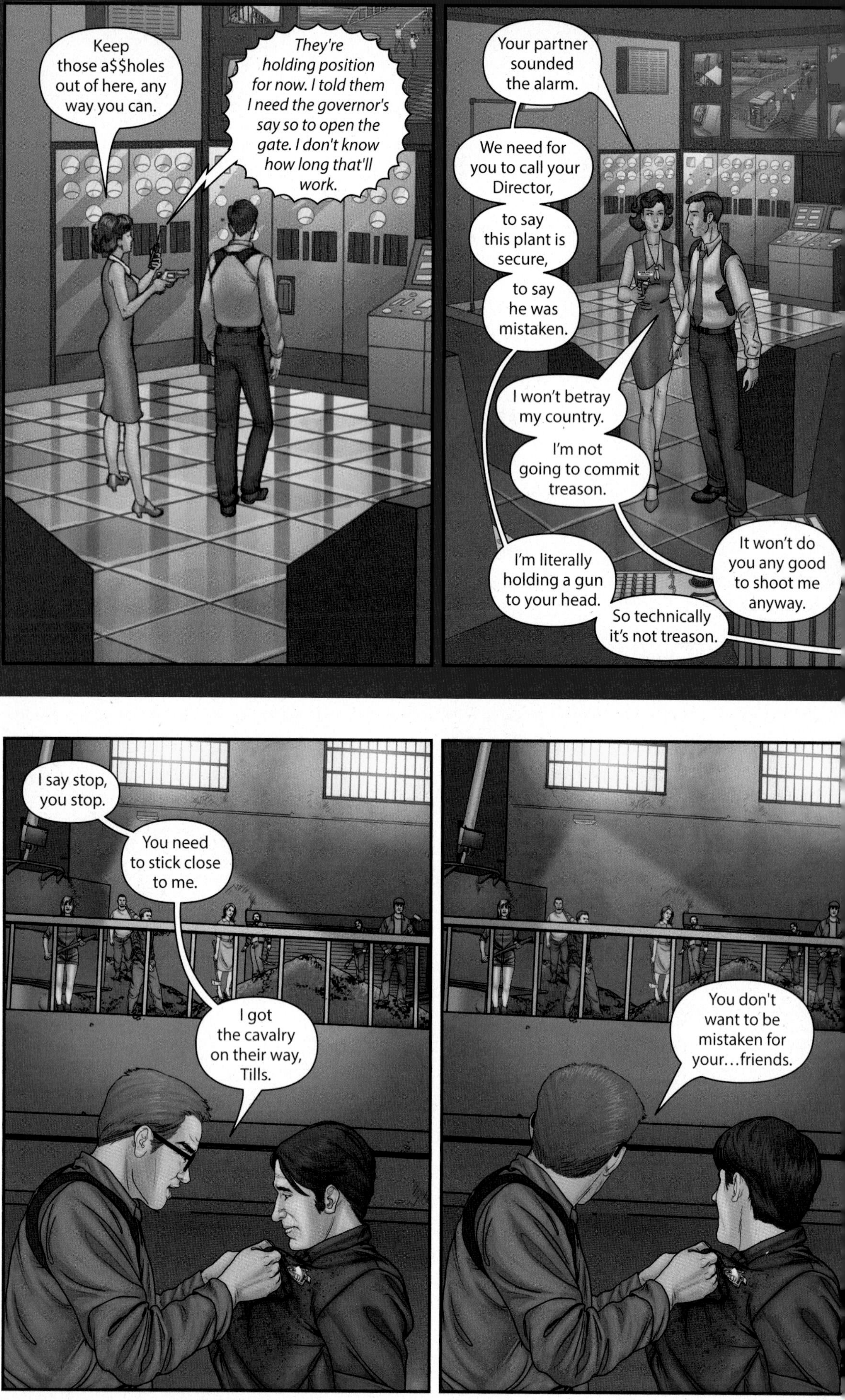

Keep those a$$holes out of here, any way you can.
They're holding position for now. I told them I need the governor's say so to open the gate. I don't know how long that'll work.
Your partner sounded the alarm.
We need for you to call your Director,
to say this plant is secure,
to say he was mistaken.
I won't betray my country.
I'm not going to commit treason.
It won't do you any good to shoot me anyway.
I'm literally holding a gun to your head.
So technically it's not treason.
I say stop, you stop.
You need to stick close to me.
I got the cavalry on their way, Tills.
You don't want to be mistaken for your…friends.

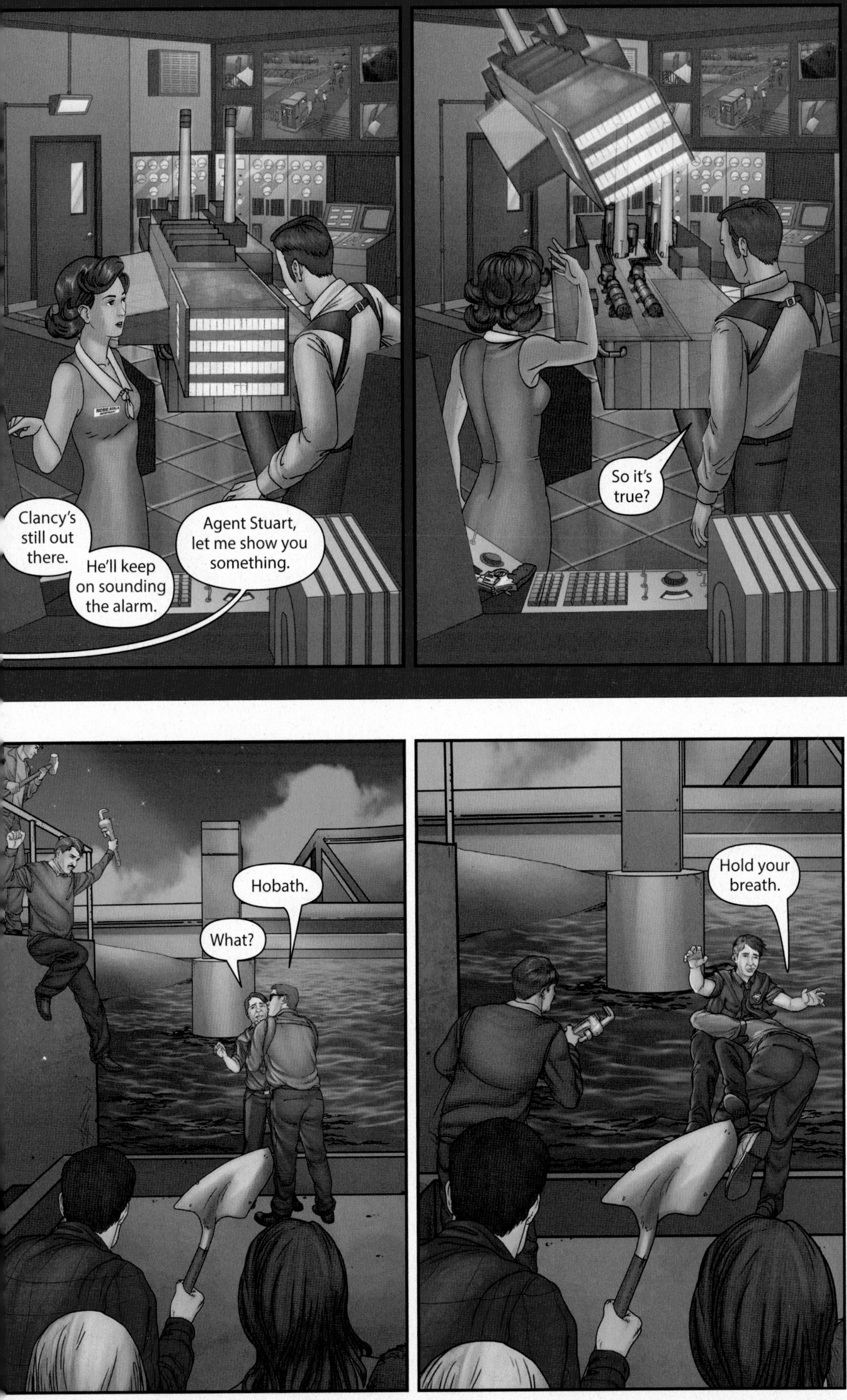
Clancy's still out there.
He'll keep on sounding the alarm.
Agent Stuart, let me show you something.
So it's true?
Hobath.
What?
Hold your breath.

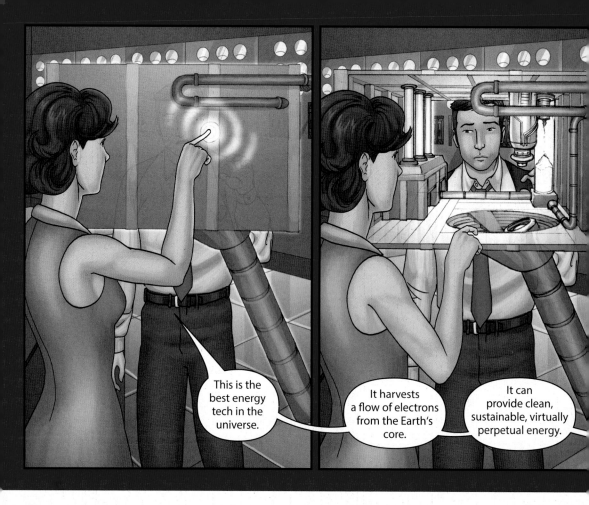

This is the best energy tech in the universe.

It harvests a flow of electrons from the Earth's core.

It can provide clean, sustainable, virtually perpetual energy.

Decorated World War II vet. Silver Star for killing six Krauts with a can opener at Bastogne. Agent of the Year for three years straight. Busted up a Russian counterfeit ring in '59. Eisenhower personally put him on the Presidential detail.

He's the real deal. A goddamn legend at the Treasury Department. Least he was until the Kennedy thing…

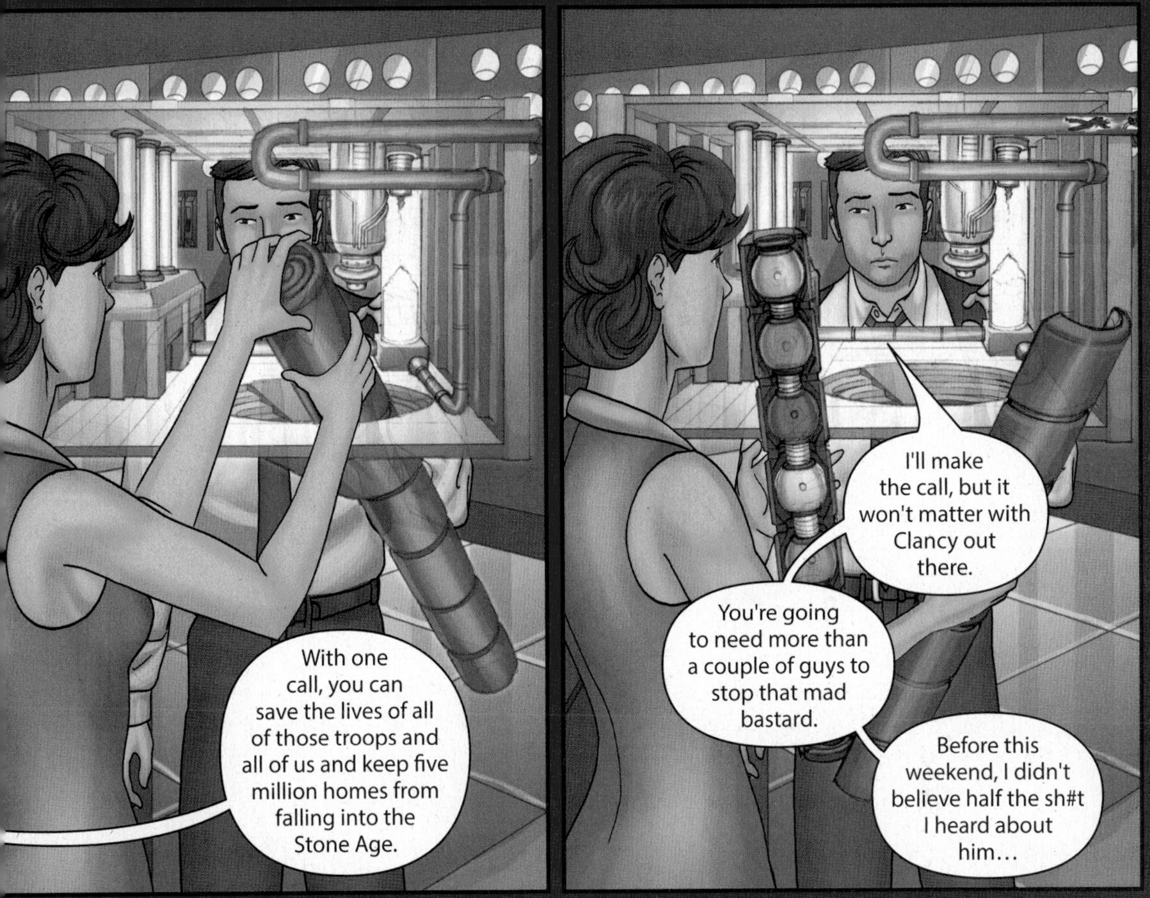
With one call, you can save the lives of all of those troops and all of us and keep five million homes from falling into the Stone Age.
I'll make the call, but it won't matter with Clancy out there.
You're going to need more than a couple of guys to stop that mad bastard.
Before this weekend, I didn't believe half the sh#t I heard about him…

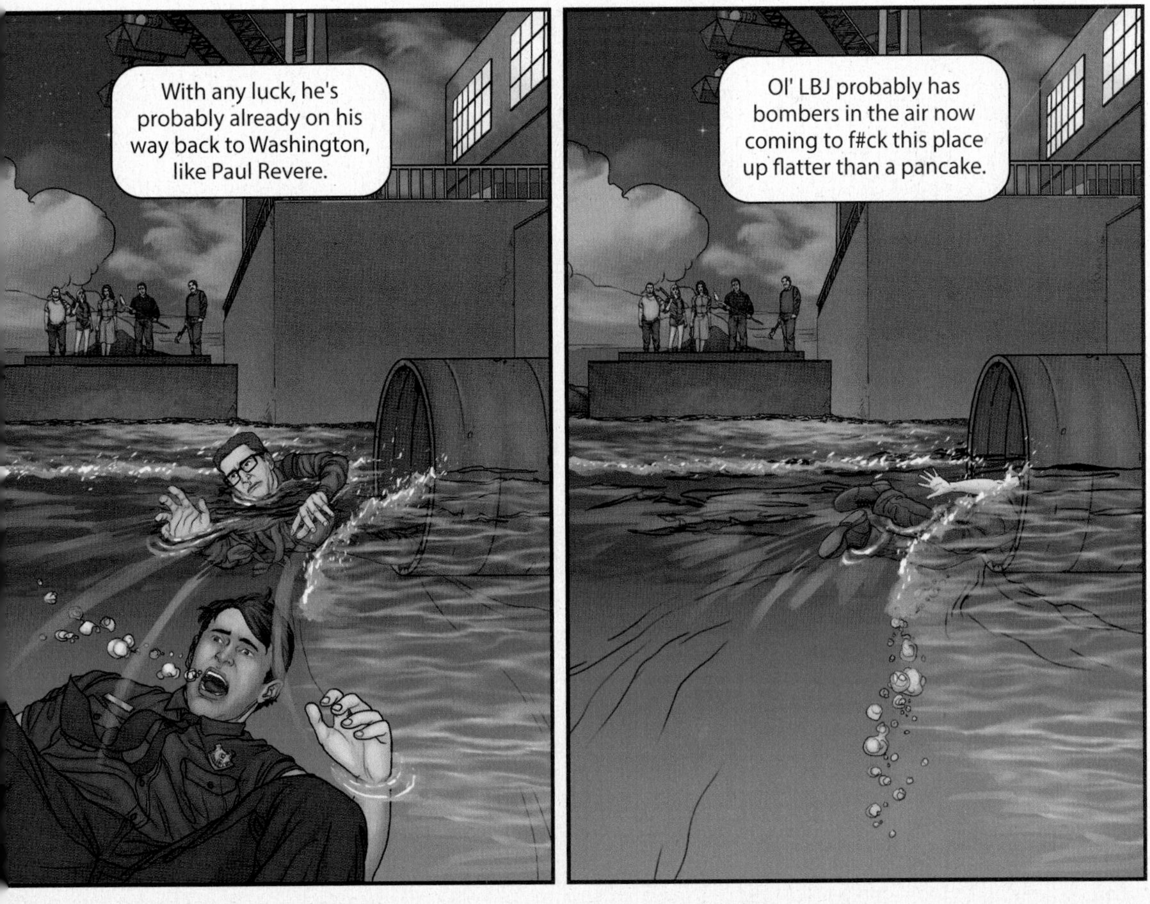
With any luck, he's probably already on his way back to Washington, like Paul Revere.
Ol' LBJ probably has bombers in the air now coming to f#ck this place up flatter than a pancake.

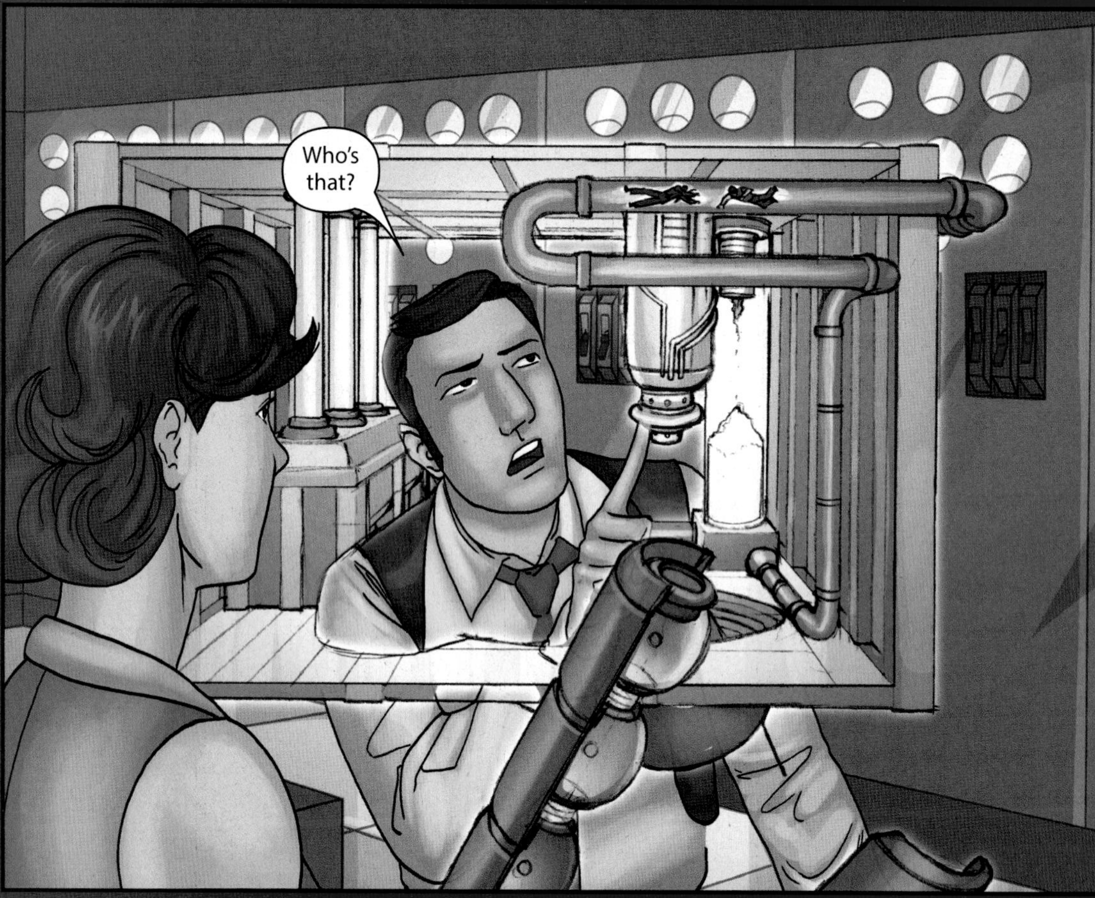
Who's that?

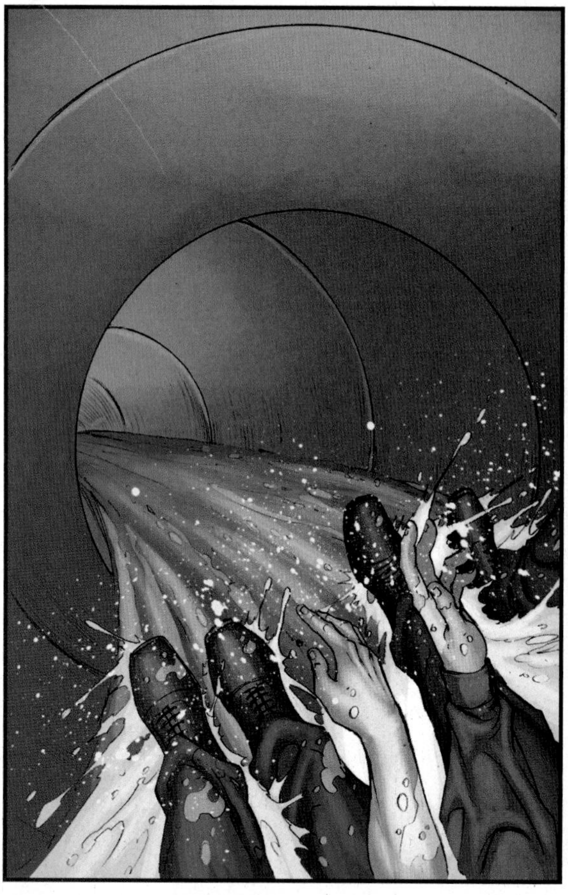

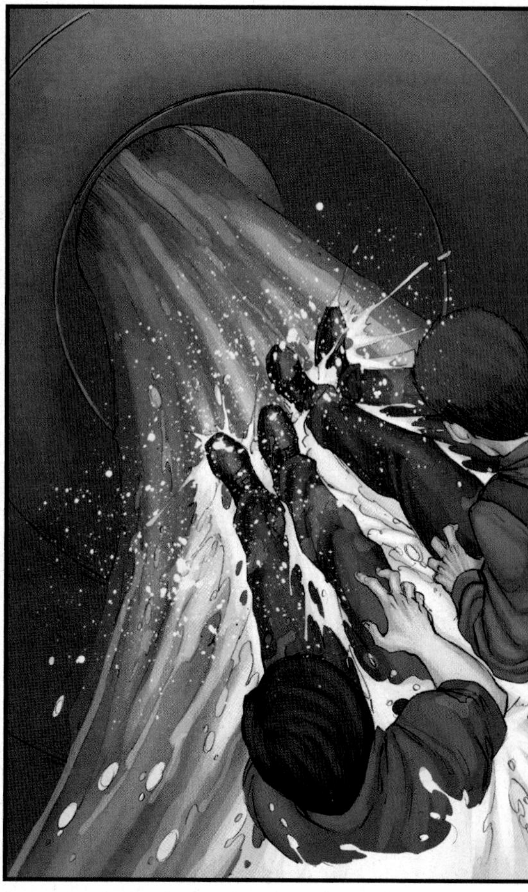

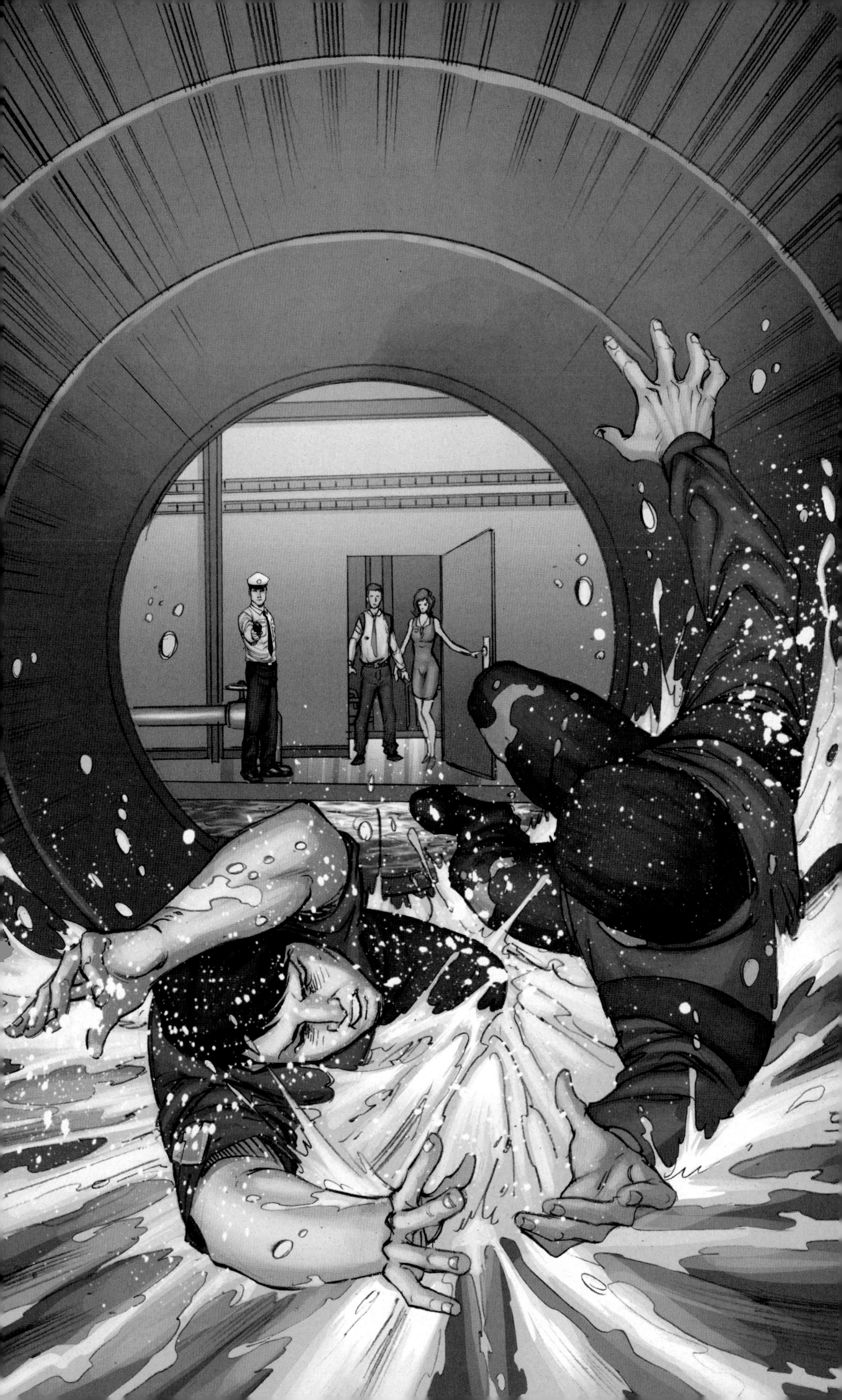

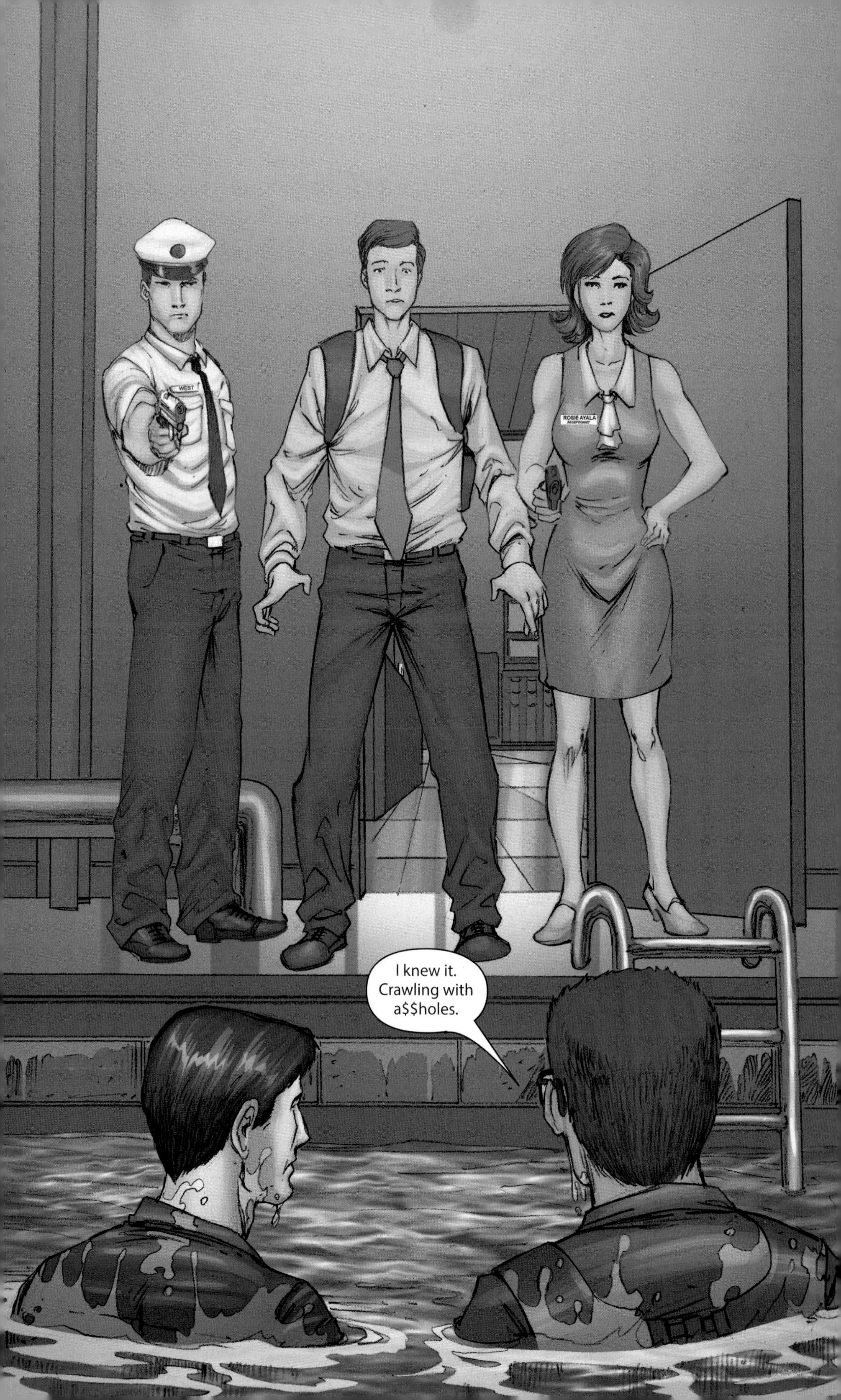
WEST
ROSIE AYALA
I knew it. Crawling with a$$holes.

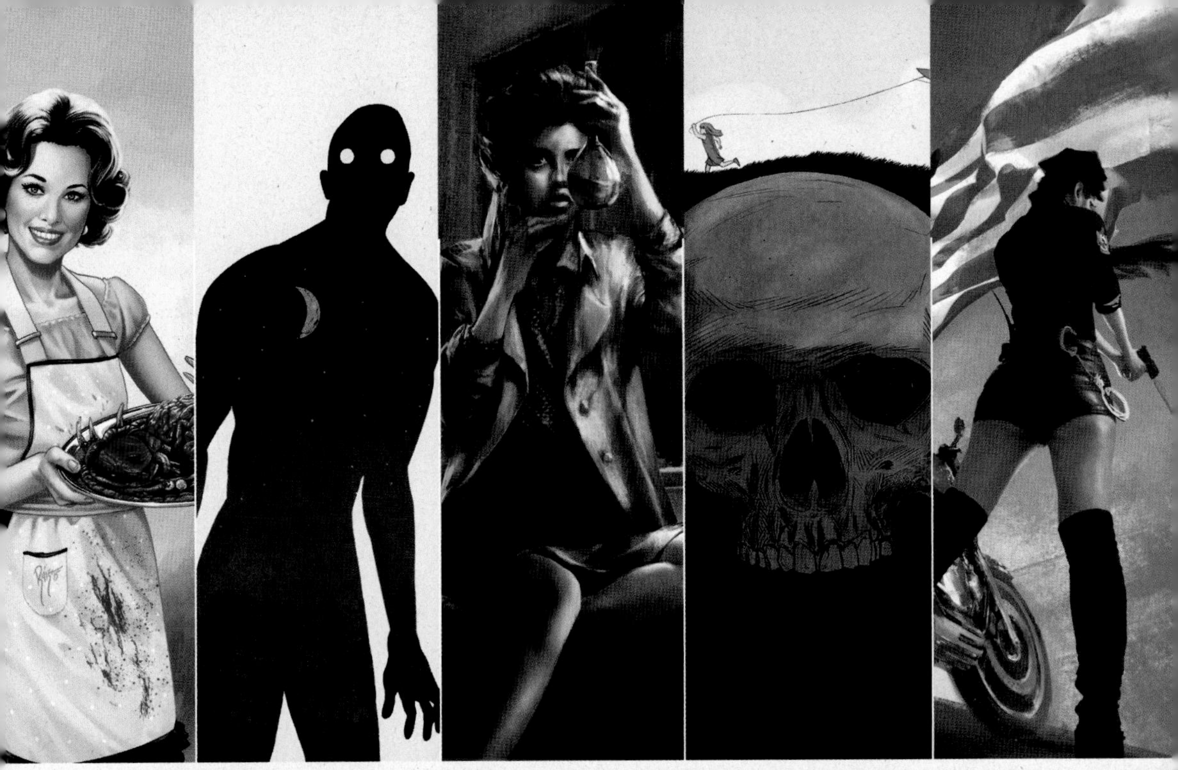

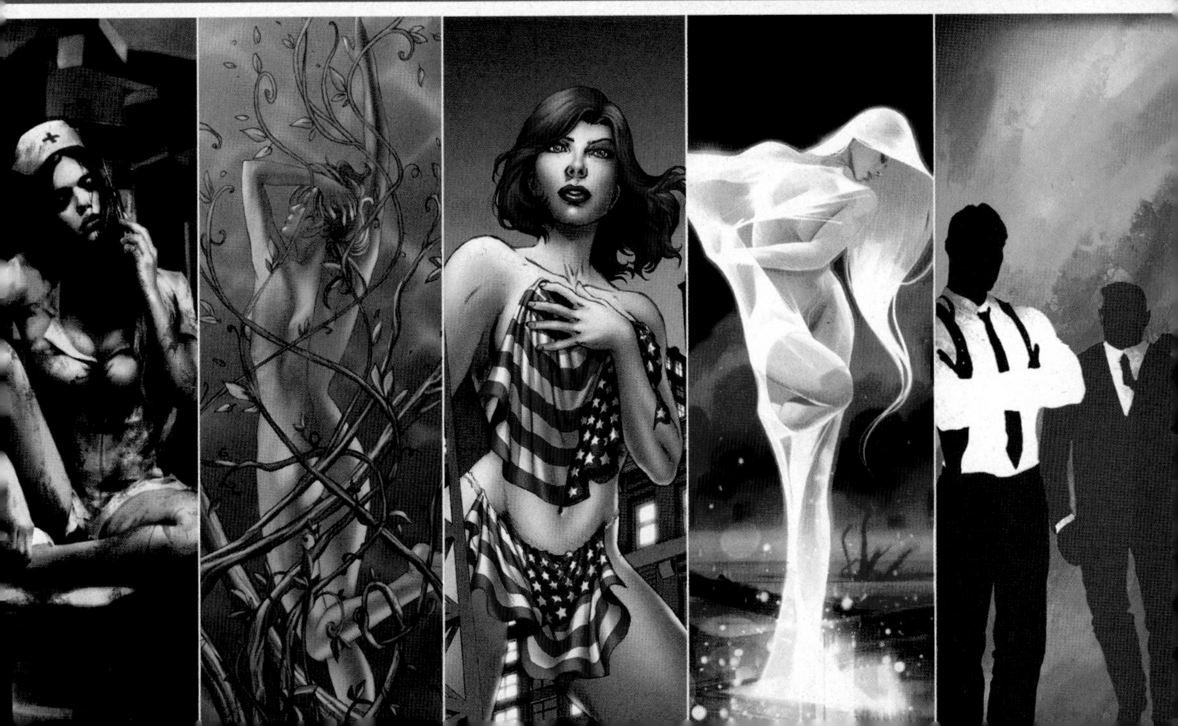

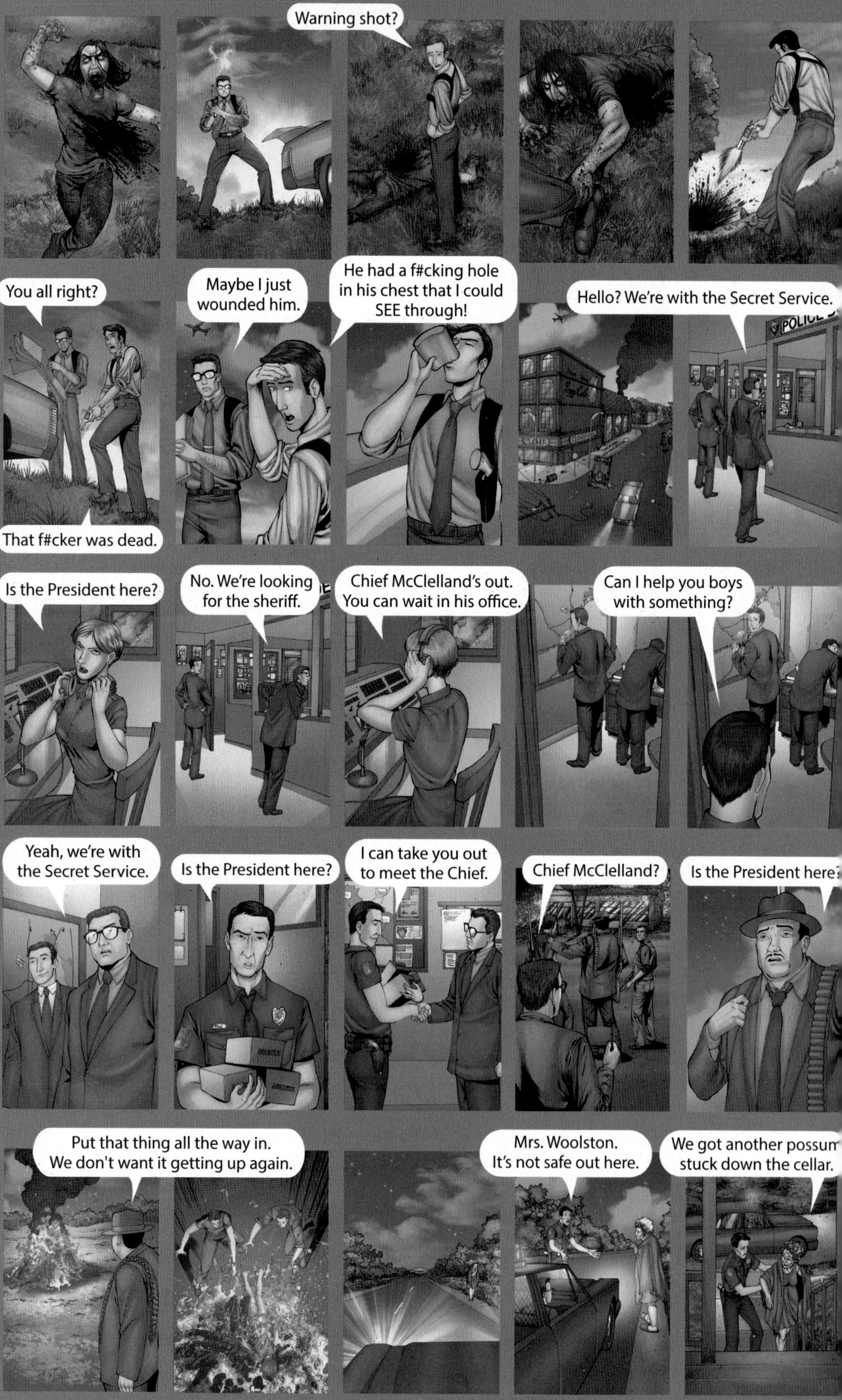

Warning shot?
You all right?
That f#cker was dead.
Maybe I just wounded him.
He had a f#cking hole in his chest that I could SEE through!
Hello? We're with the Secret Service.
POLICE
Is the President here?
No. We're looking for the sheriff.
Chief McClelland's out. You can wait in his office.
Can I help you boys with something?
Yeah, we're with the Secret Service.
Is the President here?
I can take you out to meet the Chief.
Chief McClelland?
Is the President here?
Put that thing all the way in. We don't want it getting up again.
Mrs. Woolston. It's not safe out here.
We got another possum stuck down the cellar.